Interface Collection

In the shadow of the Swastika

The *Interface Collection*, coordinated and developed by the Gypsy Research Centre at the Université René Descartes, Paris, is published with the support of the European Commission.

Some Collection titles receive Council of Europe support for distribution in Central and Eastern Europe.

Editor, Interface Collection: Jean-Pierre Liégeois

Editorial assistant: Astrid Thorn Hillig and Alice Bialestowki

Cover: Catherine Liégeois
DTP: La 13ème Heure

© 1999
Centre de recherches tsiganes (Gypsy Research Centre) and
University of Hertfordshire Press
University of Hertfordshire
College Lane
Hatfield
Hertfordshire
AL109AB - UK

Tel. +44 1707 284654
Fax +44 1707 284666

Internet: UHPress@herts.ac.uk
Web address: UHP://www.herts.ac.uk/UHPress

© 1999
ISBN 0 900458 85 2

Published 1999

Printed in Great Britain by J. W. Arrowsmith Limited, Bristol

In the shadow
of the Swastika

*The Gypsies
during the Second World War*

2

Edited by Donald Kenrick

Centre de recherches tsiganes
University of Hertfordshire Press

Giovanna Boursier was born in Turin. She is a graduate history and is a journalist. She has written articles on the treatment of the Gypsies in Italy under Fascism and is continuing her research into the subject with the organizations Opera Nomadi and Associazione Italiana Zingari Oggi.

Reimar Gilsenbach, born in Germany, is a writer and journalist. He has written many articles and books about the Romanies and Sinti. The first volume of a four-volume chronology of Gypsy history has recently been published.

Marie-Christine Hubert is a graduate in history of the University of Paris X. Her specialist subject was the Gypsies in France 1939-46 and she has since written several articles on the subject. She has recently obtained her doctorate.

Michelle Kelso is an American researcher who lived in Romania between 1994-96 while participating on the Fulbright programme. During her stay in Romania, she began examining the deportation of the Gypsies. She is an honours graduate from the University of Iowa in Iowa City.

Elena Marushiakova, obtained her doctorate at Bratislava University after graduating in Sofia. She is currently working in the Ethnographic Institute and Museum of the Bulgarian Academy of Sciences.

Vesselin Popov obtained his first degree and doctorate at Sofia University. He is currently working in the Ethnographic Institute and Museum of the Bulgarian Academy of Sciences.

Elena Marushiakova and Vesselin Popov are joint authors of the standard work on the Gypsies of Bulgaria and editors of the the journal *Studii Romani*.

Ctibor Necas is a Czech historian at the Masaryk University in Brno. He has written books and many articles on the subject of Gypsies during the Nazi occupation of Czechoslovakia.

Erika Thurner has written extensively on the camps set up by the Nazis in Austria. She is at present teaching in Innsbruck.

Michael Zimmermann is a German historian who has published several books on the Holocaust. He currently works at the Ruhrlandmuseum in Essen.

Table of Contents

III. The internment of Gypsies in France
Marie-Christine Hubert

IV. The Bulgarian Romanies during the Second World War
Elena Marushiakova and Veselin Popov

V. Gypsy deportations from Romania to Transnistria
1942-44 Michelle Kelso

VI. The Soviet Union and the Baltic States 1941-44: the massacre of the Gypsies Michael Zimmermann

VII. Bohemia and Moravia — two internment camps for Gypsies in the Czech lands Ctibor Necas

Chapter   I   translated from Italian by Donald Kenrick
Chapter   II   translated from German by Donald Kenrick
Chapter   III translated from French by Sinéad ní Shuinear
Chapter   IV   translated from Bulgarian by Donald Kenrick
Chapter   VI   translated from German by Donald Kenrick
Chapter   VII translated from Czech by Vera Taslova
Chapter   VIII translated from German by Donald Kenrick

Introduction

This second volume deals with the persecution of the Romanies and Sinti in some of the countries occupied by Germany and by its fascist allies.

In Italy there was, in fact, little centralised action against the Romanies until Berlin took direct control of their governments. We look in depth at Italy and also, later, at Bulgaria where Hitler's demands to hand over its Jewish population were resisted and measures against the Gypsies were confined to sporadic internment in labour camps.

As we saw in the first volume similar – if not harsher – measures against the Gypsies had been introduced in Austria after its annexation by Germany. The second chapter deals in more detail with the internment camp at Lackenbach.

After the declaration of war by Britain and France the German army turned its attention towards the west. Belgium, Holland and France fell by the middle of 1940.

The policy in Belgium and Holland was to be the arrest and despatch to Auschwitz of the small number of nomadic Romanies and Sinti together with such sedentaries as could be found without great effort. Belgium and Holland were seen as ripe for aryanisation and eventual incorporation as second-class countries within a German Empire.

France was a different matter. Its main role seems to have been as a provider of slave labour for the munitions factories in Germany and a place for rest and recreation for German officers. The continued internment of nomads could be seen as a security rather than a racist measure though, had the war continued, they may well have followed the Jews through Drancy on their way to extermination in the east. The third chapter is devoted to the internment camps in France.

The political changes in eastern Europe have made it possible for new research on Romania, about which comparatively little has previously been published. We can now get a more detailed picture of the mass deportations to territory annexed from the occupied Soviet Union.

Next in this volume we look at the so-called Operation Barbarossa, when in 1941 Germany attacked the Soviet Union. The killing of Gypsies alongside Jews was one of the priorities of the operation, even as the Nazi army moved forward. Documentation from this area is still thin but there is enough for our contributor to be able to give a picture of the massacres and their perpetrators.

To conclude we turn to Czechoslovakia which had been dismembered and finally occupied by the German army in March 1939. A large part of the long-established Romany community was placed in internment camps in what they had thought to be their own country, prior to deportation to Auschwitz. These camps are described by Ctibor Necas in an article largely based on Czech documentary sources.

The selection of topics in this second volume has again aimed to illustrate the various policies of internment, deportation and murder with in-depth studies, rather than to attempt to cover every aspect of the persecution.*

A chronological table has been included to show the framework of the whole Nazi era.

Donald Kenrick

---

* A concise history of the fate of the Gypsies in the Nazi period throughout Europe can be found in the *Interface* volume *Gypsies under the Swastika* by Donald Kenrick and Grattan Puxon.

I. Gypsies in Italy during the Fascist dictatorship and the Second World War

Giovanna Boursier

The amount of information gathered about the destiny of the Gypsies during the Fascist period (1922-45) and during the Second World War in Italy is still sparse and incomplete: no specific works dedicated to this subject as yet exist.

General information can be found in books by Vittorio Giuntella[1] and, more recently, Loredana Narciso.[2] They devote some space to the persecution of the Gypsies during the Second World War but make no particular reference to the Italian situation. Some interesting documentation has indeed been collected over the years by the magazine *Lacio Drom*, published by the Centro Studi Zingari of Rome. The president, Mirella Karpati, the only person who has studied the problem of the Gypsies' internment in Italy, has also been engaged with a new work which furnishes interesting ideas for further study.[3] Also Annamaria Masserini published a book that offers a good stimulus for further research.[4]

The question of race

In Italian historical writing the tendency still persists today to support the idea that the Italian Fascists were milder than the German Nazis and that the policies

13

of the Mussolini regime were a sort of surrogate or appendix to Hitler's and that the Italians cannot therefore be accused in the same way as the Germans. Similarly, it is held that the race laws of 1938 were not those of the Nazis, that many Italians acted to hide and save the persecuted Jews and that Mussolini was obliged to follow Hitler's policy, although with a less harsh approach.

In reality Fascism did tackle the question of race and racial policy which became severe when applied to the Jews.[5]

Even though it was not until September 1938 that the Gran Consiglio of Fascism[6] voted in favour of the race laws, Mussolini had said in a speech to the Party as early as the end of 1921 – some time before the Fascist Party took power:[7]

"I want to make it clear that Fascism is dealing with the problem of race. Fascists must occupy themselves with the health of the race which moulds history".[8]

This was – I reaffirm – well before Hitler came into power in Germany.

During the war in Africa the regime was already dealing with the issue of the mulattos. In this context, for example, the Royal Ordinance of April 19th 1937 defined *madamato* (relationship with African women) as being an offence against the purity and the prestige of the Italian race.

On July 14th 1938 the *Giornale d'Italia* published the "Manifesto on Race" by the race scientists in which the existence of human races was clearly affirmed. This was preceded, a few days earlier, by an appeal by the Fascist Medical Union inviting the government to use racial discrimination for "defence against the invasion of foreign professionals". In August there appeared the first issue of *La difesa della Razza* (The Defence of the Race), a racist and anti-Semitic bi-monthly directed by Telesio Interlandi.

On September 1st 1938, with the promulgation of the racial laws, foreign Jews were expelled from Italy and Jews naturalised after 1918 had their citizenship revoked. Moreover, they were excluded from attending secondary state schools while, in the primary schools, they were collected together in special classes. At the same time the Consiglio superiore per la demografia e la razza (Higher council for demography and race), the Tribunale della razza (Race Tribunal) and the Commissione per la discriminazione (Commission for Discrimination) were established.

In October, Mussolini, in the Party Order Sheet, published a signed text entitled *Declaration regarding Race* which follows the Proposals studied by the Fascist University under the guidance of the Ministry for Popular Culture.[9] It reads:

"The Supreme Council states the present urgency of the racial problems and the necessity for racial consciousness following the conquest of the Empire, and further states that Fascism is, and has been for sixteen years, taking positive action directed

14

towards the quantitative and qualitative improvement of the Italian Race, an improvement which could be gravely compromised with inestimable political consequences, by interbreeding and bastardisation. The problem of the Jews is no more than the metropolitan aspect of a problem of a more general nature."

On November 10th 1938 a further anti-Semitic law, *Measures for the defence of the Italian Race*, was issued: it prohibited mixed marriages, expelled Jews from military service, from public office, from the civil service and subjected them to severe restrictions with regard to economic activities.

Racial policy therefore, also existed in Italy: it is necessary to determine whether, and to what extent, the Gypsies were subject to it.

The Gypsy question in the first years of Fascism

From a legislative point of view at least the Gypsies did not seem to fall within the purview of the racial activities of Fascism. It is quite significant (especially if the Italian situation is compared with that in Germany) that the laws which affected the Gypsies were those concerned with public order, the prevention of criminality and keeping the rules and orders of the State.

It is useful here to remember that little is known about Gypsies in Italy before the Second World War. A small amount of data has been collected by different organisations: the one thing that is certain is that there were Gypsies living in Italy.[10] It remains very difficult to establish the exact number of them at the beginning of the twentieth century because the registers of births mentioning them date only from after the First World War. Anyway, we know that they were to be found everywhere – as we can see also from the Fascist documents concerning them which describe the Gypsies as travelling without fixed residence and begging. In fact, the Romanies in central Italy and the South practised limited nomadism within one region, while seeking work. The Sinti in the North practised nomadism over a wider area, as they worked in the circus business.

To clarify the Fascist way of thinking about the question of Gypsies it may be useful to recall the directives issued in 1926 by the Ministry of the Interior to the town halls and police superintendents, dictated by motives of "public safety and public hygiene". The one dated February 19th mentions the presence of "an infiltration of Gypsies devoted to vagrancy and begging... an infiltration which has occurred recently due to obvious neglect by the offices of Public Safety". These Gypsies were obliged to respect the laws in force at that time, laws which prevented "the Gypsies, acrobats or similar, in groups or individually, from entering our country even if in possession of a valid passport" and ordered "returning to the frontier, as quickly as possible, any foreign Gypsies on Italian territory".

On August 8th the Ministry for the Interior reaffirmed its intention

"to purge the country of the groups of Gypsies, the danger of which it is superfluous to mention with regard to public safety and hygiene due to their characteristic style of life; and to strike at the very heart of the Gypsy organism, repelling the caravans accompanied by the usual entourage of animals, carts and chattels and only allowing transit to those in possession of visas issued by the consulates of the states through which they have passed and that of their destination, and providing indications that the journey will be contained within previously defined time limits and itineraries."

It must be noted that these measures concern "foreign" Gypsies. In reality, if we take into consideration the fact that the Second World War and the emergencies which it presented were still far off, the initial intentions of the Fascist regime with regard to the Gypsies can be seen: rejection and discrimination. In fact, the expressions "purge the country of the groups of Gypsies" and, further on in the announcement, "to strike at the very heart of the Gypsy organism" were used.

The change in 1940

The racial laws of 1938 do not mention Gypsies as such. Among the *Measures relating to Marriages*, even though it was stated that "the marriage of Italian citizens of Aryan race to persons belonging to other races is prohibited" and that "the marriages celebrated in conflict with this prohibition are null", the Gypsies are not specifically mentioned.

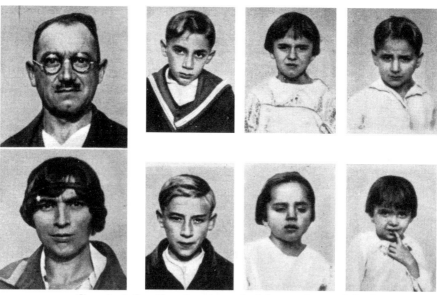

Gypsies' family photographs' from the article by Landra
in "La difesa della razza" (November 1940).

In the political dictionary published by the Fascist Party in 1940, under the entry 'Race' the Gypsies appear only in reference to the measures taken by the Nazis in Germany and, in particular, to the Nuremberg Laws.[11]

However, in November 1940, in the magazine *La difesa della razza*, an article signed by Guido Landra (director of the Race Studies and Propaganda Office) appears, dealing with the "problem of half-breeds in Europe" and pointing out the "dangers of interbreeding with Gypsies whose tendency to vagrancy and thieving are well known". Landra provides his work with many photographs of "half-breeds", among which are eleven which he describes as "Gypsies of almost pure race" and two "typical Gypsy families". He concludes by asking that steps must be taken against "these eternal vagabonds, wholly devoid of any sense of morals".[12] This is, undoubtedly, a racist point of view.

The end of 1940 seems to be the moment at which the "Gypsy Question" is given more attention by the Fascist regime. This attitude is probably also tied to the events of that time: Italy, reinforcing its alliance with Germany, had officially entered the war in June.

In May 1936 guidelines had been established for the creation of internment camps in Italy and in June 1938 "specifications for concentration camps and places of internment" were set out for the arrest of dangerous persons, both Italian and foreign, who were considered likely to disturb public order and to commit sabotage or assaults. Then, in May 1940 Arturo Bocchini, Chief of Police, sent a letter to the town halls in which he gave orders to intern, besides the foreign Jews, also Italian ones who were considered likely to undertake sabotage or spying. In September new orders extended the internment to all who were considered as enemies of the State, defined as follows: idlers, tramps, black market traffickers, and, above all, anti-Fascists and Jews. It also recommended interning them far from military or strategic centres and it asked the town halls to find suitable places.[13] As we will see now this becomes particularly interesting if compared with the orders concerning Gypsies of the same period: it must in fact be noted that in Italy, until 1943, belonging to the Jewish race was not a condition sufficient to warrant arrest, unless linked to a social danger.

Orders covering Italian Gypsies

On September 11th 1940 the first provisions were issued for the internment of the Italian Gypsies.

A circular sent by telegram from the Ministry of the Interior and signed by Bocchini to the town halls of the Kingdom explicitly refers to the internment of the Italian Gypsies, taking it almost for granted that the foreign ones must be refused entry or expelled. It said that:

Ba.

Mod. 840

Ministero dell'Interno

DIREZIONE GENERALE DELLA PUBBLICA SICUREZZA
Divisione Polizia - Sezione Terza

C O P I A del telegramma circolare n.63462/IO, in data 11 settembre I940, diretto Prefetti Regno et Questore Roma.

63462.IO- Con richiamo circolare telegrafica 11 giugno ultimo
n.IO.44509 concernente zingari et carri zingareschi comunicasi
che da segnalazioni pervenute risulta che zingari pur agendo
specialmente nei territori provincie confine sono sparsi anche
altre provincie Regno punto Sia perchè essi commettono talvolta
delitti gravi per natura intrinseca et modalità organizzazione
et esecuzione sia per possibilità che tra medesimi vi siano elementi capaci esplicare attività antinazionale virgola est indispen-
sabile che tutti zingari siano controllati dato che in istato liber
tà essi riescono facilmente sfuggire ricerche aut prove appunto
per loro vita girovaga punto Ferme restando disposizioni impartite
in precedenza circa respingimento aut espulsione zingari stranieri
disponesi che quelli nazionalità italiana certa aut presunta ancora
in circolazione vengano rastrellati più breve tempo possibile et
concentrati sotto rigorosa vigilanza in località meglio adatta
ciascuna provincia che sia lontana da fabbriche aut depositi esplo-
sivi aut comunque da opere interesse militare et dove non esistano
concentramenti di truppa virgola salvo proporre per elementi più
pericolosi aut sospetti destinazione in isola aut in Comuni altre
provincie lontane da zone frontiera aut interesse militare punto
At zingari capi famiglia potrà essere corrisposto sussidio stabili-
to per confinati comuni più una lira per ciascun componente famiglia se non potranno sostenersi con proventi lavoro come praticato-
si per quelli già assegnati at confino et seguiti da famigliari
punto Attendesi urgente assicurazione per lettera

PEL MINISTRO
F.to   Bocchini

September 11th 1940 (internment of Italian Gypsies).

"...due to the fact that they sometimes commit serious crimes because of their innate nature and methods of organisation and due to the possibility that among them there are elements capable of carrying out anti-national activities, it is indispensable that all Gypsies are controlled... It is ordered that those of Italian nationality, either confirmed or presumed, who are still in circulation are to be rounded up as quickly as possible and concentrated under vigorous surveillance in a suitable locality in every province... far from places of military interest... apart from the more dangerous or suspicious elements who are to be sent to the islands or regions..."[14]

Even if the documentation we have is still not complete, it seems the centrally-appointed mayors carried out the order by rounding up the Gypsies who were

18

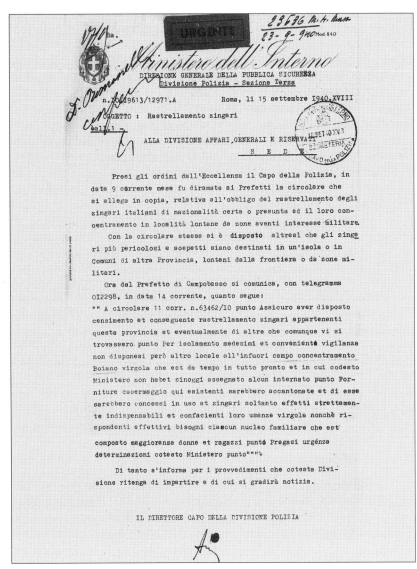

23636 M. H. Mass
23-9-940 Mod. 840

Ministero dell'Interno

DIREZIONE GENERALE DELLA PUBBLICA SICUREZZA
Divisione Polizia - Sezione Terza

n. 10/19613/12971.A   Roma, li 15 settembre 1940.XVIII

OGGETTO : Rastrellamento zingari

All.1 -

ALLA DIVISIONE AFFARI, GENERALI E RISERVATI
S E D E

Presi gli ordini dall'Eccellenza il Capo della Polizia, in data 9 corrente mese fu diramata ai Prefetti la circolare che si allega in copia, relativa all'obbligo del rastrellamento degli zingari italiani di nazionalità certa o presunta ed il loro concentramento in località lontane da zone aventi interesse militare.

Con la circolare stessa si è disposto altresì che gli zingari più pericolosi e sospetti siano destinati in un'isola o in Comuni di altra Provincia, lontani dalla frontiera o da zone militari.

Ora dal Prefetto di Campobasso si comunica, con telegramma 012298, in data 14 corrente, quanto segue:

"" A circolare 11 corr. n.63462/10 punto Assicuro aver disposto censimento et conseguente rastrellamento zingari appartenenti questa provincia et eventualmente di altre che comunque vi si trovassero punto Per isolamento medesimi et conveniente vigilanza non disponesi però altro locale all'infuori campo concentramento Boiano virgola che est da tempo in tutto pronto et in cui codesto Ministero non habet sinoggi assegnato alcun internato punto Forniture casermaggio qui esistenti sarebbero accantonate et di esse sarebbero concessi in uso at zingari soltanto effetti strettamente indispensabili et confacienti loro usanze virgola nonchè rispondenti effettivi bisogni ciascun nucleo familiare che est composto maggioranza donne et ragazzi punto Pregasi urgenza determinazioni cotesto Ministero punto"""

Di tanto s'informa per i provvedimenti che cotesta Divisione ritenga di impartire e di cui si gradirà notizia.

IL DIRETTORE CAPO DELLA DIVISIONE POLIZIA

September 15th 1940 (Boiano camp).

found in their provinces. We have letters and telegrams from the competent authorities of Aosta, Ascoli Piceno, Bolzano, Campobasso, Ferrara, Trieste, Udine and, in a somewhat less direct way, Verona, who, answering the order, demonstrate that everywhere the Gypsies were regarded as a problem which was becoming urgent and important.

Among all this correspondence that of Campobasso seems to be the most complete. It is an interesting document because it confirms, in spite of its conclusions, at least the intention to intern Italian Gypsies.

The mayor of Campobasso answered the Ministry on September 14th assuring him that he "has arranged for the census and combing out of Gypsies resorting to this province or residing here", and suggesting as a place of isolation "the concentration camp of Boiano".[15] From the second part of the letter we can understand that a detention place had just been prepared at Boiano, but – as we can deduce from the entire correspondence – not for Gypsies. On the 25th of the same month a telegram from the Ministry referring again to "the concentration camp of Boiano" asks if there is any free place to put caravans and other "interned" Gypsies' property.[16] The correspondence between the Ministry, the Mayor of Campobasso and Panariello – the General Inspector of Public Safety of Naples – continues, with them all intending to use Boiano for the detention of Gypsies. In a confidential letter on October 1st 1940 Panariello describes the place:

"The camp can be used for the internment of Gypsies. It was thought that, for that purpose, there was sufficient space for 250 prisoners. But, (considering the way Gypsies live) I have worked out that the capacity could be 300."

Despite all this, on October 6th 1940, an urgent letter from the Ministry of the Interior, to the local Police Division, informs them that Boiano cannot be used as a concentration camp for Gypsies, as it is required for other prisoners. Two days later the Ministry conveyed this in writing to the Mayor.[17] From other documents, too, we see that Italian Gypsies were to be arrested and persecuted.

On September 20th a letter from the Ministry for the Interior, dealing with the Gypsies present in the province of Udine, cites an earlier letter of the 16th from the Mayor of Udine noting that the town is located near the border and confirming that the combing out of Gypsies has been organised. He requests that "the Gypsies be removed from circulation and be sent to another province".[18]

On the same day (September 16th), the town hall of Ferrara sent the Ministry a letter which had as its subject a "Gypsy convoy led by Campanelli Giovanni, born in Gradisca di Vipacco on June 24th 1888". The prefecture points out that, in the suburbs of the city, a party of coppersmiths' had been traced, "composed of the individual in question, three women and seven children" who have been "transferred to the town of Berra, chosen for the concentration of the vagrant Italian Gypsies in the territory of this province". This place was chosen on the basis that it is "far from objects of military interest and from troop concentrations."[19] The following day another letter refers to a second coppersmiths' convoy of caravans led by Paolo Negovetic and composed of seven Italians and six Yugoslavs. The mayor, referring again to the order of September 1940, writes that, while the expulsion of the foreigners has been ordered, the Italians have been transferred to Berra, a little parish near Ferrara.

On September 17th the mayor of Ascoli Piceno writes that he has "stopped ten Gypsies, among them four children, all from Teramo and Chieti provinces, except for one who is without a fixed abode but part of the same convoy".

Considering the majority of Gypsies come from Abruzzo, the Mayor also asks the Ministry of the Interior to consider the possibility of authorising the establishment in this zone of a Gypsy concentration camp "to collect these and other Gypsies who might be stopped". Four days later, on the 21st, there is another urgent letter about "Gypsies stopped in Ascoli Piceno" that confirms the presence of nomads.

On September 22nd an urgent letter points out that in Aosta "three male Gypsies, two women and thirteen boys have been stopped" and asks, considering that this is a border place, what to do.[20] The men have been arrested. Their names are: La Fleur Matteo, Giovenale Oberto and La Fleur Natale, all of Italian nationality. Some days later the Mayor again asks what to do with these three men and the caravans.[21]

The same attitude of stopping and interning Italian Gypsies is shown by the town hall of Bolzano on September 23rd when, trying to identify right places for the internment of Gypsies, it reports that thirteen are in prison.

On September 28th also, the mayor of Trieste writes about Gypsies, informing the Ministry that two Gypsy women with four children have been arrested. The women, Apollonia Cari and Anna Caris, are described as people travelling in the country around Trieste, living without fixed residence and begging. Anna also receives a government pension: 1,760 Italian lire a year.[22]

Since on November 2nd 1940 the mayor of Verona wrote to the Ministry asking if the subsidies for prisoners' relatives are to extend also to Gypsies, we know there were Gypsies interned in Verona.

The combing out operations continued after 1940, at least in some places. On April 17th 1941 the mayor of Udine writes that on the 8th of that month three Gypsies, Giovanni Hudorovic, Caterina Bredic and Luigia Hudorovic, with her four children, were arrested and suggests, as they are "socially dangerous elements", interning them in a concentration camp. He suggests the same about eight others, all arrested on April 9th 1941.[23]

A similar deduction must be made about the correspondence referring to Gypsies arrested near Trieste on March 30th 1941. This is documented by two letters, one from the Office of Public Safety, dated April 13th 1941, and one from the Ministry of Interior to Trieste town hall. The first tells about five Gypsies arrested, one named Karis and all the others, including two children, Hudorovic. All had been imprisoned and were waiting for the answer of the Ministry before being interned, with the exception of Francesco Hudorovic who has been sent to Trieste's Military Police as he must perform military service.[24] The second, from the Ministry to the Mayor, asks if Francesco Hudorovic is still awaiting call-up for military service or if it is necessary to arrange for his internment.[25]

As we will soon see, these last documents could also be connected to the increasing presence of Gypsies in Italy since the occupation of Yugoslavia, which forced many to leave that country.

However, we will conclude this section by noting that a further letter was drawn up, dated April 27th 1941, by the Ministry for the Interior which again deals with the subject "Italian Gypsies – Internment."[26]

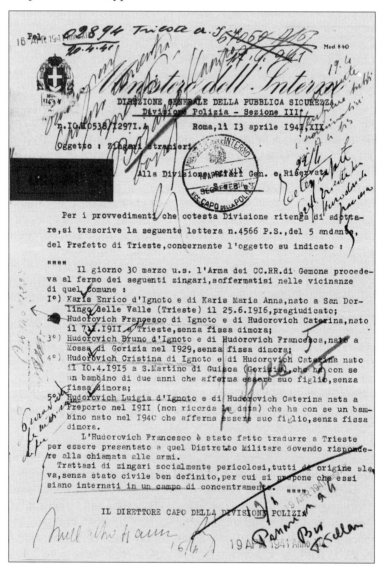

April 13th 1941 (Trieste, proposal for internment). Letter from the mayor of Trieste with the list of Gypsies arested on March 30th 1941, near the town.

Internment

Information about the existence of internment or concentration camps for Gypsies in Italy – Perdasdefogu in Sardinia, the monastery of San Bernardino in Agnone, Tossicia in the Province of Teramo – comes mainly from the first-hand testimonies of Gypsies.[27]

Rosa Raidic says:

"My daughter Lalla was born in Sardinia at Perdasdefogu on January 7th 1943, because we were there in a concentration camp"

while Mitzi Herzemberg narrates:

"During the war we were in a concentration camp at Perdasdefogu. We were terribly hungry. One day, I don't know how, a chicken got into the camp. I threw myself on it like a fox and I killed it and ate it raw through sheer hunger. They beat me and I got six months in prison for the theft."[28]

The Centro Studi Zingari possesses a copy of a letter from the Police Superintendent of Fiume concerning another Gypsy named Hudorovic.[29] Following a request for information about Giovanni Hudorovic – born in 1913 in Rudnik, Yugoslavia, and later resident at Fontana del Conte in Italy – drawn up by the VIIIth Army Group on September 13th 1940, and passed on by the Town Hall of Fiume, the Police Superintendent replied:

"Hudorovic Giovanni... Gypsy, conducted himself well in general and has no criminal or political record. The Hudorovic family was interned in Sardinia in 1938 following the well-known round-up of Gypsies."

Levakovich, born in 1902 in Croatia, but living a long time in Italy, writes that during the spring of 1938 he received a letter from his wife's sister in which she recounted that all the nomads without work had been sent by Mussolini to concentration camps in the South of Italy, to Teramo, and to Calabria and Sardinia.[30]

At Agnone the Gypsies were confined in the convent of San Bernardino. Giuseppe Goman remembers that sometimes the men were taken outside to dig holes for mines to slow up the Allied advance. The Fascist guards behaved with ferocity, inflicting severe punishment on the prisoners. Giuseppe, who at the time was only fourteen, worked in the kitchen and tried to pass food to his parents. He was taken out to be shot with some other prisoners. Fortunately, at the last minute his sentence was converted to a beating and a period of imprisonment.[31]

The allied advance and German occupied territory.

Zlato Levak's testimony confirms this:

"In Italy we were in a concentration camp... with almost no food. I was at Campobasso, with my family. There were many of us... there were also Italian Gypsies from the North near Austria... It was bad there, too. We were in a convent, all closed, with guards around like in prison. There was a Gypsy cook; but what did they give us to eat? Almost nothing. We were there almost two years. My eldest son died in the camp. He was a good painter and was very intelligent."[32]

Further to these accounts about Agnone, we have Zilka Heldt's story, quoted below, less tragic perhaps, but which nevertheless confirms what conditions were like for those who suffered internment.[33]

Those dealing with the problem of the internment of the Gypsies in Italy have generally maintained that it is probable that discrimination affected above all the foreign Gypsies present within the confines of Italy and that this was for reasons of public order: they write that it was probably the occupation of Yugoslavia and the consequent escape of many Gypsies from that country to Italy which forced the Italian authorities to intern Gypsies for security reasons.

24

It is clear that the measures taken for the persecution of Gypsies increased and became more severe following the occupation of Yugoslavia – if only because it was from there that many Gypsies escaped to Italy after the Nazi-Fascist occupation, seeking refuge and safety. We may also conclude that the internment measures for the Gypsies came to a head in 1941, when Ljubljana and its territory became part of the Kingdom of Italy and, as Masserini reports, it was no longer "tolerable that, in the new self-governing national entity, the depressing sight of travelling nomads, beggars and thieves continues".

It has been reported that the Italian authorities used to help escaping Gypsies, for example, by issuing them with documents. We can find such a story in the eye witness account of Zilka Heldt who told how Italians helped her and other Gypsies to escape from fascist persecution in Yugoslavia. Zilka, who was ten years old, reached first Ljubljana with her family, then Tolmino, where Italian authorities gave them documents. The problem was that Gypsies continued trying to go back into Yugoslavia to find and save their relatives. The consequence was that Italians deported them to near Campobasso, in an ancient monastery, where Zilka says they lived quite well; during the day they could go out to look for food. When the Allies arrived (1943), after a bombing raid in which Zilka's parents died, some of the interned Gypsies, including Zilka, fled towards the north.[34]

Rave Hudorovic, too, who, before the war, had worked with horses in Yugoslavia told how he had fled from the fascist Ustasha by hiding among the Italians near Ljubljana. He says:

"One day we were stopping at a place, Rasuplje it's called, and the Italians arrived. We were a large group of Sinti, fifty people... they came in lorries and said: "Get ready we are going to Ljubljana". Everyone prepared his bundle and off we went. We were happy, why not?... In Ljubljana they put us together with many others. We were in Ljubljana for a week and then we went by train to Tossicia near Teramo. I don't remember exactly which month it was, but it was the summer, maybe July. We stayed at Tossicia for eighteen months. Anton was small... At Tossicia all the Sinti were together. Even if it was a concentration camp, it was like a village. They gave us food and clothes and we slept indoors as if in barracks. At that time the people of the town were good to us. There were a few police here and there were guards but we were not locked up."[35]

In his story Giuseppe Levakovic tells of his escape from Yugoslavia together with other relatives.[36] It is an interesting testimony because it offers a somewhat different description of the life of the Gypsies in Italy during the war to the preceding one. Levakovic escaped and could not rest anywhere: first he was in Friuli, then in Veneto, and then in Ferrara and Bologna. As he was entering Pistoia two police stopped him to check his documents:

"A warrant-officer came in the evening accompanied by a policeman and checked the documents again. He recognised me as a nomad and asked me the reason why I was not in the concentration camp... At Foligno, for the first time in the whole trip, I met a family of Gypsies who spoke my language. The head of the family... told me that there was a concentration camp for Gypsies at Teramo... we moved on to Teramo where we stayed..."

After numerous contacts with interned Gypsies, one day, escorted by a policeman, Levakovic obtained permission to visit the camp:

"The Gypsies held there lived under terrible conditions, in huts, and they slept on the floor. There was little food and it was rationed but fortunately the lieutenant allowed the elder women to go to mang(beg) in the bordering towns... There were half-naked children in a miserable state."

Levakovic's journey kept pace with the war. Once again he went to Trieste:

"That was where I first realised that the Germans respected nobody...Everyone spoke about this, all had brothers or fathers who had been sent to Germany and this made me understand the situation even more clearly."

During his continual journey from one place to another Levakovic met the partisans and narrates his activities in the Osoppo Brigade and of the leader, Commander Lupo, who, hearing himself called boss had asked us peremptorily "to call him comrade and not boss".

In addition to the eyewitness reports and in contrast to the situation regarding other camps, for which documentation is still very scarce and contradictory, Tossicia is the only camp for which relatively certain datas exist. The papers and documents in the communal archives state that it was operative from October 21st 1940, set up for Jews, stateless people, and, 116 Chinese travelling tie salesmen. From the summer of 1942 there were also Gypsies. On May 12th of that year, in fact, the Ministry for the Interior ordered the Chinese to be transferred to the Isola del Gran Sasso to allow space for the Gypsies.

The conditions in the camp give us an idea of the general situation in these camps. The manager of the camp and the health officer complained in 1942 that the situation, which was already absolutely unbearable, had degenerated even further with the arrival of the nomads:

"The number of different elements in the colony at Tossicia is more than just deplorable. Whereas before, the camp was composed only of civilised citizens, today there are naked Gypsies who, due to their mentality, do not seem European nor even of our time. But more than this the women with their incorrigible ignorance and their numerous children love the chaos. But the thing which worries me personally more than anything is the lack of toilet facilities."[37]

In August 1942 a list of the interned Gypsies given a daily allowance, which varied between one and seven lire, was compiled: 107 people, mainly belonging to the Hudorovic extended family, followed by the Levakovic's and Brajdic's as well as nine children born between August 1942 and September 1943, eight

Rivista Abruzzese di studi storici
dal fascismo alla Resistenza
Anno VI N. 1

Tossicia concentration camp
List of subsidied Gypsies in August 1942

Hudorovic Giovanni
Hudorovic Francesco
Hudorovic Francesca
Hudorovic Ida
Hudorovic Peppino
Hudorovic Frida
Hudorovic Carlo
Hudorovic Silvestro
Hudorovic Giovanni
Hudorovic Dora
Hudorovic Milan
Hudorovic Hazi
Hudorovic Giuseppe
Hudorovic Dora
Hudorovic Antonio
Hudorovic Carlo
Hudorovic Antonio
Levakovic Lisca
Levakovic Rodolfo
Levakovic Anna
Levakovic Bogomil
Levakovic Mirco
Levakovic Elena
Levakovic Amalia
Levakovic Edeva
Levakovic Giuseppe
Levakovic Luigi
Levakovic Luigia
Levakovic Maria
Levakovic Misca
Brajdic Francesco
Brajdic Francesca
Brajdic Aloisio
Hudorovic Michele
Brajdic Angela
Hudorovic Olga
Hudorovic Pola
Hudorovic Ida
Hudorovic Minica
Brajdic Carlo
Hudorovic Maria
Brajdic Benito
Brajdic Stefano
Brajdic Felice
Brajdic Giovanni
Brajdic Zilca
Hudorovic Stefano
Brajdic Olga
Brajdic Giulio
Hudorovic Emma
Brajdic Marian
Brajdic Antonetta

Levakovic Michele
Hudorovic Caterina
Levakovic Francesco
Levakovic Antonio
Levakovic Giovanni
Levakovic Tencka
Levakovic Giuseppe
Levakovic Sonia
Hudorovic Matteo
Hudorovic Zora
Hudorovic Stefania
Hudorovic Teme
Hudorovic Luisa
Hudorovic Vittorio
Hudorovic Maria
Hudorovic Antonia
Hudorovic Angela
Hudorovic Lorenzo
Hudorovic Stanko
Hudorovic Stefania
Hudorovic Antonio
Hudorovic Francesca
Hudorovic Antonio
Hudorovic Maria
Hudorovic Antonio
Hudorovic Giovanna
Hudorovic Albina
Hudorovic Ignazio
Hudorovic Giuseppe
Hudorovic Antonio
Hudorovic Rodolfo
Hudorovic Mario
Hudorovic Antonio
Hudorovic Angela
Hudorovic Antonio
Rajhard Pietro
Rajhard Sinchiumiro
Rajhard Antonio
Rajhard Sofia
Hudorovic Angela
Malovac Ovetka
Malovac Justa
Malovac Maria
Malovac Angela
Malovac Olga
Malovac Elcha
Hudorovic Slaker
Hudorovic Zorka
Hudorovic Orelia
Hudorovic Lorenza
Hudorovic Ivana

Gypsies born in Tossicia in 1942-43

	Date of birth
Hudorovic Benito di Lorenzo e Ivana Hudorovic	11. 08. 1942
Hudorovic Orelia di Slates e Zeraglia Hudorovic	19. 08. 1942
Hudorovic Orlanda di Antonio e Maria Hudorovic	07. 09. 1972
Hudorovic Maria di Stefano e Olga Brajdic	28. 10. 1942
Levakovic Stefania di Michele e Caterina Levakovic	02. 12. 1942
Hudorovic Emma di Michele et Angela Brajdic	10. 12. 1942
Hudorovic Pasquale di Antonio e Luisa Levakovic	22. 04. 1943
Hudorovic Carlo di Giovanni e Angela Hudorovic	05. 09. 1943
Hudorovic Maria di Carlo e Stefania Hudorovic	06. 09. 1943

List of interned Gypsies from "Rivista abruzzese di Studi Storici".

Hudorovic and one Levakovic.[38] Following the liberation, the surviving Gypsies fled. From a report by the warrant-officer of the police at Podestà of September 27th 1943 it is known that survivors fled heading north, "making no noise because none had shoes". In the last months it seems that there were no variations in the number of interned Gypsies: there were 118 on June 23rd 1943 and 119 three months later, perhaps due to the birth of a child.

One of the most revealing testimonies, though short, is that of Antonio Hudorovic:

"Once, when we were at Tossicia, a German official came. He measured us, even our heads. He said that it was so that they could give us a suit and a hat."[39]

Sporadic testimonies mention other places of detention: Celeste Casamonica, in a recent interview, says she was deported with her family to Pieve, a little village near Viterbo, "in a big house where we spent a terrible time". She remembers a morning of September 1943, "when we got up and saw there were three or four military lorries... They were Fascists as they spoke Italian and wore black shirts... They were looking for Gypsies... just Gypsies. They said we should get in a lorry and they took us to a little town near Viterbo, Pieve, about twenty kilometres from Viterbo. We were there five months."[40]

Pasqualina Di Rocco narrates that there were many Gypsies at Montopoli Sabina, while Silvio Di Rocco was at Collefiorito near Foligno. Thulo Reinhardt says that he was deported with his family and other gachkané Sinti to the Tremiti Islands.

The presence of Gypsies in camps not specifically set up for them is also mentioned: places like Poggio Mirteto near Rieti, or Ferramonti di Tarsia, in the province of Cosenza, that existed from July 1940 to September 1943 and was one of the biggest Italian concentration camps. From the register of the camp, we know that on June 22nd 1943 eight Gypsies coming from Viterbo were imprisoned: they were the Kwik and Philipoff families, with their children, born in Italy. On May 26th 1944, twenty-two Gypsies are noted leaving the camp, perhaps the Kwiks and Philipoffs with their relatives.[41]

This is also independently confirmed by a certificate (still in the possession of the family) from the Commissariat for Public Safety of the Cosenza Police Superintendent's office dated October 31st 1943 which reads:

"This is to certify that Miss Philipoff Kwik... and Philipoff George, born 10/3/1922 and 1/6/1914... in Italy by order of the Italian Ministry of the Interior were interned from June 21st 1943 to September 3rd 1943 in the concentration camp of Ferramonti-Tarsia (province of Cosenza). The internment ceased in accordance with Art. 3 of the Armistice Convention between the Allied Powers and the Kingdom of Italy of September 3rd 1943."

Also, since we now know that the Philipoffs were not Italians, it is interesting that the Italian authorities apparently registered the internment of two Gypsies "born in Italy". In reality they were Anna Kwik, born 1922 in Warsaw, and George Philipoff, born 1914 in Southend on Sea (England), who had at that time two children, Paula, born in Messina in 1939, and Joseph, born in Tuscany in 1940. They could also have been among the Gypsies leaving Ferramonti on May 1944 as we see, in another document, this time from the British Consulate of Bari, dated February 21st 1945. George Philipoff wanted a passport and obtained a substitute one as the first, "issued – the document says – by the British consulate on March 2nd 1937 and in which was included his wife, Mrs Anna Kwik Philipoff... was taken from Mr Philipoff... for (sic) his internment". Italian Gypsies were also deported to Austria. On November 1st 1941 the entry registers of Lackenbach camp indicate twenty Italian Gypsies coming via Innsbruck whose prisoner numbers ranged from 2518 to 2537.

After the Armistice of September 1943

On the basis of the conditions of the Armistice of September 8th 1943, signed between Italy and the Allies, many camps in southern Italy were closed and Gypsies then fled, spreading out over the mountains and, in some cases, joining up with the partisans.

Amilcare Debar — 48th Garibaldi Brigade, 1944.

Amilcare Debar on the mountain.

Amilcare Debar told of having been a dispatch-rider in the area around Cuneo:

"The Fascists captured me and put me to the wall with eighteen partisans. At the last moment the order was given to let me go. I escaped to the mountains where I stayed with the partisans until the end of the war."[42]

Walter Catter was hanged as a partisan in Vicenza. His cousin had died just before in a guerrilla action in Liguria: he was twenty years old. "His father went up there and found him dead in the mud and carried him step by step to the cemetery on his shoulders."

Giacomo Sacco, a Sinto Gypsy, who died in 1988, left this testimony:

"They captured me together with another seventeen people while I was going to mangel. At the Turchino pass the partisans freed us. I saw the partisans' desire to end the abuse by the Fascists so I decided to stay and fight for the liberation of Genoa. I was the only Gypsy in the entire brigade but it was pleasant because we had a common ideal, that of fighting the Fascist and Nazi forces occupying our country. It was hard to maintain contact with my family... we were almost always in the mountains. My work consisted in riding with dispatches between one group and another. Later I learnt of another Sinto man living in the mountains who may have been a chief because he directed the attack operations. All our work was directed to preparing the offensive which took place from April 25th to May 15th in Genoa... only thirteen of us managed to survive... The period in which I was a partisan was very important because I took part in the liberation of Italy... If I had to I would do the same again, even at the cost of risking my life."[43]

This did not mean the story of the deportation of Gypsies was finished. Even though the camps in southern Italy were dismantled by the Allies entering Italy, those in the occupied North were put into operation at that time as places for collection and transit to camps in Germany.

Arcangelo Morelli, a Gypsy man from Abruzzo, was tortured in the mental hospital of Aquila, which had been transformed into the Gestapo headquarters. We know also about Gries near Bolzano, that existed from August 1944 to April 1945, as an antechamber of the German camps, set up for anti-Fascists condemned by the Salo Republic.[44] A partisan, Laura Conti, interned at Bolzano, spoke about "children imprisoned in that camp, coming almost exclusively from Gypsy, Jewish or Slav families" and "male and female Gypsies who spoke only their own tongue, which made it therefore difficult to get information about them."[45] In the same camp of Bolzano a Gypsy Sinti woman, Edvige Mayer, was also imprisoned. She also died there. This is confirmed by her two brothers Viktor and Franz who succeeded in surviving the war as soldiers in the German army by hiding their origins.[46]

We know from Levakovic about some Gypsies who arrived in German camps in this period: Levakovic's wife, Wilma, with another two Gypsy women, Muja and Mitska, were deported to Ravensbrück and from there to Dachau.[47]

Conclusion

The history of the persecution of the Gypsies in Italy during the Second World War has for the most part still to be written.

It is, moreover, difficult to follow the story because of the lack of documentation and because research is just beginning.

Current research into the sources do not supply us with sufficient information to enable us to fully understand the reason for the persecution of Gypsies by Fascists and, consequently, what would have been the future for them after a victorious war within the Italian boundaries.

In particular, too little is known about the Italian Gypsies, those who had lived in Italy for almost 400 years by the time the war broke out. Somewhat more is known of the Fascist policy regarding the foreign ones who penetrated Italy. As I said above, this is partly owing to the fact that, until now, those dealing with the subject of the persecution of Gypsies during the Second World War have generally maintained that discrimination involved mainly foreign Gypsies and not Italian ones. But, considering in particular the order of September 1940 – to round up and detain the Italian Gypsies in controlled places and to continue, probably on the basis of the norms of 1926, to expel foreign Gypsies – and the further order of April 1941, we have to note here that these two orders resulted from a wish to also intern Italian Gypsies. We can, moreover, imagine, just considering the documentation here presented, that it was the general intention to persecute Gypsies all over the country, with the Ministry of Interior, town halls and police all involved.

In spite of this, we cannot yet really say if the internment of Italian Gypsies did effectively take place and, above all, to what extent. From the documents we see Gypsies were arrested but we really do not know anything about the practical organisation of the detention centres, except for Boiano, which in the end was not established as a camp for Gypsies.

The main sources where we learn of Gypsies being interned are the oral testimonies. In Levakovic's letter about his internment in 1938 there are no particular references to different nationalities; Levak explicitly says that in Agnone there were also Italian Gypsies who, at the outbreak of war, had already been living in Italy for a long time. But some others, for example Zilka Heldt, speak only about Gypsies who have arrived from Yugoslavia.

What we need now is a check, place by place and name by name, in all municipal and local archives, to find supplementary information to what we have in oral and written documents.

Correspondence in archives, if compared with oral witnesses, could also give us something else to consider: it would be interesting to find out if the names of places of internment remembered by Gypsies could be related to the written documentation about internment of Italians. For example, to find out if the Agnone mentioned by Levak could be the camp we saw the Fascist authorities try to install in Boiano, as both of these places are near Campobasso, or if Tossicia could be the concentration camp which the mayor of Ascoli Piceno asked to be installed in Abruzzo.

In our documentation names of places of detention about which absolutely nothing is known have also appeared: thus for example, in the letter from the mayor of Ferrara to the Ministry for the Interior it is stated that "the town of Berra has been chosen for the concentration of the vagrant Italian Gypsies in the province", but nothing further is known of this place. Celeste Casamonica said she was deported to a place near Viterbo but for this too we have no other data. Silvio Di Rocco was imprisoned along with his family in the concentration camp of Collefiorito near Foligno and this place too is not mentioned in written records.

Masserini writes that it is contradictory to speak of concentration camps and that the large-scale round-up of Gypsies mainly concerned foreign ones who had entered Italy illegally and were arrested only for reasons of security, deported to Sardinia but later released upon arrival there.

As far as it is possible to determine from the information available up to now it seems that already in 1938 some were indeed interned at Perdasdefogu and that, at least from the end of 1940 onwards, methodical discrimination and persecution of the Gypsies, including those from Italy itself, were practised to a certain degree. As we have seen, the occupation of Yugoslavia (April 6th 1941) and the situation which was created in Croatia in particular as a result of the creation of the Pavelic government, Artukovic's racist decrees and the Ustasha violence with the consequent flight of many Romanies towards Italy and further the annexation by Italy of most of Slovenia (May 3rd) must have caused a further control over the measures for the internment of the Gypsies in Italy. As for the hypothesis about the saving of Gypsies arriving in Italy from Yugoslavia, nothing at the moment shows the slightest intention by the Fascists centrally to protect the Gypsy people and we have not yet found any official order to confirm this attitude as being general, rather than the result of individual initiative.

The picture which emerges is one of a confused situation. The descriptions of internment also give contradictory data. With Zilka Heldt, or Rave Hudorovic, we find a description of a quite good situation, and Karpati describes Ferramonti as an "oasis of peace", but in other cases, as in the testimony of Levakovic or Levak, we find a terrible reality of detention, hunger, terror and death.

We know almost nothing about what happened after the fall of Fascism (July 25th 1943), the Nazi occupation and the constitution of the Salo Republic. As Liliana Picciotto Fargian shows, referring to Jews: "The Republic gave formal legitimacy to the extermination of the Jews, and substantial power to its police to give the Nazis the necessary help for deportations."[48]

It is probable also that we have to think about what this occupation meant for Gypsies. An important fact is the deportation of some Gypsy children to the camp of Gries at Bolzano. These internees probably ended up in the German concentration camps, victims of mass extermination by the Nazis. There can be no mitigation of guilt as the Gypsies interned in north Italy eventually reached Germany, just like the Jews, when the concentration camps were turned into antechambers to the extermination camps.

Finally, it is above all necessary to clarify whether the persecution and internment of the Gypsies in Italy was only due to reasons of public order and safety or heralded intentions of a racial nature. Some hypotheses have been put forward, supporting the first reason, maintaining that in Fascist Italy there are no grounds for the identification of a Gypsy question similar to that of the Nazis in Germany and therefore there is no reason to define the persecution of the Gypsies as racial.

Even if it is true that all that concerns the internment of Gypsies here mentioned has been found in the archives under the rubric "Public Safety", we have also to note and consider the fact that nomads are always called Gypsies (Zingari) as a well-determined category or group of persons. So in the letters from Udine town hall of 1941 we read they are to be interned as Gypsies and, for this reason, dangerous. Moreover, in the order of September 1940 it is true that one of the reasons expressed by the Ministry for their internment is that "there are elements capable of carrying out anti-national activities", for example espionage, but it is also said that "they sometimes commit serious crimes due to their innate nature and methods of organisation". And by "innate nature", as is well known, is not meant actual behaviour at all, but a predetermined fact.

So, we cannot yet be so sure that in Italy there was no racial persecution or at least such an intention. We know that in Germany, at the beginning, Gypsies were interned as 'asocial' and, for Italy too, we still need to study this problem in depth.

A final problem is to understand what campo di concentramento meant for Italy. To resolve this question we would need a general study about the reality of concentration camps in Italy, often requested by historians but not yet existing. Perhaps it would be better to call the places of detention internment camps, but we find the term "concentration camp" in official documents as, for example, in the correspondence referring to Boiano.

Conclusion

In the time between preparing the draft of this text and its publication I have continued my research on the treatment of the Gypsies in Italy under Fascism. So, I am able to add here a resumé of new data and conclusions[49] which are essentially based on the search of individual personal files reserved in the State Central Archive. They form part of correspondence between the Ministry of the Interior, town halls and polic concerning some Gypsies (Rosina, Michele, Giuseppe and Giovanna Hudorovic, Angela Levakovitch and others) in the years 1928-1943, i.e. under Fascism and before the German occupation of Italy.

Even a partial analysis of this new documentation gives us new data concerning the destiny of Italian and "foreign" Gypsies living in Italy under Fascism.

Above all, thanks to the police reports on Gypsies who were stopped on the road or arrested, we can visualise them as nomadic persons who were working in Italy in traditional Gypsy occupation, as traders, breeding horses, selling baskets or making pots.

But, above all, we can now be sure that the Fascist regime introduced controls on Gypsies and the restriction of their freedom, provisions for which two phases must be distinguished - the first until 1940 and the second between 1940 and 1943.

In the first phase, the policy regarding Gypsies was limited to their arrest and expulsion, generally into Yugoslavia. This was officially aimed at foreign Gypsies but in some cases Italian Gypsies were also affected. In the second phase the expulsion policy became an internment policy which affected all Gypsies, foreign and Italian, who were subjected to the general rules of internment in Italy that prescribed detention in a concentration camp or so-called free internment, compulsorily staying in a particular place[50].

Last but not least, this new documentation enables us to state positively that internment of Gypsies was in fact put into practice in some places.

Besides Vinchiaturo (near Campobassso) and the Tremiti Islands, for which we have isolated cases - in addition to the testimony of Thulo Reinhardt for (Tremiti) - the internment of some Gypsies in Boiano has now been documented. In fact, contrary to what the documentation available so far seemed to show, there is clear evidence of the presence of some Gypsies, at least in summer 1941, when all the prisoners were probably transferred to a new camp. At Boiano Gypsies were interned in an old factory, in five cold and damp buildings, where the poor living conditions forced the Fascist authorities to transfer some prisoners even before that summer, but not the Gypsies, who stayed there until the closing of the camp.

What also emerges from these documents are further references to internment in two other camps which were mentioned in the body of the article; Tossicia and Agnone. Tossicia was one of the worst camps in Abruzzi. All the prisoners were crammed into three houses and the one called Casa Mirti was reserved for Gypsies, in intolerable conditions. The buildings were tumble-down and windowless. There was no water and the drains overflowed in the camp daily.

The camp at Agnone was outside of the town in a village some 50 metres high in the convent of San Bernardino. The documents confirm the presence of Gypsies there and could lead us to suppose that from a certain time, the camp was reserved for them alone.

Finally, there is the story of a family in "free internment" - the Levacovic's (mother, father and eight children) and were interned in Ravenna from 1938 to 1944 when they were all transferred to Germany, in order, as the file says, "to make them work."

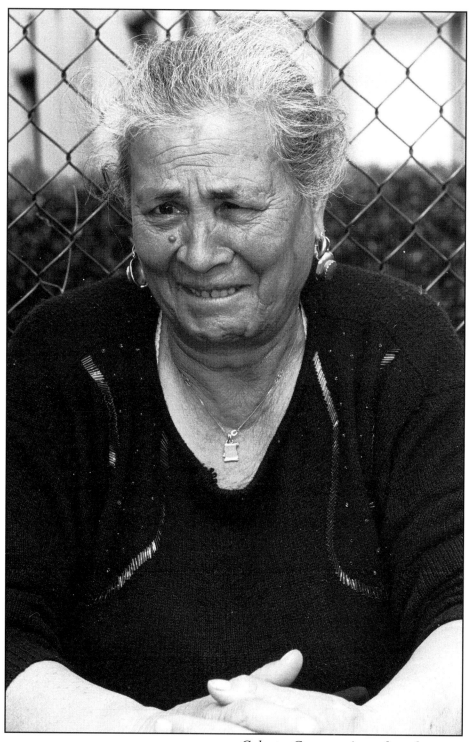

Celeste Casamonica after the war.

II. Gypsies in the Austrian Burgenland – the camp at Lackenbach

Erika Thurner

Introduction

Burgenland, in eastern Austria, was the region where the greatest number of sedentary Gypsies lived. The largest Gypsy camp in Austria was to be erected by the Nazis on the soil of Burgenland.

The theme of this chapter will be more than just the Lackenbach camp. It will also cover the National Socialist solution of the so-called Gypsy question in Burgenland, the central Nazi policy of persecution and its adaptation to the circumstances of Burgenland and, finally, the influence of the actions in Burgenland on central policy.

The percentage of landworkers and daily labourers was comparatively high in this region which remained predominantly agricultural. It was the poorest and most backward part of the Austrian republic until after the Second World War. In the whole period between the First and Second World Wars a tense situation prevailed in the labour market. The poorer sections of the population possessing no property depended on mobility and flexibility as an essential part of securing their livelihood. Burgenland Gypsies were part of these poorer sections of the population.[1] The first attempts to settle these nomads had been made by Maria Theresa and Josef II. In general, the liberal assimilationist programme of these Habsburg monarchs was doomed to failure. Nevertheless, it formed the prelude to a large influx of Gypsies, fleeing from persecution elsewhere, and the establishment of settlements, the so-called Gypsy colonies. Marginalisation and a worsening of the economic situation in the inter-war period drastically reduced the possibilities of earning a living for the Gypsies. They could not earn their living either in traditional occupations or in other professions. Begging and petty theft from the fields was the only way to survive for many of them.

In the 1930s there were 7,000-8,000 Romanies in Burgenland, 2.5-3% of the population. In the rest of Austria some 3,000 nomadic Gypsies – Sinti as well as Kalderash and Lovari – were registered.

Burgenland Gypsies lived in relatively few areas but in many districts of the Oberwart region and southern Burgenland they formed from a quarter to a half of the population. Their settlements were seldom in the villages themselves but on their fringes – often well outside the boundary of the village. In Burgenland, as elsewhere, the dominant policy was the traditional one of trying simultaneously to make Gypsies settle and to drive them away.[2] In general, dislike and mistrust of the Gypsies, together with discrimination against them, was so strong in every day life that, when the National Socialists came to power, the Gypsies merely suffered the extreme culmination of this previous policy. All the measures that could now be carried out under Nazi rule had already been formulated as ideas in Burgenland. The demands and published proposals to "solve the problem" included, for example:

"Separation and internment in forced labour camps, expulsion from the country...extermination through sterilisation – placing them without fail on the same level as the Jews."[3]

In a region which had undergone a series of economic crises and which had a relatively high percentage of non-German speaking minorities, the National Socialist Party was able to make significant advances in the beginning of the 1930s. A possible union with Germany gave hope to some sections of the community. The local administration, rural constabulary and police were soon infiltrated by National Socialists. This meant that marches by the uniformed SA (Storm Troopers), mass spreading of propaganda and other activities could be carried out in spite of the national ban on the Nazi Party.

On the eve of March 11th 1938, Burgenland found itself to be one of the first regions of Austria to be in National Socialist hands. Tobias Portschy – a leader of the banned Nazi Party and later Deputy Governor of Steiermark – took an authoritative part in the almost trouble-free seizure of power. The first victims to be targeted were the Jews and Gypsies. Under his rule persecution was faster, more brutal and more complete than elsewhere.[4] These two minorities – Jewish and Romany – had little in common until the Nazi period. The National Socialist policy of persecution and extermination gave them interlocking destinies. That meant that both groups faced discrimination, expulsion, isolation, removal of rights, imprisonment and forced labour, sterilisation and being used as objects of experiments and extermination.[5]

The theoretical basis for this was the Nuremberg racial laws that became operative in Austria as well as Germany from March 1938. The so-called "racially unworthy, criminal and antisocial Gypsies" caused problems for the Nazis as they should have counted as Aryans because of their Indian origin. So they were first of all classified in the group of "antisocials" and, in the framework of the relevant cleaning-up operations, placed in concentration camps. There was a permanently established Race Research Hygiene Centre in Berlin whose task was to produce a scientific basis for further measures against Gypsies and a draft Gypsy Law. Without waiting for this Law, the persecution continued in Greater Germany and, during the whole Nazi era, remained part of the sphere of authority of Heinrich Himmler as overall chief of the police.[6]

In March 1938 the first independent measures of persecution started in Burgenland. After forbidding school attendance and the playing of music as a profession, came the removal of voting rights and restrictions on movement and then the duty of compulsory labour under the watch of the SS and SA. That happened even before the setting up of internment camps and before the issue of Himmler's relevant decrees – the Circular of December 12th 1938 and the Settlement Decree of October 17th 1939.[7]

Only Burgenland Gypsies were affected by the Preventive Measures for Fighting the Gypsy Plague in Burgenland – the name given to the first large deportation of some 3,000 Romanies to the concentration camps of Dachau and Ravensbrück in June 1939. The Burgenland authorities had made good preparations. The State Police Administration Centre in Eisenstadt was able to pass on a Gypsy card index that contained some 8,000 names.

The next step, the deportation of all Gypsies from Austria and Germany to Poland in the autumn of 1940 had nevertheless to be delayed. Transport capacity was insufficient for all the "foreign people". As a temporary solution guarded internment and labour camps were set up.

The creation and expansion of the Lackenbach camp

On November 23rd 1940 the Gypsy camp in Lackenbach in central Burgenland was opened. In accordance with a Decree of the Ministry of the Interior in October 31st 1940, the district councils of Bruck an der Leitha, Eisenstadt,

Lilienfeld, Oberpullendorf, St Poten and Wiener Neustadt, as well as the Central Administration of Vienna, agreed to take responsibility for bringing together and maintaining the Gypsies living in those areas[8]. For this purpose a disused farm belonging to Count Esterhazy was rented. When the first transports followed in November 1940 the area chosen for the family camp was still in a terrible state. Apart from the walled storage buildings that were taken over by the camp administration there remained only stables that had to serve as living and sleeping quarters for the detainees. Families who were brought to the camp in their caravans could for the time being live in them and were therefore better accommodated. The sleeping places in the stables were completely sodden with damp and rain. As more and more arrived, 200 people were pushed into one room. There was a lack of water and there were no sanitary facilities. Almost everything was lacking. The inmates had to clean the latrines with their bare hands.

The conversion of this old farm into an internment camp was only possible by setting the prisoners to work immediately on building works. As in other camps, buildings for the camp leadership and administration took priority. So the office building was in place long before barracks were constructed for the prisoners. It was only the outbreak of a typhus epidemic at the end of 1941 which also threatened the camp guards that gave the impetus for a small improvement in living conditions. Three dormitory barracks and one sanatorium were erected, toilet and washing facilities were installed and the conditions then at least resembled those in the other Gypsy internment camps.

The barracks were burnt down in 1945 and recently the last relic – the office building (see illustration) was also pulled down. This building, was used after the war first as an office and then as a private house. Numerous documents from the camp leadership and administration were found in 1981 after the removal of its ceiling and several walls. There were some 300 index cards

The one time Administration Building of Lackenbach in 1978.

preserved, memoranda between the camp administration and the Police Headquarters in Vienna, as well as with officials elsewhere in Austria; also work contracts, salary slips, descriptions of wanted persons and similar documents. From these documents it has been possible to extend our knowledge of the conditions in the camp.

The camp administration

The administration of the camp was under the Criminal Police HQ in Vienna, Inspectorate IIb, under its then chief, Criminal Director Kapphengst. Active officers from the criminal investigation department in Vienna with the rank of lieutenant and sub-lieutenant in the SS filled the top posts including that of camp commander and his deputy. The most important administrative posts were filled by officials from Vienna.

The first camp commander, SS Sub-lieutenant Hans Kollross was a victim of the typhus epidemic in January 1942. His successor was Franz Langmüller whose period in charge until September 1942 was the most dismal period of the history of the camp.

From the Central Office in Vienna orders were issued that escapees were to be especially harshly treated and that beatings were to be used as a punishment. The rules, however, were so generally ignored that the prisoners were to a great degree at the mercy of the camp commander. Franz Langmüller was so brutal that he was put on trial and condemned after the war.

Der Angeklagte Franz L a n g m ü l l e r ist schuldig, er habe in Lackenbach im Burgenland in den Jahren 1941 und 1942, zur Zeit der ns. Gewaltherrschaft, unter Ausnützung dienstlicher Gewalt, Menschen, nämlich Zigeuner, in einen qualvollen Zustand versetzt und empfindlich misshandelt und in ihrer Menschenwürde gekränkt und beleidigt.
Er hat hiedurch das Verbrechen der Quälerei und Misshandlungen nach § 3 KVG., sowie das Verbrechen gegen die Menschlichkeit und Menschenwürde nach § 4 KVG. und wird nach § 3 KVG., 265a StPO. und § 34 StG. zur Strafe des schweren Kerkers in der Dauer von
e i n e m (1) J a h r ,
verschärft durch ein hartes Lager vierteljährlich und gem. § 389 StPO. zum Ersatze der Kosten des Strafverfahrens verurteilt.
Auf diese Strafe ist die Haft vom 27. VII. 1948, 8 Uhr, bis 15. X. 1948, 14 Uhr, gem. § 55a StG. anzurechnen.

Extract from the judgement of the Vienna Court against Frantz Langmüller (which found him guilty and sentenced him to one year hard labour, August 15th 1948).

Through the trial of Langmüller some of the cruelty and bullying in Lackenbach came to public notice. As well as beatings, official disciplinary measures included solitary confinement, being deprived of food, and hard labour in the open air, again without food.

Langmüller's successor, SS Lieutenant Fritz Eckschlager, renounced any form of beating as a punishment. This improvement was continued by the last camp commander SS Sub-lieutenant Julius Brunner from September 1943, with further relaxation of the regime.

The camp Chief however only had the overall responsibility for supervision. Just as in the concentration camps there was also in Lackenbach camp an inner structure following the principle of so-called self-government. The responsibility for carrying out orders was further delegated to prisoners. For the keeping of camp discipline camp Elders or Kapos were responsible.

Arrest and internment in the camp

The Police Headquarters in Vienna was responsible for the deportations to the camp. Transports by other police and constabulary posts could only take place after agreement from headquarters in Vienna. Internment followed a decision to arrest the particular individual by the Gypsy Department of the Vienna Police Headquarters and the National Centre for Fighting the Gypsy Menace in the Criminal Police Headquarters in Berlin.

Suspected persons were arrested and their identity investigated. Indications of their origins might be "typical Gypsy name" or "typical Gypsy occupation". If the investigated person proved to be a Romany, "Gypsy origin" was added and this was a ground for internment, whether or not the person arrested possessed a fixed address or work place. Rudolf Weinrich told the early researcher Selma Steinmetz:

"I was a young healthy lad when I was taken to the camp. I lost my youth and my health in Lackenbach. We were taken there from our settlement in Bruchhaufen, from our clean houses and caravans into poverty and dirt..."

Often the simultaneous arrest and internment of whole families and extended families took place. There were women and children in the camp from the very beginning. Many families, however, had by this point already been separated, and so it sometimes happened that children whose parents had already been sent to concentration camps arrived at Lackenbach on their own. Often all the inhabitants of a settlement were removed, after which the buildings were razed to the ground.

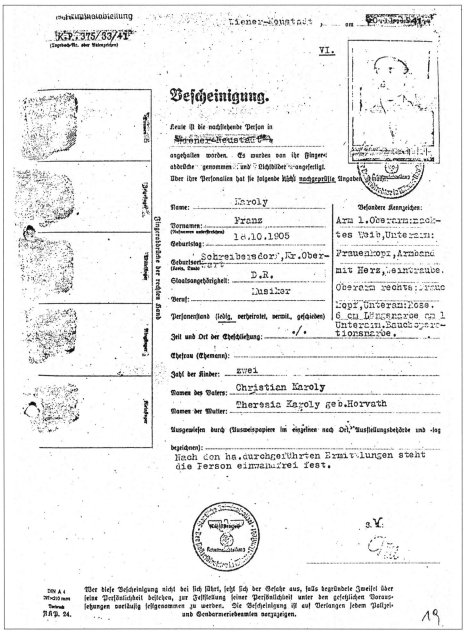

Identification document of Franz Karoly.

Two survivors spoke about their experiences of that time. Rosalia Karoly said:

"We were about ten families in Mörbisch. There were about a hundred of us living by the lake. On one Sunday in August 1941 we were arrested. I will never forget that day. As early as five o'clock in the morning we were dragged away from our homes. There were police and SS men from Mörbisch with weapons."

Forced deportation of Gypsies into the camps.

Julius Hodosy recounts:

"One night the SS came to the village. Lorries were driven up and whole families were loaded in without any choice... After that almost all the Gypsies fled from the village. I went to Giesshubel near Vienna... in 1941. I was arrested by the Gestapo with my wife in Giesshubel. We were sent to the Reception camp in Lackenbach in Burgenland."

Composition of the prisoner population

The great majority of the interned Gypsies came from Burgenland, which at that time had been divided and formed into two administrative districts in the Niederdonau and Steiermark regions. Burgenland Romanies formed the majority of the internees. Apart from them there was a large number of Sinti Gypsies in Lackenbach. Apart from the transports from Vienna, arrivals from Carinthia, Upper Austria and a few from Salzburg were recorded. The last were mainly German Sinti from the area of Wurtemberg who had left Germany itself before the beginning of the war and had been temporarily interned in a camp in Salzburg. Smaller groups also came from Hungary and Italy.

Zugangsliste: Einweisungen ins Lackenbacher Lager im Jahre 1941 (Transporte mit mehr als 10 Personen)

Datum:	Lager-stand:	Zug.-Menge:	Ort/Umgebung:	Lagernr.:
6. 4.41	591	398	Mattersburg u. Umgebg.	214- 612
30. 4.41	603	14	Ritzing	623- 636
9. 5.	620	18	Gend.Posten St. Martin	637- 654
29. 5.	639	11	Wien	673- 683
30. 5.	654	15	Lager Wepersdorf	684- 698
6. 6.	676	14	Gend.Posten St. Martin	705- 718
4. 7.	770	64	1. Wiener Transport	737- 800
6. 7.	833	58	Wiener Zigeuner	805- 863
9. 7.	916	83	"	864- 946
12. 7.	1017	103	"	947-1049
30. 7.	1016	11	"	1053-1063
31. 8.	1280	287	Eisenstadt	1067-1354
2. 9.	1299	15	"	1358-1372
19. 9.	1431	296	St. Pölten	1393-1689
21. 9.	1756	333	Bruck/Leitha	1690-2023
26. 9.	1631	18	"	2027-2044
2.10.	1657	11	Wien (Pol.-Gefängnis)	2052-2062
26.10.	1975	268	Oberpullendorf	2087-2356
29.10.*	2260	79	über Wien aus KL Mauthausen	2357-2435
29.10.	-	13	Gend.P.Bruck/Leitha	2439-2451
31.10.	2318	65	Kripo Villach	2453-2517
1.11.	2335	20	" Innsbruck (aus Italien)	2518-2537
4.11.	1629	301	Kripo Linz (für Lodz)	2541-2848
		-1000	Lodz	
7.11.	628	-1000	Lodz	
18.11.	591	14	Kripo Klagenfurt	2857-2870
19.11.41	609	24	Gend.P. Hollabrunn	2871-2895

Liste erstellt aufgrund der Eintragungen ins Lagertagebuch/ DÖW-Akt Nr. 11340.

*Hierbei handelte es sich zum Teil um Häftlinge, die bereits eine Haft in Dachau und Buchenwald hinter sich hatten, die also gleich bei den ersten Verhaftungen dabei waren.

Transports (of over 10 persons) into Lackenbach in 1941.

Arrivals

Because the new arrivals were numbered consecutively we know that altogether 4,000 Gypsies were interned in Lackenbach. The largest variation in the total numbers came in the first six months.

When the camp opened there were already Austrian Gypsies who had been interned in the concentration camp in Mauthausen and they were brought to Lackenbach and given jobs as trustee prisoners. In the first months until April 1941 the number of prisoners grew slowly to around 200. Mass internment began with a large transport on April 6th 1941 and these larger transports continued to the middle of that year.

With the arrivals of April 6th 1941 the total number of prisoners in the camp was 591. The table shows five further large transports while most were small, comprising between ten and one hundred persons. The October arrivals from Mauthausen included prisoners who had previously been held in Dachau and Buchenwald and were amongst those who had been arrested in 1939. Apart from that there was the continuous arrival of individuals and families.

On November 1st 1941 the largest total of internees recorded was reached with 2,335 persons, just before two transports to Lodz in Poland. In the beginning of 1942 the Camp Diary showed a total population of 572 prisoners. Apart from the deportations to Lodz the reduction also reflected the many deaths from an epidemic that followed the arrival of some internees from the Salzburg camp.

Afterwards the number of internees varied between 600 and 900 of whom a third were children.

In the following months new arrivals came only in small groups. This was partly because the larger settlements had already been broken up and partly because the Auschwitz Decree came into force, so that from spring 1943 most of those arrested were deported directly to the Gypsy Family Camp in Auschwitz-Birkenau and only a few individuals were sent to Lackenbach.

At the beginning of April 1943 the camp in Leopoldskron (Maxglan) in Salzburg was closed and almost all the prisoners from there were sent to Auschwitz. A small group however were transported to Lackenbach. Amongst them were Josefa and Anna Reinhardt. They received the numbers 3074 and 3057.

There were also additions to the numbers through births in the camp and transfers from other camps or prisons.

Transports out

For the majority of the internees Lackenbach was only a transit camp. As the administrative official Josef Hajek said in a statement:

"The Gypsy Internment camp in Lackenbach was also a so-called Transit camp for Gypsies some of whom, following instructions from Vienna, were delivered to us and then, following further specific instructions from Vienna, were collected for further transports."

The largest transports out of the camp were the two deportations to Lodz, each with 1,000 persons on November 4th and 7th 1941[9]. The sources lead us to conclude that the decisive criterion for selection was unsuitability for work. It was above all small children – more than half were children – old persons and others unable to work who had to leave Lackenbach for a journey which went via Lodz to the Extermination camp in Kulmhof (Chelmno). Afterwards some smaller groups or individuals from Lackenbach were sent to other concentration camps.

Deaths

Only after the war were families able to erect gravestones and memorials for their deceased relatives.

As revealed by the available sources i.e. the Camp Diary, Register of Deaths and records of the Lackenbach Registry Office, there were 237 cases where death was the reason given for removal from the camp register. Eye witness accounts and survivors' stories suggest that there were even more deaths. The sources are full of gaps when it comes to the registration of births in the camp and the death of newly born children.

An epidemic which broke out in the camp at the end of 1941 alone caused between 250 and 300 deaths. Officially the Camp Diary noted the outbreak of

47

Post	Tag	bezeichnung des Wohnortes (Gasse, Hausnummer)	und Stellung im Berufe	Religion	Stand	Tag und Jahr der Geb.	Geburtsort, Verwaltungsbezirk, Land
198	12.41	*Gizela* Papai Lg. N° 3239 Zigeunerankatlelager, Lackenbach	Zigeuner	r. kath.	verwitwet	30/8. 1875	Zigeusdorf
199	25.41	*Julius* Baranyai Lg. N° 3085 Zigeunerankatlelager, Lackenbach	Zigeuner-kind	r. kath.	ledig	19/X 1941	Lackenbach Ob. O.
200	41.42	*Franz* Hodosi Lg. N° 3254 Zigeunerankatlelager, Lackenbach	Zigeuner	r. kath.	ledig	16/XI 1910	[illegible]
203	3.42	*Elisabeth* Papai Lg. N° 3108 Zigeunerankatlelager, Lackenbach	Zigeuner	r. kath.	verwitwet	70 Jahre	[illegible] Ob. O.
204	41.42	*Moritz* Prochar Lg. N° 1758 Zigeunerankatlelager, Lackenbach	Lagerin-sass.	r. kath.	verh.	12/X 1993	[illegible]

Entries in the Register of Deaths
(showing that even before the camp was isolated, 60% of deaths had taken place without any treatment by a doctor).

Zuständigkeitsort, Bezirk, Land	Gestorben (totgeboren) am	Todesursache (Grundleiden und unmittelbare Todesursache)	Tag der Beerdigung	Behandelnder Arzt
D. Reich	31/XII. 41 20 Uhr 15 Uhr	Grippe	3.I.42 Lackenb	ohne
D. Reich	2/I. 42 5 Uhr 40 früh	[illegible] Lungenentzündung	3.I.42 Lackenb	[illegible]
D. Reich	2/I. 42 8 Uhr 15 früh	Grippe [illegible]	3.I.42 Lackenb	ohne
D. Reich	2/II. 42 20 Uhr 30	Grippe	4.I.42 von	ohne
Protektorat	3/I. 42 24 Uhr 25	Lungen-entzündung Herzmuskel	6.I.42 Lackenb.	D. Gelichart

Zum Zeitpunkt dieser Eintragungen wurde das Totenbuch bereits im Lager deponiert. Lediglich die drei Rubriken — Todesursache, Tag der Beerdigung, behandelnder Arzt — wurden bis zum 4.1.42 noch von Dr. Beilhart ausgefüllt. Ab 6.1.42 wurden auch diese Eintragungen vom jeweiligen Schriftführer vorgenommen.

an epidemic on January 6th 1942, when the first camp commander SS Sub-lieutenant Kollross was taken into a Vienna hospital and typhus was diagnosed. On the same day the complete isolation of the camp was ordered and the camp guards and officials were put in quarantine.

The prisoners were locked in the camp and left to face the disease on their own. Only the Lackenbach village doctor, Dr Georg Blihart, who had looked after the camp inmates until then, gave some medical attention. Gypsies who had been working outside the camp were recalled from their places of work, placed in the camp and thereby exposed to the danger of infection. Finally, the guards on the perimeter of the camp were strengthened and the order was given "that anyone attempting to escape would be shot" according to the Camp Diary entry for January 6th 1942.

Through these measures the camp guards, officials and the inhabitants of Lackenbach were to be protected. The mass deaths in the sealed-off area were of interest only when they became a danger for the non-Gypsies.

By October 1941 the epidemic had claimed many victims and it continued until spring 1942. In the first months it was mainly babies and young children who died. At the turn of the year the death rate amongst the adults also rose rapidly. After the end of the epidemic the death rate in the camp fell sharply. The dead Gypsies were buried in the nearby Jewish cemetery in mass graves. It was not until after the war that some families erected gravestones and memorials for their deceased relatives

Attempts to escape

The "continual possibilities of escape" and occasional release from the camp led to a decrease in the number of prisoners, according to the camp commander, Julius Brunner.

For many it was an examination of their parentage which led to their release, for example, non-Romanies and those of mixed race with a majority of German blood. Others were able later to establish the basis for being released by reclaiming their Hungarian nationality.

The most common reaction to the inhuman conditions in the camp was flight. As in the concentration camps, the commanders in Lackenbach were determined through terrifying punishments to discourage inmates from even thinking about escape. Josef Hodoschi reported:

"I was delivered to the Lackenbach camp on September 19th 1941. From the very beginning I was hit with a rubber truncheon. When my wife died a few months later from typhus I could stand it no longer and I ran away. But they caught me in Oberpullendorf and I was brought back to the camp. The punishment was twenty-five strokes with the so-called rubber sausage."

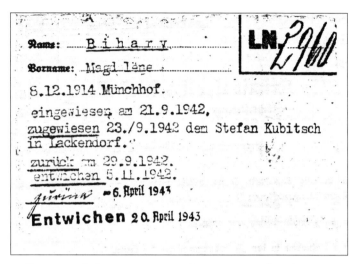

Report of the recapture of an escaped prisoner.

Unsuccessful escapers were punished by the camp guards with various penalties, beating with a stick, solitary confinement, being deprived of food, and/or hard labour. Nevertheless, many detainees were not frightened by this and tried more than once to escape. In many cases recaptured prisoners were sent to a concentration camp. There were many opportunities for flight but without outside help it was very hard to slip away from the well-organised searches for wanted persons.

Julius Hodosi, who succeeded in hiding for a time, described his flight from Lackenbach:

"I was working on road building. We took breakfast near a wood. An opportunity did once arise and I fled into the wood. After three minutes my absence was noticed, they set out after me but I was able to hide my traces. During my flight I came on to Hungarian territory... got through to Mattersburg where I took the train to Vienna, illegally of course."

He was captured later and sent with his wife and two children to Auschwitz.

In the period for which the Camp Diary is legible there were 170 attempted escapes of which sixty-four were successful. However, it is not possible to establish whether the escapers were recaptured and sent back to Lackenbach or to another camp.

Conditions in the camp

The conditions in the camp in the first eighteen months after Lackenbach was set up as an internment camp were particularly hard. Daily life in the camp was marked by hard work and a lack of facilities, with personal freedom restricted to the bare minimum. Men, women and children had to suffer the same horrors and oppression as prisoners in a concentration camp: beatings, standing for hours at roll call, removal of food and slave labour under the hardest conditions.

Only gradually, with a reduction in the numbers of inmates and the creation of more space, were there attempts to set up an efficiently functioning camp. With the removal of corporal punishment and the improvements that the camp commanders Eckschlager and Brunner introduced, the conditions reached a level which was better than deportation to a concentration camp.

The daily routine

The daily timetable was based around the prisoners' work. Those who were working outside the camp left early and did not return until the evening. The only ones present for the midday meal were those who were working in the camp or in the dairy. Food was delivered to the working parties in the vicinity of the camp. There was no work on Saturday and Sunday. On those days, however, there were jobs to be done such as washing clothes and collecting wood.

Leaving the camp was only possible with a permit, which was issued for a short leave in exceptional cases and for a particular purpose. Visits took place only under the eyes of guards in an area outside the camp. Entry to the camp was forbidden for visitors. Written contact with the outside world was possible although all letters and packets were censored. Any large sums of money had to be deposited in the administration office.

Life for the small children was arranged differently. As the mothers were allocated to working parties, a prisoner supervisor looked after the smallest children who were, in this way, somewhat shielded from the reality of the camp. The life of the older children resembled that of the adults. They had work allocated to them.

Food

On arrival in the camp the inmates had to give up their ration books. This was followed by the organisation of communal catering. The food was not only poor but insufficient. Apart from the statements of the prisoners, entries in the Camp Diary paint the same picture, for example:

"9.8.1941 – Today the food question became very urgent and took a long time and great effort to solve."

The situation only improved when more inmates were working with outside firms and farms and were partly fed by the employer. Camp commander Brunner also tried to increase the amount of food available by adding some from the camp's own farm.

Most meals consisted, as in other camps, of various soups and stews. In their memories of the camp ex-prisoners speak of potatoes, turnips, bad cabbage, inedible cheese, as well as peas and beans full of maggots.

Clothing

The prisoners in Lackenbach did not have any sort of uniform. The camp administration was pleased when people brought their own clothes with them. If not, then clothes were to be provided by the camp but there was so little available that, for example, children had to collect wood in the winter in their bare feet.

Making money from the prisoners' work

In the decree which set up Lackenbach it was assumed that the camp would be self-supporting through the work of the Gypsies themselves. It was the intention to place the men in particular in workplaces outside the camp. Women and children would take over suitable activities and work inside the camp.

Marching off to work.

The situation at the beginning was, however, that nearly all the inmates were required to stay in the camp in order to build the camp itself. Then there was work in the camp's own agricultural enterprise and the sawmill. The approach roads and later the accommodation had to be built or renovated. Women and children were also employed in this work. "Even my small brothers and sisters had to carry the stones from the Jewish synagogue up to build the camp barracks," recounted Rosilia Karoly who was twelve years old at the time.

With the continuation of the war the demand to recruit workers from the Lackenbach prisoners increased. Even more Gypsies were allocated to outside work places. Many were taken back to the sort of job they had done before they were interned. They were labourers in the construction industry and the firms which supplied building material; some worked on the land, in the forests and also in various private firms; others were "loaned" out as domestic help, in restaurants or to farms. Women were also employed building motorways and streets. Many firms could keep their businesses going only with the assistance of Gypsy labour[10].

Work conditions

Work each day lasted between eight and eleven hours. Keeping guard over the work place were members of the camp staff and Gypsies who were appointed as foremen. Strict discipline was observed during the work period. For example, talking was forbidden. Breaking the rules could lead to maltreatment and harassment by the employer, the foremen or the senior prisoner.

Conditions were generally better for the prisoners who worked outside the camp.

Wages

The firms had to pay the regular local wages for the Gypsies. Farmers who took prisoners to work on their estates had to pay between ten and twenty marks to the camp monthly. The amount for children was relatively smaller, between five and eight marks. The workers should have received 10% as pocket money while the other 90% went to the camp account. From the preserved accounts of a building firm which paid relatively high wages, it seems that their men should have received twelve marks pocket money and women ten marks.

Ex-prisoners recounted, however, that they received nothing apart from three or four marks each month which was just enough to cover the three cigarettes they were allowed per day. The camp authorities took the rest.

Contracts were made between the camp staff and the employers with the conditions carefully laid out. The employer, by his signature, committed himself

Lackenbach, am 14.Juni 1944.

Arbeitsvertrag

Arbeitgeber: T h e r e s i a W I E D E M A N N

Wohnort: Lackenbach,Berggasse No.26

Art des Besitzes: Landwirtschaft

Flächenausm: 7 ha

benötigt für die Zeit vom 15.Juni 1944 bis auf weiteres nachstehend angeführte Arbeitskraft (xxxxxxx)

Zugewiesen wurde (x) Lg.Nr. 3124 Johann H o r v a t h ,

am 2o.6.1932 im Walde bei Dreieichen

Ich verpflichte mich als Arbeitgeber am 15. eines jeden Monates RM. 5.-

in Worten: Reichsmark: f ü n f ----------- an die Lagerkasse zu bezahlen. Als Taschengeld habe ich wöchentlich RM.0.5o (fünfzig Pfennige) dem (xx) Arbeiter (xx zu verabfolgen, sowie für Bekleidung u.Verköstigung aufzukommen.

Ferner nehme ich zur Kenntnis, daß jeder Verkehr der Arbeitskraft mit den deutschen Volksgenossen verboten und die zugewiesene Person (ex) abgesondert zu verpflegen und unterzubringen ist (xxx).

Wiedemann Therese
Unterschrift des Arbeitgebers.

hier unterschreiben
Zurück senden

Brunner
Unterschrift des Lagerleiters.

SS Untersturmführer und Lagerleiter.

Work contract between the camp and an amployer.

"to feed and house separately the person allocated to them and hinder any relationship with German citizens."

Children's work

Apart from the very youngest, children were also compelled to work. They had to make themselves useful in the camp or carry out some work in the barracks. In general, employers did not have to pay any wages to the camp for children but had to provide them with board and lodging instead. Boys and girls aged between ten and thirteen went to work on farms, digging ditches or working in the silk-worm industry.

Mrs Karoly remembered her sad childhood in Lackenbach:

"I was then twelve and a half... I was given a set of overalls and clogs and we had to work on the irrigation channels. I was given a pickaxe that was bigger than me. Already on the first day I came back to the barracks with a bloody face. I had been hit so much. I always had to work with the adults but I was only given a child's portion of food."

The transports to Lodz

The physical extermination of the persecuted Gypsies began with five transports, each of 1,000 persons, to the Jewish ghetto of Lodz. From the preserved records of the so-called Jewish Council there, we learn of the arrival of 2,000 Gypsies from Austria. From other sources we know that there were altogether 5,007 Gypsies brought to the ghetto. It is not yet clear if they all came from Austria. Two of the transports, each of 1,000 Romanies and Sinti, were certainly assembled in Lackenbach.

In Lodz a section of the Jewish ghetto was set aside as a Gypsy quarter. A double line of barbed wire separated the two ghettos. The conditions were terrible and in the first two months 613 people had died or been killed

After an outbreak of typhus only Jewish doctors and grave diggers were allowed into the quarter.

At the beginning of January 1942 the survivors were transported in lorries to the Extermination camp of Chelmno and the "ghetto within a ghetto" disappeared. Gassing of Jews had already begun in Chelmno in December 1941. On March 19th 1942 the Regional Office for Oberwart informed all mayors that regarding any enquiries about Lodz it should be announced that no visitor's permits would be issued. This was at a time when all those who had been "resettled" were dead. We know the administration of Lackenbach had kept exact records for, in later years, the camp staff was able to answer requests for information about when and under what reference number a particular person had been "resettled" in Lodz.

Apart from those names on the evacuation list of November 4th 1941, nineteen more names can be established from camp numbers and card index entries.

From the "Final Solution" to the liberation of Lackenbach

Lackenbach camp was kept open until the end of the war. It was not closed when Himmler's Auschwitz Decree of December 1942 made closure a possibility[11]. Over 20,000 Romanies and Sinti were deported from all the countries occupied by the Nazis to the Gypsy Family Camp in Auschwitz-Birkenau (BIIe). The majority died in the gas chambers or as a result of conditions in the camp. The number of persons from Lackenbach deported to Auschwitz is not known because there is insufficient documentation for that period.

The number of persons in the Austrian camp was kept at around 500-600 until the end of the war. It looks, therefore, as if thinking sensibly about the needs of industry – or more likely the critical economic situation – put a stop to the pointless policy of extermination, at least in the final years of the war. A small

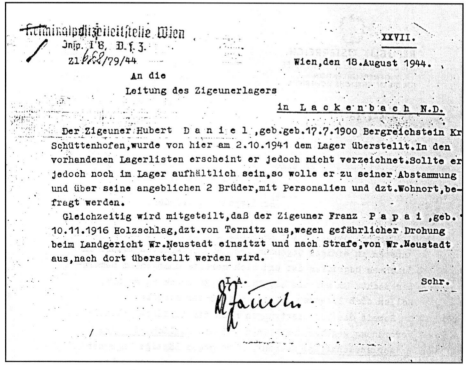

Letter relating to the deportation of Hubert Daniel to Lodz.

number of Romanies and Sinti were in this way spared from the gas chambers. What was seen as a temporary solution became a permanent factor. Other exceptions to deportation to Auschwitz, on racial or social grounds as outlined in Himmler's Decree, were only on paper and saved very few Gypsies from persecution.[12]

The change in the conditions in Lackenbach camp towards the end of the war, the partial improvements in the living conditions and the dropping of corporal punishment have obscured the cruelty of the early years. The fact remains that in this camp – which was not recognised as a concentration camp – the first steps of the National Socialist persecution of the Gypsies were cruelly carried out and that in Lackenbach, in the appalling conditions at the time it was opened, there was a hint already of the system that was to rule in Auschwitz and the extermination camps – slave labour and speedy death.

Lackenbach, den 28. August 1944.

KPIST.Z.L. 17/44.

An die

Kriminalpolizeileitstelle Wien
Inspektion I B,D.f.Z.

in W i e n .

Betrifft: Zigeuner Hubert D a n i e l , Aufenthalt.
Bezug: Dortiges Schreiben Zl.688/79/44, v.18.8.44.

Hubert Da n i e l , geb. 17.7.1900 Bergreichenstein, wurde am 2.10.1941 unter der Lg.Nr. 2052 aus St.Pölten in das Lager eingewiesen und wurde im Jahre 1941 unter der Kontr.Nr. 423 nach Litzmannstadt umgesiedelt.
Ueber seine 2 Brüder sind ho. keine Vormerkungen vorhanden und konnte auch durch Umfrage bei den hiesigen Lagerinsasse über dieselben nichts in Erfahrung gebracht werden.

Letter from the camp relating to the deportation of Hubert Daniel to Lodz.

Conclusion

Over two thirds of the 11,000 Romanies and Sinti in Austria were murdered in the Nazi period. Many went to their death via the Lackenbach camp[13].

Studies of anti-Semitism and the Nazi persecution of Jews in Vienna give clear parallels with the persecution of the Gypsies in Burgenland[14]. Just as the anti-Jewish policies in Vienna – through the intensity and brutality of their anti-Semitism – gave an impetus to the policies of the German State, so can we discern the same picture for the Nazi Gypsy policies in Burgenland. The radical "proposals for a solution" of Tobias Portschy and others, together with his petition to the Nazi officials, influenced the National Socialist programme of persecuting the Gypsies; indeed they demanded that measures and steps be taken. The different measures of discrimination and marginalization anticipated the central government's programme. Burgenland ran ahead of Germany itself.

The persecution of Gypsies and Jews under the Nazi Empire was a process that developed its own momentum and evolved as it went on. Although the general direction was established, the details, the timetable, the means and finally the degree of intensity and brutality were not thought out in advance. The earlier "mild" forms made the escalating drastic nature of the Holocaust possible. Carrying out orders from above was possible because ideological discrimination – in the case of the Gypsies as antisocials and racially inferior – had sunk deep into the population over the centuries[15]. To some extent the Gypsy policies of the Nazi Empire can be traced back to the social situation in Burgenland.

There is no doubt about the importance of the ideological and psychological causes of Gypsy persecution, but these cannot be detached from the economic causes, both local and regional, in Burgenland. The political uncertainties and the economic poverty of the majority of the population provided the social and political dynamite that was to explode against the Gypsies with great hatred and severity as the National Socialist power system opened the floodgates.

III. The Internment of Gypsies in France

Marie-Christine Hubert

Introduction[1]

From France's declaration of war against Germany on September 3rd 1939, Gypsies were progressively excluded from French society – a process which culminated in October 1940 with the German occupying forces issuing an order for their internment. Abandoned by the French authorities who implemented this order, and by public opinion which had never displayed the least interest in their fate, the Gypsies knew no "Liberation" until 1946 when, in an atmosphere of continuing indifference, those who still had the means to do so took to the roads again, while others became sedentary. This indifference persisted until very recently. The internment of Gypsies in France does not figure in the national memory and gets no mention in history textbooks.

Despite this public apathy, French Gypsies, unlike those in other occupied territories, suffered neither mass deportation nor extermination. This paradox stems from a law dated July 16th 1912, the sole purpose of which was to regulate the movements of Gypsies on French territory. In so doing, it defined them by behavioural characteristics (in the official view Gypsies were, above all, nomads) rather than by racial criteria as was the case in Germany. This conceptual difference prevented the German occupying forces from singling out Gypsies by their own definitions, and consequently from applying in France the racial policies that elsewhere led to the extermination of this people.

A tradition of hampering movement

As from 1912 French legislation and administration officially dropped the use of *Bohémiens and Romanichels* previously employed to designate Gypsies, replacing them with the single term, *nomades*. This new terminology was introduced in the Law of July 16th 1912, *On the Exercise of Itinerant Trades and the Regulation of the Movements of Nomads*, the purpose of which was to control and curtail the movements of those practising itinerant trades in rural areas and to reassure public opinion, alarmed by the arrival of groups of Gypsies from Eastern Europe in the late 1800s. Official census figures in 1897 gave an estimated 400,000 itinerants, of whom 25,000 were described as "nomads travelling in caravans", on French territory[2]; Criminal Investigation Department figures a few years later mentioned from 9-10,000 *Romanichels*.[3] All this sowed confusion in the public mind. Media coverage, expanding on existing fears, added to the confusion:

"These new arrivals, whether *Romanichels, Zingari, Tziganes* or even Frenchmen, are particularly dreaded, for their passing through is always accompanied by depredations of every sort. Guilty of every kind of misdeed, they are robbers of washing spread out on the hedges to dry, of chickens pecking in the fields, of rabbits from insecurely fastened hutches; incendiaries of barns they are forbidden to enter; satyrs exploiting the isolation of a woman or young girl in field or farmhouse to appease their brutal passions."[4]

Thus from 1907-12, Parliament considered how to put a halt to this "scourge of the countryside".

The Law of July 16th 1912

Under the letter of the law, Gypsies could not be arrested for vagrancy or begging. Nor could they be deported to their countries of origin, since they had no documentation by which their identities, and thus their nationalities, could be established; moreover, neighbouring countries had taken to expelling Gypsies from their own territories at around the same time. Since Gypsies did not come under any existing legislation, Parliament had no choice but to create new legislation aimed specifically at them. This approach demanded a neat, precise definition of the target group, but parliamentary debate revealed that no viable definition could be applied: Gypsies shared neither nationality nor customs nor social behaviour. Moreover, French parliamentarians refused to consider criteria based on physical characteristics or "a sign of race" as advocated by Deputy Fernand David in particular.[5] In the end, the government

60

took as its determining criterion a behavioural characteristic shared by the majority of Gypsies: nomadism and, in particular, the absence of a fixed abode (caravans not qualifying for this designation).[6] Parliament was now in a position to legislate in relation to Gypsies, although the criteria adopted applied to all itinerants whether Gypsies or not.

Thus on July 16th 1912 a law regulating the exercise of itinerant trades and the movement of nomads, was passed. It differentiated three distinct categories of itinerant tradesmen, travelling showmen, and nomads.

Article 1 - All individuals domiciled in France, or possessing a fixed abode therein, whatever their nationality, wishing to exercise an itinerant trade, business or profession, are obliged to make a declaration to this effect at the office or deputy office of the district in which they are domiciled or in which their fixed abode is located...

Article 2 - All individuals of French nationality who possess neither fixed abode nor domicile, wishing to travel about the territory of France in order to exercise the trade of commercial or industrial showman[7] must request an identity card carrying their particulars backed by a photograph and listing their name, first name, place and date of birth, last domicile/place of residence, and indicating the type of commerce or trade in which they intend to engage...

Article 3 - Under the terms of application of the present law, the designation "nomad" shall apply to all persons of whatever nationality travelling France without fixed abode or domicile, and not coming under any of the categories specified above, even if they possess resources or claim to exercise a trade. These nomads must carry an anthropometric identity card.

Nomads who are in France when the law comes into operation must, within the period of one month, submit a request for the identity card specified in the preceding paragraph, be it to the mayor of the principal district of the department or to the deputy mayor in the case of other districts.

Nomads coming in from abroad shall not be permitted to travel in France save under condition of proof of certain identity certified by producing authentic documentation for themselves and all persons travelling with them. They shall address their request for the requisite identity card to the office or deputy office of the border district in question.

Under no circumstances shall the authorities be obliged to honour an application for an anthropometric identity card. This shall in no way impede the implementation of the provisions of the Law of December 3rd 1849 on French residence for foreign nationals, nor the exercise of local authorities' recognised rights under laws and regulations relating to camping by nomads on the territory of their districts.

All nomads stopping in a given district must, upon arrival and again on departure, present their identity cards for stamping, to the commissioner of police if there is one in the district or, in the absence of a commissioner, to the superintendent of the local rural police or, in the absence of a police office, to the mayor.

The holder must produce his anthropometric identity card whenever requested to do so by a member of the police force or of the public authorities.

All infractions of the terms of the present article shall be punishable by the penalties specified under enactments applying to vagrancy.

Article 4 - Anthropometric identity cards apply to individuals. At the same time, the head of family must also obtain a collective identity card covering all members of the family...

From the legislative point of view, Gypsies were categorised as nomads. This is not, however, apparent from a reading of Article 3, in which "the nomad" is defined by default as any itinerant not coming under the previous two categories. The first of these allows for no ambiguity, as its determining criterion, a fixed abode, is clear and precise. The dividing line between categories two and three is, by contrast, much more fluid. In effect, no one was in a position to state that a Gypsy could not exercise the profession of "commercial or industrial showman", as this was not clearly defined. Under which category were Gypsies working in circuses, or exhibiting trained bears at fairs, to be classed? This was the weak point of the legislation, and the Gypsies were to rush into the gaps. Some rented accommodation in which they did not live, but which entitled them to claim a permanent abode, while more still declared themselves as travelling showmen. Over the years following the passing of the law, the administration issued numerous circulars warning those responsible for issuing the different kinds of identity cards, to be on the look-out for ploys of this kind. It was precisely this legal loophole which was to enable the Germans to intern travelling showmen under the same terms as applied to "nomads".

The reason why so many Gypsies were anxious to avoid classification as nomads was because this category of itinerant was subject to significant constraints, including the legal obligation to carry a special type of identification – the anthropometric identity card. Supplementary legislation dated February 13th 1913 specified additional details to be included in this document: marital status, height, chest circumference, breadth of shoulders, length and circumference of head, bizygomatic index (span from cheekbone to cheekbone), length of right ear, length of middle and little fingers of left hand, length from elbow to fingertips of left arm, eye colour, fingerprints, and two photographs (full face and profile) of holder. The head of the family or company was also obliged to be in possession of a collective identity card naming all persons travelling with him, including all children under the age of thirteen not in possession of identity cards of their own. All vehicles belonging to nomads required a special registration plate, also recorded on the collective identity card. The obligation to have this stamped every time they moved, and to produce it on demand for every official who asked to see it, subjected nomads to ongoing verification of their identity. These constrictive measures enabled the public authorities to identify and trace with precision the itineraries of nomads (including Gypsies), thus fulfilling the principal objective of the Law of July 16th 1912.[8]

Despite these measures regulating nomads' movements, mayors and mayors (préfets et maires) retained the power to impose further restrictions on, or even to prohibit outright, the camping of nomads in the territory under their jurisdiction. Thus, "the length of the roads, and on the outskirts of every city and town, stood signposts displaying notices reading NOMADS PROHIBITED".[9] In the Indre-et-Loire department for example, in the 1930s, 106 local authorities issued decrees prohibiting camping by nomads. "These measures disrupted an economic mobility dictated by the rhythms of country life (fair days, harvesting, etc.) and the imposition of fines strained incomes which fluctuated by nature. As a result, families that had been travelling for over a century gave up life on the road".[10] Notwithstanding the stemming of the influx of Gypsies from abroad and the tight surveillance of Gypsies travelling the national territory, the French population, despite being accustomed to their passing through, continued to view Gypsies with an undiminished negativity.

Assigning a place of residence in wartime

Tolerated in peacetime, nomads became undesirables in time of war, and were subjected to the coercive measures inherent in such a context. During the First World War, enemy subjects, including those from Alsace and Lorraine (annexed by Germany in 1871) were held in French internment camps because of their nationality. "But a mob of individuals, of every sort of background, are going to end up in preliminary sorting camps – and some of them in camps for suspects – for all sorts of reasons having – in principle – nothing to do with their nationality. Expelled by the armed forces, or by police headquarters in Paris, they are deemed 'suspicious' or 'undesirable'."[11] Nomads came under both headings, in a number of ways: suspect due to their frequent moves, undesirable because they had no steady work (and on this basis considered "useless mouths to be fed"). In effect, "certain trades are undesirable behind the lines". A note issued by General Headquarters and dated 16th June 1915 reminds all units that Article 5 of the Law of August 9th 1849, *On States of Siege*, empowers the military authorities "to expel from the war zone all nomads therein or who may seek to enter. This applies in particular to peddlers, rag-and-bone men, basket-weavers and other itinerant tradesmen."[12] Generally speaking, evacuees from the war zone ended up in interment camps.[13] As no research on the situation of nomads at this time has been undertaken, no figures are available on how they were affected by this imprisonment.

France repeated this process of exclusion during the Second World War. For example, as early as September 1939, newly installed local authorities in the Indre-et-Loire department undertook the expulsion of nomads.[14] On October 22nd of that year a military decree based on Article 5 of the Law on *States of Siege* prohibited nomads from travelling eight departments in the Poitou-Charentes region as well as their camping in the Indre-et-Loire and Maine-et-Loire departments.[15]

A Statutory Decree passed on April 6th 1940 prohibited nomads from travelling anywhere in metropolitan France[16] for the duration of hostilities: the Gypsies were, as ever in time of war, suspected of being spies:

"In wartime the circulation of nomads, wandering individuals generally without domicile, homeland or any real profession, constitutes, with regard to national defence and the maintenance of secrecy, a danger to be removed."

A Circular from the Minister of the Interior, dated April 29th 1940, specifies the terms of the Decree. In Article 3 of this Circular the Minister requests mayors to assign nomads to a place of compulsory residence, but opposes their being gathered together

"in a sort of big concentration camp, which would entail the double disadvantage of bringing back together bands that the services had succeeded in splitting up, and creating awkward problems associated with accommodating, feeding and guarding them, entailing disastrous expenditure."

There was, therefore, no question of interning nomads under this legislation. Assigning them a place to live was intended, among other things, to stabilise

"the wandering bands which constitute a definite danger from the social point of view, and to give some of them a taste for, or at least the habit of, regular work."[17]

Officially, the Decree was passed for reasons associated with military interests; unofficially, the goal was settle Gypsies as a step towards their absorption into French society. Having first identified this mobile population, and kept it under surveillance, the authorities envisioned controlling and channelling its behaviour.

The mayors charged with implementing the Decree ordered an immediate census of all nomads in their respective departments. Stage two was the publishing of an order assigning a place of compulsory residence; the police then proceeded to arrest nomads and to bring them to the area to which they had been assigned. As the State took no responsibility for their welfare, nomads were authorised to work within a zone to be defined by the local mayor. Implementation of the Decree was uneven: many nomads evaded police surveillance, and the German invasion prevented its being applied at all in many departments. Nonetheless, months before the Occupation began, Gypsies were already being counted and forced to settle. Although they could no longer travel, they were not yet being locked up in internment camps under constant surveillance.

Internment: decided by the Germans, carried out by the French

On May 13th 1940 German troops invaded France and advanced without significant difficulty. A month later – June 14th – they entered Paris. On June 17th Marshall Pétain, head of the French government, requested an armistice. The Franco-German Armistice was signed on June 22nd 1940. The Germans, as victors, dictated the conditions for peace. The partition of French territory was one of these conditions. France was thenceforward divided into seven zones, each with its own administrative relationship with the German occupying authorities.[18] The Coastal Zone, a strip of territory ten to twenty kilometres wide stretching from the Belgian border as far as Hendaye, was off limits to everyone but residents and persons in possession of a German pass. As of August 14th 1940 a decree from the German Army High Command had all "undesirables" (English, Jews and Gypsies) expelled from this zone. The Northern Zone (comprising the departments of Pas-de-Calais and le Nord) was administratively attached to the German Military Command in Belgium and for four years remained totally isolated from the rest of France. The Forbidden Zone, demarcated by the Green Line, also known as the Führer's Line, covered the departments of l'Aisne, the Ardennes, la Meuse, Meurthe-et-Moselle and Vosges; French citizens were not permitted to travel freely here, and it was off limits to returning refugees. Alsace-Lorraine (Haut-Rhin, Bas-Rhin and Moselle) was effectively annexed into Germany proper on 15th July 1940, cutting off the area to "undesirables" who had fled for refuge to "the interior" when war first broke out, and leading to the expulsion of some 100,000 locals, deemed to be "unassimilable", towards the Southern Zone. The Occupied Zone had a 1,000-kilometre frontier stretching from the Swiss to the Spanish border, and was under the direct control of the German Military Command in France. The Unoccupied Zone, also known as the "Free" or Southern Zone, was under the Vichy Government. On November 11th 1942 German troops invaded this zone in reprisal for the Allied landing in North Africa, but the French continued to govern here. The Italian Zone, initially limited to the border region, was extended after this occupation of the Southern Zone to include seven departments (Haute-Savoie, Savoie, Drôme, Hautes- and Basses-Alpes, Var, Alpes-Maritimes) as well as part of Isère and of Vaucluse. On September 8th 1943, following the Italian armistice with the Allies, it too was occupied by the Germans.

The expulsion of the Gypsies from Alsace-Lorraine

The Gypsies of Alsace-Lorraine were the first to be affected by German measures. The disputed frontier region had been returned to France in 1918, only to be re-annexed by Germany in 1940. As of July 1940 the occupying forces aimed for the expulsion of "undesirables", including Gypsies[19], from the region. In September of that year 160 Gypsies and "antisocials" were evacuated from the Haut-Rhin; in December the annexed region expelled a further 146 men and 403 women and children classed as "antisocials". It should be noted that the Nazis did not intern these Gypsies in internment camps, as was already being done in Germany proper, instead Gypsies, like Jews, were initially expelled towards the Free Zone. It appears that the Nazis' first concern was to purge those territories attached to Germany proper of individuals deemed to be "undesirable".

Internment in the Free Zone

Gypsies from Alsace-Lorraine were scattered all over France. From October 1940 nearly 600 of them were interned in camps in the Free Zone, initially at Argelès-sur-Mer, then transferred to Barcarès and Rivesaltes in the Eastern Pyrenees. In November 1942, they were all brought together in a camp at Saliers in the Bouches-du-Rhône.

In March 1942 the Vichy Government undertook an initiative to set up a model camp for nomads in response to criticism in the foreign – particularly the Swiss – press, denouncing the existence of camps in the south of France. The architect was instructed to make it a showcase for government propaganda. Following these guidelines, he situated it at Saliers near Saintes-Maries-de-la-Mer (site of an annual pilgrimage attracting Gypsies from all over Europe) and drew inspiration from local building styles and materials, including their characteristic reed-thatched roofs and whitewashed walls. Saliers was meant to be a model camp where nomads would feel at home. It was a total failure, proving uninhabitable for a number of reasons: the beaten earth floors dissolved into mud whenever it rained, the cabins were crawling with parasites, etc. Internees escaped en masse. In August 1944 all the remaining inmates took advantage of bombardments to get out of the camp for good.[20]

The Free Zone had two camps exclusively for nomads: in addition to the one at Saliers, there was another at Lannemezan in the Hautes-Pyrénées; the internment of Gypsies in the latter is described in two works by the Gypsy author Matéo Maximoff.[21] The writer and his family, of Russian origin, were assigned a place of compulsory residence at Tarbes on August 8th 1940; on April 1st 1941 French military police brought them, and other Gypsies living in the region, to the Lannemezan plateau, where they lived under constant police surveillance and extremely precarious conditions until they, and a small number of other families, were gradually released to specified places of residence beginning in December 1943. These two cases of internment aside, however, the Vichy Government contented itself with applying the Decree of April 6th 1940, and did so with no particular zeal; there is, nonetheless, evidence of Gypsies having been interned for various periods in the camps at Gurs, Noé, Brens, Agde and Nexon, all in the Free Zone. German occupation, when it did come about, had no impact on Gypsies there.

The German decree of October 4th 1940

In the Occupied Zone, by contrast, Gypsies were locked up in internment camps in an atmosphere of total indifference from the public at large. On October 4th 1940 the German Military Command in France ordered that:

Gypsy internees at the Rivesaltes camp.

"1. Gypsies *(Zigeuner)* in the Occupied Zone must be transferred to internment camps under the surveillance of French police officers. Details to be worked out by the German military authorities.

2. Crossing the demarcation line into the Occupied Zone is forbidden."[22]

On October 21st 1940 the Field Commander of the Eure department explained to the local mayor how the decree was to be interpreted:

"a) all persons, whether of French or foreign nationality, without fixed abode and wandering the Occupied region according to the habits of the Bohemians (nomads, travelling showmen) shall be considered Bohemians, whether or not they are in possession of an identity card or anthropometric identity card.

b) these measures shall be carried out by the French authorities.

c) persons under arrest must, pending their transfer to a secure place of detention, be brought to the main town of the department in question, and lodged there. Members of the same family must not be separated. Their surveillance and maintenance are the responsibility of the mayor, who must also ensure that the children attend school.

d) the question of camps will be sorted when the number of persons to be interned is known."[23]

In contrast to the French, the Germans classed travelling showmen and nomads under a single heading, on the grounds that they were all Gypsies. As a result, a number of showmen were incarcerated in internment camps under the same terms as nomads. In April 1941, the Germans justified this decision by officially eliminating the category of "travelling showman". Those formerly classed in this manner had either to prove that they had a fixed address – in which case they were reclassified as "itinerant tradesmen" – or, if unable to do so, were relegated to "nomad" status.[24] It was therefore the German authorities who took the decision to intern the Gypsies.

In mid-October 1940 the Field Commanders in charge of implementing these measures ordered the mayors of the Occupied Zone to organise the internment process. On October 24th, the mayor of the Vendée department issued a decree that all nomads in the jurisdiction were to be brought to the quarries at Monsireigne, explaining in the preface that he was acting in accordance with German orders:

"In view of instruction no. 606 of October 13th 1940 from the Field Commander's office, issued in application of orders emanating from the military administration in France and prescribing that all nomads within a given department must, by November 1st 1940, be assembled in a camp under the surveillance of the French police..."[25]

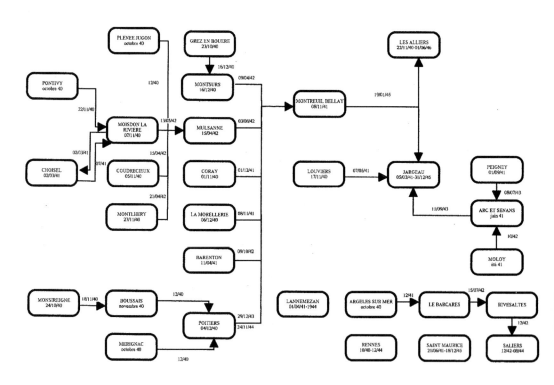

Diagram of internment camps for nomads, 1940-46. Dates given in boxes indicate the arrival of the first nomads and the departure of the last nomads, respectively. Dates associated with arrows indicate transfers.

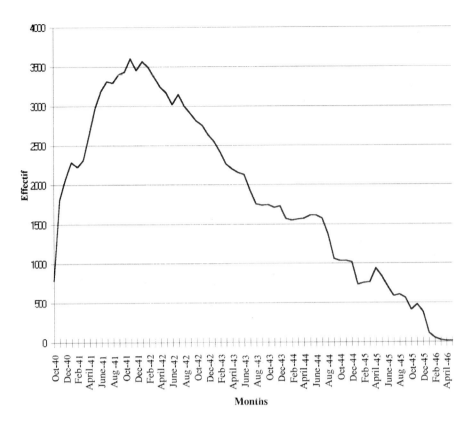

Numbers of nomads interned in France, 1940-46.

The process was always identical: the local Field Commander ordered the mayor – rarely in writing – to take all necessary measures with a view to interning nomads, that is, to count them, locate an internment camp for them, and then to carry out the internment. Once the military police had found a camp, the mayor issued an order legalising the internment of nomads. Edmond Duméril, formerly an interpreter at the Loire-Inférieure department office, explains the process:

"In order to avoid outraging public opinion, decisions taken by the Germans at these conferences had to be transformed into orders from the mayor without the slightest trace of foreign interference. The purpose of this subterfuge was to ensure that the French authorities took the blame for unpopular measures dictated by an occupying force which liked to think of itself as benign."[26]

Despite being the driving force behind this internment, the Germans refused categorically to carry it out themselves:

"The surveillance of nomads is a political measure incumbent upon the French administrative authorities. This is why the costs associated with interning nomads are borne by the French administration as police measures undertaken by the French state, even when the internment takes place by order of the German authorities."[27]

69

In legalising the internment of Gypsies by issuing an order from the mayor, the French state became, logically, the sole body responsible for their internment, and for this reason was also obliged to accept all the consequences thereof. The French authorities, for their part, were willing to take on organisation and management of the internment process, drawing the line only at bearing the associated costs. Until October 1942 the two sides passed the buck from one to the other and it was the nomads who suffered the consequences (dilapidated camps, no provisions). Finally, in 1942, running costs were charged to account number 38-05, to be paid under the heading of occupation costs.[28]

The first internment camps for nomads

From October to November 1940, anywhere that nomads were interned called itself a camp. In reality, nomads were gathered together in isolated, delimited areas within which they continued to travel in search of work; as at Monsireigne in the Vendée, no provision was made for feeding them in these early months. The first step, then, was to gather them together, waiting to be transported to a real internment camp. Only a small number of nomads – about fifty per department – were affected.

On October 14th 1940, nomads at Morbihan were brought together at a disused castle in Pontivy before being transferred a month later to Moisdon-la-Rivière in the Loire-Inférieure department. At Grez-en-Bouère in Mayenne, they were packed into an old quarry before being transferred, on December 16th, to the camp at Montsûrs. Forty nomads were brought together at Plénée-Jugon in the Côtes-du-Nord, awaiting transfer. In Eure, from November 17th 1940, some sixty nomads were held in the Plumet quarry at Louviers. The precarious nature of these "camps" was specific to the internment of nomads: they were to be set apart at any price, and to achieve this were simply herded into isolated spots with no regard for sheltering them from the wind and rain or consideration of how they were to obtain food. It must be borne in mind that this internment affected entire families, most of them with numerous dependent children and no possessions. They had no savings on which to draw and no relatives on the outside to offer support.

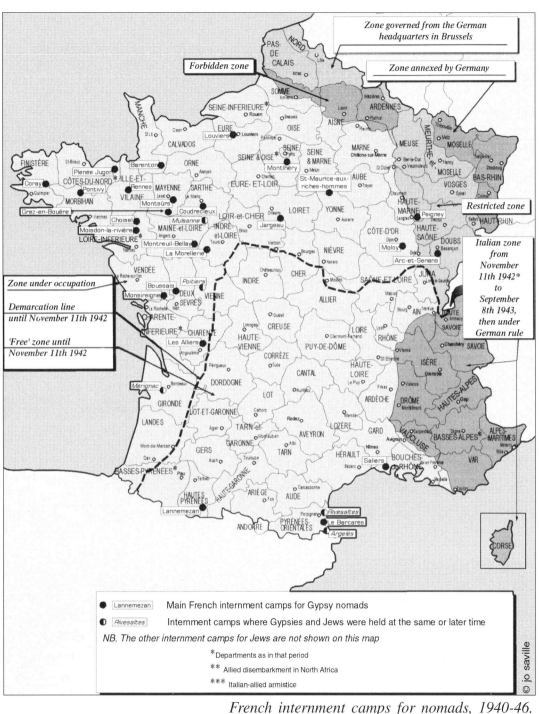

French internment camps for nomads, 1940-46.

In November 1940, only five proper concentration camps for nomads were in existence.

*In Gironde, the camp at Mérignac took in Jews and nomads from the month of October; the nomads were transferred to Poitiers in December.

*On November 5th the nomads of Brittany and Sarthe were interned at La Pierre at Coudrecieux (Sarthe) where they were accommodated in an old glass factory.

*The camp at Moisdon-la-Rivière in Loire-Inférieure took in its first nomads on November 7th. They were accommodated in an abandoned iron ore forge encircled by barbed wire and kept under permanent guard; the Germans closed the camp five months later on health grounds.

*From November 1st 1940 – December 1st 1941, the nomads of Finistère were held at an old cinema at Coray. They were not fed by the administration.

*Up to December 1944, the nomads of Ille-et-Vilaine were interned at Margueritte camp on the Rue Le Guen de Kérangal, Rennes.

CAMP DE MOISDON - LA - RIVIERE
27 janvier 1941
(AN : 72 AJ 283 : A2 I)

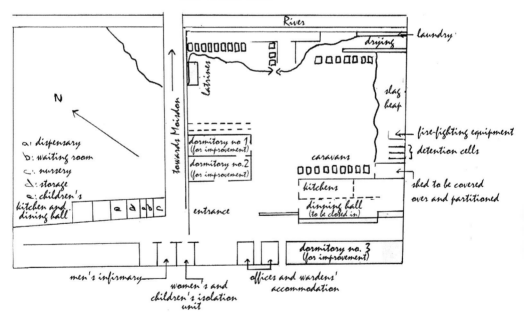

Plan of Moisdon-la-Rivière Camp, January 27 th 1941.

Existing transit camps disappeared under German pressure. In effect a decree issued by the occupying forces on November 22nd 1940 prohibited the exercise of mobile trades in twenty-one departments of western France; itinerant tradesmen, travelling showmen and nomads all came under the ban.[29] In the remainder of the Occupied Zone, the practice of these trades was subject to obtaining prior authorisation. The consequences were immediate: the Germans expelled all itinerants from the Coastal Zone and interned them in camps.

On November 22nd 1940, nomads travelling in Charente and Charente-Inférieure were directed to Les Alliers camp at Angoulême.

On November 27th, 201 nomads rounded up in Seine-Inférieure were taken to Linas-Montlhéry camp in Seine-et-Oise.

On December 4th, 204 nomads expelled from the southwestern coastal regions were assigned places of compulsory residence in the Vienne department. They were sent to the camp at Poitiers the following day.

On December 6th, Morellerie camp in Indre-et-Loire took in its first nomads, as did Jargeau in Loiret on March 5th 1941 and La Mine camp at Barenton in la Manche on April 11th in their turn.

Camp at Saint-Maurice-aux-Riches-Hommes (Yonne department).

*Main entrance to the Route de Limoges Camp at Poitiers
(Haute-Vienne department).*

By the end of December 1940, approximately 1,700 nomads and travelling showmen were interned in ten camps throughout the Occupied Zone.

In eastern France, organising the internment of nomads began on April 12th 1941, the date on which the head of the German military administration of Region C (northeastern France) ordered mayors in the jurisdiction to assemble the nomads of each department into camps.[30]

In June 1941 the ancient royal saltworks at Arc-et-Senans provided lodgings for the nomads of Doubs, followed by those from the occupied departments of Côte d'Or, Haute-Marne, Saône-et-Loire, Jura and l'Ain. On September 11th 1943 the 168 nomads still interned there were transferred to Jargeau.

On June 21st 1941 nomads travelling in Yonne, le Nord, l'Aube and Deux-Sèvres were interned in the courtyard of a disused railway station at Saint-Maurice-aux-Riches-Hommes.

These camps were of every size (Barenton held fifty internees, Moisdon-la-Rivière, 400) and description: a manor in Indre-et-Loire, an historic monument in Doubs, a mine in la Manche, a railway station in Yonne. Other camps (Jargeau, Choisel, Montsûrs) had been purpose built in 1939 to shelter refugees fleeing the Civil War in Spain. Some nomads ended up interned alongside

74

Barracks set aside for interned nomads, Poitiers.

political prisoners (Choisel), "undesirables" (Rennes), Jews (Poitiers) and prostitutes (Jargeau).

Setting up regional camps

These large numbers of small camps, some properly organised, others less so, posed massive administrational problems. By 1941 the Germans decided to reorganise the lot:

"Reorganising the camps...will be undertaken with the twin aim of preventing different categories of internees from sharing camps, and of reducing insofar as possible the manpower tied up in guarding them. This will be achieved by setting up large camps to take over from those currently operating, the great number of which increases demands on supplies and personnel."[31]

Thus on November 8th 1941 the regional camp at Montreuil-Bellay[32] (Maine-et-Loire department) opened its gates, taking in 258 nomads formerly interned at La Morellerie camp. Those from other camps which were dissolved followed in turn – Coray (December 2nd 1941), Montsûrs (April 4th 1942), Mulsanne (August 5th 1942), Barenton (October 9th 1942) and Poitiers (December 27th 1943). With 1086 internees by August 1942, Montreuil-Bellay was the biggest of the internment camps for nomads.

75

Mulsanne, in Sarthe department, was another regional camp. It took in the nomads from Coudrecieux (April 15th 1942), Montlhéry (April 21st) and Moisdon-la-Rivière (May 13th).

In order to estimate the numbers interned in the thirty camps for nomads operating in France 1940-46, we must examine figures camp by camp, taking account of gaps in the information available for some, and being careful not to count anyone – notably those transferred from camp to camp – twice. This gives us a minimum figure of 4,657 nomads interned in the Occupied Zone and 1,404 in the Free Zone: a total of 6,061. Therefore, between 6,000-6,500 individuals were interned as nomads in French internment camps.

90% of the nomads interned were of French nationality: for example, of the 504 nomads interned at Poitiers, 457 were French, and forty-seven of other nationalities, while at Mulsanne in June 1942 the ratio of French to foreign was 564:47. There were thus very few foreign nomads to be found in these camps; they included Belgians, Italians, Germans, Spaniards, Czechoslovaks, Poles, Russians and stateless persons. According to Matéo Maximoff, a number of foreign Gypsies would have succeeded in crossing over into Spain within a very short period of the outbreak of hostilities. It is also possible that they were interned in other camps, classed as foreigners rather than Gypsies; it is thus almost impossible to trace them.

The camp at Montreuil-Bellay (Maine-et-Loir department) in 1944.

There were a great many women and children in these camps. Women often outnumbered men, and children made up 30-40% of internees. This made conditions all the more unbearable.

Daily life of the internees – health hazards, cold and destitution

At Peigney in Haute-Marne, nomads were housed in a disused fortress bereft of doors, windows, and running water. The barracks at Mulsanne were roofed with sheet metal, making them as glacial in winter as they were stifling in summer. Camps were often built in flat, open country or on hillsides at the mercy of the elements. Nomads preferred to live in their caravans than in barracks ill-suited to their way of life.

Internees fought a losing battle with the cold. The winters of the war years were particularly harsh and, where coal and wood could not be got, internees burnt everything they could get their hands on including (at Moisdon-la-Rivière) the floorboards of their own barracks. Their clothing was inadequate for winter conditions: most of them had had to abandon their meagre possessions when arrested. For example, Montlhéry internees arrested at Darnétal in Seine-Inférieure were forced to leave their caravans and all their personal effects behind them.

Interior of barracks at Mérignac camp (Gironde department).

All heads of camps noted the nomads' destitution in their reports. At Montsûrs, in January 1942, "the adults have no shirts, and wear jackets next the skin."[33] Children went barefoot in the mud and women cut up clothing to improvise bedcovers as protection from the cold. Underwear was nonexistent. The nomads had no change of clothing, nor money with which to buy any. Heads of camps tried their best to obtain clothes for the inmates but due to lack of funding could not pay suppliers. They also deplored the inaction of charitable bodies, notably the Red Cross and the Secours National[34], which occasionally sent small batches of secondhand clothing – never enough to meet needs. In October 1942 nomads at Les Alliers camp got clogs and clothing from the Secours National, but had to pay for these with cash or clothing ration points: "One nomad, who got a waistcoat in mediocre condition and a pair of trousers in a very bad state, had to give twenty-four points for them; this was quite excessive."[35]

Poor hygiene, hunger and isolation

Camps, being unpaved, were habitually muddy. Accommodation quickly became uninhabitable, especially in winter: there were neither mattresses nor blankets and the barracks were crawling with fleas and lice. The heads of camps denounced what they called "a repulsive state of filth"[36] for which they held the internees responsible. Delousing was a rarity, as were showers; what sanitation was provided was dilapidated and inadequate. The camp nurse at Saint-Maurice deplored the fact that "the lack of towelling makes it impossible to dry the children, to warm them up".[37]

Nomads had also to do battle with hunger. In some camps, such as the one at Coray, the administration made no provision for feeding internees, instead authorising them to leave the camp to procure their own supplies. In March 1942, Doctor Aujaleu, of the General Camps Inspectorate, remarked that the internees at Moisdon-la-Rivière were getting a mere 1400 calories per day, i.e. 300 less than the absolute minimum required to maintain the body in a resting state, and 1,000 less than required by an active adult male.[38] In April 1941 the internees at Mulsanne had had no breakfast for over a week; according to the camp doctor, the food was wholesome, but "inadequate for people used to living in the open air, and with good appetites".[39]

The following letter was written at Montlhéry, November 29th 1941:

From all the nomads of the camp, to the Superintendent

We have the honour of writing these few words to you, that is the whole lot of us here in the camp, that is on the subject of bread. We have been patient up to Friday as you had promised us there would be a change in the bread, we counted on you. But we see that there has been no change, we have a right to 253 grams of bread per person and we only get 175 grams. You understand that we are obliged to ask, seeing as we are not getting our share. We have been putting up with this business for a good while now and it cannot go on so I am announcing if this continues no one will go to work anymore owing to weakness. We are asking simply for our share and no more. That way everybody will be happy because it is you who are there to check on what goes on in the camp.

With sincerest good wishes.[40]

Funding never reached the camps, or got there too late to pay off suppliers. As everywhere, there was theft and black market activity. The nomads' main disadvantage was that they, unlike other internees, had no supplementary sources of food such as parcels from outside. Many charitable bodies provided assistance to Jewish internees, but no one looked after the nomads; their only chance was if the camp head took pity on them or some religious body made an effort to improve their situation.

Illness and death

In spite of everything, nomads proved more resistant than other groups to the rigours of prolonged internment. In 1942 Doctor Aujaleu noted that cachexia and oedemas, so widespread in other camps, were rare among these internees. He explained their resilience as being due to the fact that conditions in the camps were not very different from those in which they normally lived, and this opinion was shared by all the camp heads.

There were, nonetheless, fatalities due to malnutrition and various diseases. The death rate was highest amongst children, the elderly and lone adults. Diseases were treated at the camp infirmary, if there was one or, if not, at the nearest hospital, as was the case at Montsûrs. Babies were born in the camps, too: as expectant mothers refused to go to hospital, they gave birth inside the wire.

School for the children, work for their parents

The authorities denounced the idleness of nomads and made a point of sending the children to school and parents to work. As a result, some Gypsies learned to read and write while interned. Children interned at Montsûrs had to attend the village school "but were often unable to do so due to lack of shoes and shirts".[41] Elsewhere, barracks were transformed into one or more classrooms and teachers (evacuated Alsatians, Lorrainers or members of religious orders) appointed to instruct the children in the rudiments of French and mathematics. For example, at Coudrecieux, in January 1942, fifty-eight children were attending courses which, due to the lack of electricity, had to take place by natural light alone: mornings from 10-11:30 and afternoons 14:00-17:00. Sometimes, as at Saliers, they were removed from the "bad influence" of their parents by being temporarily placed in institutions run by religious bodies.

79

Interned children playing in front of the school building at Jargeau camp (Loiret department).

Adults were, naturally enough, put to work at the usual tasks such as tidying the camp and collecting firewood, but were also employed in more lucrative endeavours such as the making of objects in wickerwork or, as at Montreuil-Bellay, subcontracted to make camouflage nets for a local firm. At Jargeau, internees worked in carpentry, shoe repair, basketry and rope-making workshops and at the camp barbershop; at Arc-et-Senans they were employed as agricultural labourers and by the Department of Water and Forestry. In the Sarthe region nomads were employed at the Renault factory at Mans for a few weeks before being let go on the grounds that they produced too little and quarrelled too much. In fact, they did not fit into the industrial scene: they were "lazy and unskilled".[42] But work was meant to educate them.

Nomads were also employed in German industries located in France, notably the Todt plants at La Rochelle, Saintes and Champagnole.[43]

Compulsory Work Service (STO)

As ever-greater numbers of men were mobilised, German industry suffered a shortage of labour and Gypsies in France were – like all citizens and resident foreigners – subject to conscription to fill the gaps: workers from all the occupied countries were sent to Germany to labour in the armaments industry.[44] In France, the Germans began by hiring volunteers but there were not enough of these. From September 1941 to March 1942 14,000 volunteers left France for Germany; in March 1942 the Germans issued an appeal for a further 300,000 workers, 150,000 of them specialists, to report for duty by September of that year. In June 1942 Pierre Laval[45] launched Operation Relief: Germany promised to release one prisoner of war for every three specialists to volunteer. From June 1st to September 1st, only 17,000 workers volunteered to leave for Germany; by December 31st 1942 the number had risen to 240,000, 135,000 of them specialists. Now embroiled in Russia, Germany was once again short of manpower; at the beginning of 1943, a new appeal was launched, this time for a million workers, 250,000 of them French. On February 16th 1943, a new law instituting Compulsory Work Service (Service du Travail Obligatoire, colloquially known as STO), was passed.

"Applied in accordance with date of birth, as if it were military service, it lasted for two years. Its requirements could be fulfilled by remaining in the employment in which one was engaged when called up, if this was deemed to be in conformity with the country's needs."[46]

The first recruitment drive targeted males born between 1920-22 – years when the birth rate had been particularly high. A census was taken of all young men, and these were at first strongly encouraged, and in time physically forced, to leave for Germany; the occupying forces went as far as round-ups and arbitrary arrests. STO very quickly became unpopular, and numbers dodging it rose despite the reprisals carried out against their families. 250,259 French workers, 157,020 of them specialists, were working for Germany by March 31st 1943.

Gypsies were sent to Germany both under Operation Relief and STO, some voluntarily, others not. The first nomads to leave for Germany (internees from the Saint-Maurice camp) went with the February 1943 batch of deportees; in his monthly report, the camp director noted that:

"Fifteen inmates were designated to leave for Germany. Of these, G. Pierre and K. Emile escaped while in transit between Sens and Laroche, despite the presence of two guards. Moreover a further two inmates, T. Louis and G. Michel, escaped after they had been handed over to the German authorities at Dijon."[47]

During the month of June, two men left the camp to work for the Germans in separate establishments at Sens. In October, "a nomad who had gone to work in Germany was sent back, declared unfit for work."[48] At no point were many Gypsies involved in these schemes as the Germans were wary of taking on this unqualified, "workshy" manpower.[49]

The camp at Poitiers was a tragic exception. On January 13th 1943, seventy men aged sixteen to sixty were transferred out of the camp to work in Germany, as the director's report confirms.[50] Traces of them are to be found at Royallieu camp at Compiègne (Oise department) from which sixty-six of them were transported, on January 23rd, to Oranienburg-Sachsenhausen camp in Germany.[51] On June 23rd 1943 a further twenty-five men left Poitiers for Compiègne camp; three days later twenty-three of them were transferred to Buchenwald. By

81

August 4th 1943, only six of these men (four from the first lot, two from the second) had returned to Poitiers; unlike their companions, they had never left Compiègne.[52] Nothing more was ever heard from the remainder of the Poitiers deportees.

These Gypsies appear to have been sent to work in Germany, apparently delivered by the French authorities to avoid local youths from having to go. Their transfer to Nazi concentration camps remains inexplicable to this day.

Escape

There were a great many escapes among the nomads who found internment unbearable and did not understand why it had been imposed on them. Being prevented from travelling was insupportable. They were isolated, illiterate for the most part and with no outside contacts to help them. To these difficulties must be added the fact that they had little hope of being set free.

As a further letter from Montlhéry, November 22nd 1941, states:

To the mayor

I have the honour of sending you this letter in the name of all my colleagues who are interned with me at Montlhéry and ask you to excuse our using these rough words to write to you but under the circumstances they are necessary. You know that it has now been exactly a year that we have been interned at Montlhéry for what reason we still do not know because we have never killed nor robbed and yet for the year we have been interned. We have been supplied with neither clothing nor shoes and we are absolutely cut off from the rest of the world. There are about 200 of us here and at least 80% of us are barefoot and you could also say without clothing because when we left Darnétal we only had an hour to make our preparations. So we weren't able to bring a lot and the little that we did have is now completely worn out. So here we are reduced to the state of vagabonds while in our caravans our clothes are rotting and we have money we cannot use. Sir, you are a Frenchman, you have a human heart, and maybe a father's heart, so, try to put yourself in our place! If you were shut up in a camp with your wife and children and you saw them crying out of misery, what would you feel! Sir, we are all fathers here and every day for the past year we see our wives and children who, most of the time, hide themselves away to cry, so as not to add to our sufferings. So Sir, is that any way to live? No it is not. Make a decision but do not leave us suffering this way. Let us go get our things from our caravans and put us in a different camp because the situation here is unbearable. Otherwise let us go we will accept any conditions at all even if we have to buy houses and report to the local town hall every day.

I hope, Sir, that wretchedness as great as ours will touch your heart because we have been suffering like this for a year now.

In the hope of a reply which I hope will be positive, Sir, we remain very sincerely yours,

The nomads of Montlhéry camp.[53]

A small number of internees enlisted the aid of solicitors who had great difficulty in getting them out except under conditions along the lines of owning a house or possessing a certificate of accommodation, being accepted by the local authorities in the area where they were to live, having demonstrated good conduct while in the camp, getting the go-ahead from the mayor in the department they were leaving and in the department they were moving to, and sometimes from the German authorities as well. Once let go, they were assigned a place of residence and remained at the mercy of the local authorities who could send them back to camp.

There were a lot of escapes during transfers. Women and children were kept as hostages, especially when the men were sent to Germany, but that did not stop men from escaping, nor from coming back to camp to free their families. Release was a rarity and so nomads tended to escape en masse, in family groups, bringing with them even the aged and the very young. They used every possible means: jumping the walls, bribing the guards, not coming back from hospital, seizing the opportunity of an outing. Most were caught within a few days but, once back in camp, they tried again at the first opportunity: some escaped four or five times.

Liberation – but not for everyone

On June 6th 1944 the Allied landing in Normandy established a presence that went on expanding but which the Germans were able to contain until July 25th, when the Allies broke through the front at Avranches and surged westwards towards the Loire and Seine, driving the enemy from the whole of northern France. The Franco-American landing in Provence on August 15th achieved far quicker results: in less than a month they had spread northwards, linking up with troops from Normandy on September 12th, near Dijon, and forcing the Germans into a rushed evacuation of central and southwest France to avoid encirclement. Nazi troops retreated towards the east and north; by November 1944 they remained in control of only a couple of pockets of territory on the Atlantic coast at Dunkerque and Colmar.[54]

In December 1944 nomads were still being interned in five camps: Les Alliers, Montreuil-Bellay, Rennes, Jargeau and Saint-Maurice. By January 1st 1945 no more nomads were interned at Rennes. A few weeks later – January 19th – 172 of the nomads interned at Montreuil-Bellay were released and the remainder transferred to the camps at Jargeau and Les Alliers.

On May 8th 1945 Germany capitulated. The war was over on French territory.

The French State was no longer in existence; France was administered by the Provisional Government of the Republic with General de Gaulle at its head.

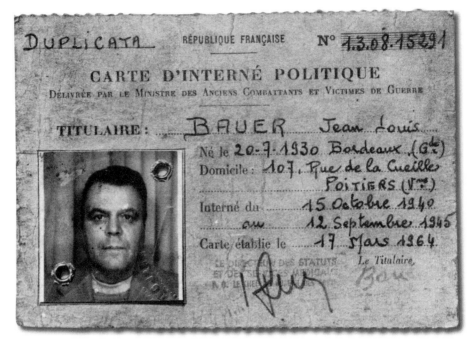

Jean-Louis Bauer's political internee's identity card.

In a memorandum dated July 18th 1945 the Administrative Services Monitoring Board noted that 675 nomads were still interned in France and queried the legality of this internment.[55] On September 15th 1945, the Director of the Criminal Investigation Department authorised their release while advocating that they be assigned a place of compulsory residence within their department of origin and recommending that minute investigation be undertaken beforehand.[56] The Decree of April 6th 1940 remained operative despite the fact that hostilities had ceased and the military considerations cited in justification of the Decree were no longer relevant.

On September 26th 1945 the Minister of the Interior finally came out in favour of the "release pure and simple of those nomads who are not subject to expulsion orders"[57] and to their being assigned a place of residence without undergoing scrutiny of their records, this process being deemed too heavy handed. The last nomad internees were freed from Saint-Maurice camp on December 18th 1945, from Jargeau on December 31st 1945, and from Les Alliers on June 1st 1946.

The Law of May 10th 1946, fixing the legal date of the cessation of hostilities, abrogated the Decree of April 6th 1940, yet even then nomads' liberty was not restored in its entirety. On July 20th 1946 the Minister of the Interior recommended the "severe [application] of the measures provided for under Articles 3 and 4 of the Law of July 16th 1912 vis à vis nomads who do not acquire stability and who do not demonstrate a willingness to integrate into the sedentary population."[58]

Once released, nomads picked up the pieces of the travelling life as best they could. They were often poorer than they had been before the War: their meagre savings depleted during internment, their caravans gone. This is how Jean-Louis Baucr describes his release from Jargeau camp in September 1945:

"When we got out, no one helped us. We were alone on the road and we walked from Jargeau to Poitiers, with nothing, in abject poverty."[59]

Families were broken up. Even in liberty, they remained under surveillance and subject to the measures of the Law of July 16th 1912. For all these reasons some nomads had no option but to settle down when they were released from French internment camps.

Deportation to Auschwitz – the convoy of January 15th 1944

Many aspects of the subject of this chapter remain unknown. The deportation of Gypsies from Belgium to Auschwitz is, however, well documented.

When we consult *Memorial Book, the Gypsies at Auschwitz-Birkenau*[60], a work listing all 20,943 Gypsies interned at this camp, we find the names of 145 French Gypsies (seventy-four women, seventy-one men) who arrived on January 17th 1944. Their presence at Auschwitz comes at first as a shock for in all our research in the national and regional archives of France we have found no documentation attesting to this deportation. Nor do the archives of French internment camps for nomads ever make mention of any departure for Auschwitz. So how did these people get there?

An answer is to be found in José Gotovicht's article[61] on the extermination of Belgian Gypsies. The Northern Zone of France was administratively attached to the German Military Command in Belgium and was effectively cut off from the rest of the country. The number of Gypsies travelling Belgium at the time was estimated as 200-300 persons.[62] Gotovicht's article reproduces a statement issued by the Belgian Ministry for Public Health and the Family[63] listing the 351 Gypsies who made up Z Convoy.[64] It proves that these French Gypsies, arrested in the Northern Zone and in Belgium proper, were indeed part of that convoy which departed Malines for Auschwitz on January 15th 1944. The history of these French deportees is thus linked with that of the Gypsies of Belgium.

"In 1933 the Aliens Office [in Belgium] decided to establish [Gypsies'] identity by photographing and fingerprinting them. They were then issued with a travel pass valid for three months. Tolerance of camping was left to the discretion of the local authorities, who were empowered to curtail or overturn the 48 hours rule generally applied."[65]

The Nazi invasion of Belgium in May 1940 sent two million refugees, Gypsies among them, pouring over the border into France. With the fall of France, some of these – like the Annies, Bourquin, Czardas, Modeste, Peterbost and

Toloche families – stayed where they were, while others – among them the Galut, Gorgan, Kall, Karoly, Keck and Modis, families – returned to Belgium. Others split up: members of the Maitre, Taicon and Vadoche families were to be found on either side of the border.[66]

The occupying forces in Belgium passed only one official measure against the Gypsies: the decree of November 12th 1940 prohibited itinerant trading throughout Flanders and in the area around Antwerp. In December 1941 the Aliens Office introduced the "nomads' identity card" to replace the "travel pass". From 5-20th January 1942 all rural constabulary brigades were requested to arrest and detain all Gypsies they came across to ensure that they received their new cards. From January 21st 1942 all nomads over the age of fifteen were required to carry this card. According to José Gotovicht, Gypsies were allowed to carry on without major hindrance until 1943, travelling as usual throughout the region, including the Northern Zone of France. A small number were arrested for infractions of the decree of November 12th 1940.

In late October 1943 "brutal mass arrests got under way throughout Belgium and the Northern Zone"[67]: Himmler had given the order for the arrest of all Gypsies in these territories. The first known mass arrests occurred at Tournai in Belgium on October 22nd. "Over the month of November, up to December 6th, more arrests were carried out in rapid succession: Tournai again, Hasselt, Brussels, Arras and Roubaix"[68] (the last two named are in northern France). On December 6th 1943, 166 Gypsies were interned at Dossin Barracks at Malines. Some, like Paprika Galut, arrested with his family at Hénin-Liétard in the Pas-de-Calais department of northern France, were held at Loos prison in Lille for a few days before being transferred to this central holding facility. On December 9th an additional 182 Gypsies arrived at Malines.

"At Dossin Barracks at Malines, the Gypsies were to live in appalling conditions for one or two months as the case might be. Locked up in three rooms at the end of the courtyard, deprived of everything, totally isolated from both the outside world and the Jewish prisoners, they were allowed only two hours of fresh air per day."[69]

On January 15th 1944, 351 Gypsies were handed a single loaf of bread each and loaded onto cattle cars for transfer to Auschwitz; their hellish journey lasted two days. On arrival they were shaved, tattooed and put into quarantine; the time for their extermination had not yet come. Once the quarantine period was over, they joined the rest of the Gypsies in the Family Section set aside for them. This was where Angélika Schmidt was born on March 6th 1944; the Nazis registered her as Z 10 029. Ten days later, she died, as did many of her compatriots: eight in February, twenty-two in March, thirteen in April, six in May, five each in June and July and another twelve that year for whom no exact dates are known. 49% of French Gypsies at Auschwitz died within six months of arrival. The main cause of this high mortality was typhus which ravaged the concentration camps. On April 15th 1944, 1,357 Gypsies were transferred to other camps: 884 men (fifteen of them French) to Buchenwald,

473 women (nine of them French) to Ravensbrück. Of the 351 Gypsies deported from Malines only twelve survived.

We have established that some of these Gypsies had been interned in French camps prior to their deportation: for example, French citizens Marie and Joséphine Boudin (Z 9910 and Z 9911 respectively) spent 1940-43 in Montlhéry, Mulsanne and Montreuil-Bellay. Their names also figure on the previously named list of Belgian internees[70], compiled on September 29th 1942[71]; forty of the fifty-nine names on that list are later to be found on the register at Auschwitz.[72] Having fled the German advance in May 1940 these Belgians were interned in Montlhéry camp in November of that year by the German authorities, and later transferred to Mulsanne and Montreuil-Bellay; they were released from the latter in 1943 and settled in the region. The Toloche and Boudin families set up home at Cersay in the Deux-Sèvres department[73]; it appears that they decided to return to Belgium where they were picked up in mass arrests.

As far as we know, these were the only Gypsies to have been deported from France on racial grounds.

Other deportations

Only at Auschwitz were Gypsies given "Z" (for Zigeuner – Gypsy) classification numbers. Generally speaking, it is difficult to identify the Gypsies elsewhere among the other categories of internees. In fact, German camp records – with the exception of Auschwitz – make almost no mention at all of Gypsies as a category prior to 1944.[74]

It does appear that French Gypsies were also deported to other camps: some individually, on racial grounds, some for working with the Resistance or for other reasons.

When this subject is brought up among Gypsies today, they all say they know, or knew, someone who was deported from France to Nazi concentration camps. It is impossible to trace these individual deportations in the archives; our only possible source of information is personal testimony and there is still very little of this.

We also know that Gypsies were deported to Nazi concentration camps for other reasons. For example, in 1943 twenty-three "French Gitans" were deported from the Northern Zone for political reasons and a further six as members of the Resistance.[75] A proper history of Gypsies' role in the Resistance remains to be written; all we have so far are scattered personal testimonies.

Conclusion

I think that the reason why French Gypsies were not deported was partly because the Germans were unable to apply their racial criteria here. French legislation had always had the eradication of nomadism as its sole objective; Gypsies who took up permanent accommodation, or who were recognised as travelling showmen, were left in peace. The majority of Gypsies were categorised as nomads but not all Gypsies were nomads, nor were all nomads Gypsies. As many memoranda attest, the Germans attempted in vain to impose their own criteria of classification[76] but were unsuccessful, not least because they insisted that arrests and internment be carried out by the French police who limited their attentions to carriers of anthropometric identification cards. Others were left in peace provided they behaved discreetly.

Where the Germans handled arrests themselves, they rounded up everyone indiscriminately – but they did not often do so, and when they did the French authorities secured the release of those who did not come under Article 3 of the Law of July 16th 1912. Given the non-homogenous nature of the population in question, the Germans could not order the deportation of all Gypsies living in France; inevitably, some would have slipped through the net. However, this is just one of several theories put forward to explain why Nazi policy was so different in France from in other occupied countries.

IV. The Bulgarian Romanies during the Second World War

Elena Marushiakova
Vesselin Popov

Introduction

People who called themselves *Roma* and were known to the Bulgarians as *tsigani* have inhabited Bulgarian lands for centuries. The first wave of Gypsy migrations reached the Balkan peninsula in 11th and 12th centuries A.D. and the first Gypsy settlements on the territory of contemporary Bulgaria date from the 13th and 14th centuries A.D.[1] The centuries of coexistence between Gypsies (especially the sedentary groups) and the surrounding population brought about a gradual effacement of their particular social structures and forms of social life.

Gypsies in Bulgaria in the 1940s

In the 1940s in Bulgaria there was a large Gypsy population, belonging to different groups.[2] There is no exact information about the number of Gypsies for the years immediately preceding the Second World War. The last pre-war census information dates from 1926 when 135,000 Gypsies were said to live in Bulgaria – 32,000 in the towns and 103,000 in the villages. This was 2.5%

89

of the country's population. The next census taken in 1946 registered 170,000 Gypsies, of whom 50,000 lived in towns and 120,000 in villages. This information, however, is not entirely credible and it would be unwise to draw any serious conclusions from it, considering the unreliability of similar population censuses with regard to Gypsies.

Measures against the Jews and Gypsies

The situation of the Gypsies in Bulgaria during the Second World War was very complicated, even though they were not explicitly mentioned in the *Law for the Protection of the Nation* (passed in 1940 by the 25th National Assembly and signed by King Boris III by Decree No. 3 on January 21st 1941). According to this law (directed especially against the Jewish population) the Jews in Bulgaria were restricted to specific regions – they could not vote or be elected, be employed as state and civil officials, marry (or live together without official marriage with) people of Bulgarian origin, have Bulgarian names, possess farming lands or a permanent residence in Sofia and other big cities.

As stated above the Gypsies were not mentioned explicitly in the Law for the Protection of the Nation (LPN), but Decree 4567 of the Council of Ministers was published in the "State Gazette" of August 29, 1942, approving the special Regulation assigning the Law to the Council of Ministers "to take all measures to settle the Jewish issues and the issues related to it." According to Article 24 of this Regulation, Article 21 of the Law was changed as follow:

"Jews are prohibited... from having marital or sexual relations with people of Bulgarian or similar origin; such marriages concluded after this law is enacted with be considered invalid.

Note: The regulation refers to the marriages of Gypsies to people of Bulgarian or similar origin."

There is no information on how this part of the regulation was observed in respect of Gypsies (and if it was ever applied), but it is quite indicative of the way of thinking of the Bulgarian authorities in respect of the Gypsies.

New Anti-Jewish laws and decrees followed: a new tax paid on one occasion only, a curfew, restriction of free movement to specific places and the obligatory wearing of the Jewish star (the Star of David). As a result the Jews from Sofia and other big towns and cities were relocated to some villages and small towns in the countryside.

The authorities also imposed severe restrictions on Gypsies. In Bulgaria, as elsewhere in Nazi-dominated Europe, they were treated as an element to be eradicated. Particular attention was given to their segregation. The most drastic measures were taken to prevent the Gypsies from continuing their nomadic

90

way of life so that they could be more easily seized by the authorities and used for compulsory labour or placed in internment or concentration camps.[3]

As early as May 1942 a decree was issued which provided for the compulsary employment of Gypsies, mainly in public works. Apparently this decree was not applied with the necessary stringency for a year later it was announced that "all Gypsies between sixteen and fifty years of age found idle will be mobilised for the harvest." The Bulgarian authorities, however, needed several months to carry out this measure. In August, the Sofia newspapers *Dnes* and *Dnevnik* reported that police had searched the capital and all the larger Bulgarian towns for idlers. Restaurants, coffee-houses, milk bars and taverns were raided. All Gypsies unable to prove employment of one kind or another, were deported from the city to work on the harvest or on roads, railways and other public utilities.[4] The *Dnes* newspaper of August 14th 1943 stated that thousands of Gypsies had already been sent out of Sofia alone.[5]

On August 25th, under the pretext that Gypsies were spreading contagious diseases, especially typhus, the Bulgarian Ministry of the Interior ordered district and regional authorities to restrict the free movement of Gypsies living in twelve regions. They included the Sofia area where there was a very large Gypsy population.

Food rations for Gypsies were sharply reduced: for example, an instruction issued on March 7th 1943 by the district authorities in Razgrad prescribed 200 grams of olives and 500 grams of sugar for Bulgarians, 100 and 200 grams respectively for Jews, and fifty grams of each for Gypsies.[6]

Those who were allowed to stay in Sofia were forbidden access to the central parts of the city and the use of trams. Several other restrictions were also applied in regard to their language, names and the performance of Muslim religious practices. Manush Romanov[7] recalls that, on January 19th 1942, the police surrounded the Gypsy neighbourhood of Faculteta in Sofia, and all the Gypsies living there were herded out with fire hoses to a nearby church where they were "baptized" and given new, Bulgarian names.[8]

There is reason to believe, although it is not confirmed by any official written records, that the Bulgarian government seriously considered the possibility of deporting the Gypsies from Bulgaria, together with the Jews, to Nazi concentration camps where they were to be annihilated. Many eyewitnesses from this time remember that Gypsies from Sofia were expelled, together with Jews, to Dupnitsa.

"Uncle" Nano from the Sofia quarter, Faculteta, spoke about that time:

"We used to live in Koniovitsa then, near the Jewish quarter Yuchbunar. The Jews were taken to Dupnitsa (later called Stanke Dimitrov) because they were not supposed to live in Sofia and many of our people went with them. I was there too. I was little.

91

Our parents did any kind of work; there was great hunger, so we ate bread made from chick-peas. They deported more than 200 families. Many young people became friends there and got married. Many poor Jewish girls without a dowry married Gypsies; they were ashamed in front of the other pure Jews, but in front of us they were proud of their Jewish blood. There were more than a hundred such families in Faculteta after the war and we called them *Zhutane Roma*; they lived separately on Sredna Gora Street. Now they have all gone to Israel, although one or two families have remained."

Thus, gradually, a new, separate Gypsy group was formed, the so-called *Zhutane Roma* (i.e. Jewish Gypsies) – descendants of mixed marriages between Gypsies and Jews, most of whom later emigrated to Israel.

In many places throughout the country temporary camps were created to house Gypsies and in some of them Gypsies from the region were held for some time.

On February 23rd 1943 an agreement between the Bulgarian Government Commissioner for the Jewish Question, Alexander Belev, and the special delegate of Germany, SS Lieutenant Theodor Daniker, was signed. According to this agreement Bulgaria would deport not only the Jews from the newly annexed territories (Macedonia and Thrace) but also "a certain number of Jews from the old boundaries" to reach the fixed number of 20,000 people. With decree No.127 of March 2nd 1943 the Bulgarian Government approved this agreement and elaborated seven further decrees paving the way for the prepared deportation. According to decree No.116 all people of Jewish origin were deprived of Bulgarian citizenship. In March 1943 Bulgaria deported Jews from the newly annexed territories in Macedonia and Thrace (about 12,000) but there are no known written sources about a simultaneous Gypsy deportation which has, however, been reported by eye-witnesses from the Gypsy community.

An elder, Emine from Kyustendil, remembers that time:

"The Gypsies from Bitolya suffered the most. They were brought here and couldn't save themselves, and were sent to Poland. Many people were taken away who never came back. Whoever could hid with their relations in Bulgaria and lived there. I got married here and my brothers hid in the mahalla (Gypsy quarter) where no one could find them, and after the war they went back to Macedonia, but many people I knew died."

The existing historical sources such as the *Law for Protection of the Nation*, passed in 1940, as well as other laws and decrees, show that usually Gypsies were not specifically mentioned in official state documents as a community destined for deportation to Nazi concentration and extermination camps. But the actual events suggest that Bulgarian officials were ready to take advantage of the possibility of deporting at least part of the Bulgarian Gypsies together with the Bulgarian Jews. In this sense the Gypsies in Bulgaria were fortunate because, under the influence of public opinion and political pressure from some directions, the Bulgarian government had resisted deporting the Jews from "Old Bulgaria".

As a result the Gypsies were spared together with the Jews (in spite of the fact that nobody took any special notice of the former). The averted deportation of the Bulgarian Jews also saved the Gypsies, but memories of the hardships and of their salvation have been preserved in a legend, collected in the town of Assenovgrad:

That happened in the time of the King. The King decided to exterminate all the Gypsies and said to himself: "Today I'll kill them!", but he lay down and went to sleep. Then his wife went to a meadow where she picked lots of different kinds of flowers and returned to the King. She woke him up, and when he saw the flowers she told him: "There are lots of different flowers just as there are lots of different people. Don't kill them!" So the King decided to spare them and ever since the Gypsies paint their houses in different bright colours.[9]

Gypsy participation in Anti-fascist resistance

The Gypsies in Bulgaria were searching for their own place in the social and political structure of the majority society where they lived. Some of the Gypsies in Bulgaria joined with the local population and took part in political movements against fascism. The first Gypsies fighting actively against fascism were those living in rural regions who had been settled farmworkers for centuries. Although they did not own any land, they had an interest in agricultural reform. In the 1920s the government of the Bulgarian Agricultural People's Union led by Alexander Stamboliyski passed a law giving land to some landless Gypsies. After a fascist coup on June 9th 1923 and the assassination of Alexander Stamboliyski, there were uprisings in some villages and four Gypsy participants were killed in the region of Pazardjik. In the autumn of the same year the September Anti-fascist Uprising broke out in some regions. It was organised by the Bulgarian Communist Party and joined by many supporters of the Bulgarian Agricultural People's Union. Seven Gypsies were killed in North-eastern Bulgaria where the uprising was at its the most effective.

Later some Gypsies fought actively against fascism later during the Second World War. In the years 1941-44 a number of Gypsies participated in the partisan movement organised by the Bulgarian Communist Party (BCP). During the war the town of Sliven – the town which had the largest Gypsy proletariat of any town in Bulgaria – saw some twenty Gypsies arrested as political prisoners for supporting the BCP. The Gypsy partisan, Yussein Kamenov, was killed in the region of Vratsa in 1944. Velichka Drumcheva, Mustafa Yovchev and Yussein Mussov, were also among those who died in the resistance movement. Bulgarian Gypsies also participated in the partisan movements of other countries; among them was Dimitar Nemtsov from Sliven who was a soldier in the Bulgarian occupation forces in Yugoslavia and ran away to join the local partisans.[10]

The number of Gypsies who participated directly and actively in the anti-fascist movement in Bulgaria was relatively small. There were about twenty who were named Active Fighters against Fascism – an official title given to them after the war in the Socialist period. Although they represent only a small part of the total Gypsy community they nevertheless deserve a special mention.

V. Gypsy deportations from Romania to Transnistria 1942-44

Michelle Kelso

Introduction

The long history of Gypsies in Romanian territory is little known, despite their arrival in the region around the thirteenth century. Persecuted and enslaved, emancipation for Gypsies in Moldova and Wallachia came only in 1855-56. While a handful of books on the origins of the Gypsies appeared in the last century, relatively few works have since been published on the history of the Gypsies in Romania.[1] Contemporary Gypsy history has been little researched by scholars.

Perhaps the most controversial contemporary historical period in Romania is that of the interwar and the Second World War, especially when researching policy concerning national and ethnic minorities. Although few have examined policy regarding the Gypsies, the Jewish policy has been under investigation since the war and continues to divide scholars vehemently. One theory suggests that Marshal Ion Antonescu's regime espoused and implemented Hitlerian policy by adopting the final solution in the deportation of Romanian Jews. Another theory contends that Antonescu rejected Germany's directives and opted for emigration of Jews from Romanian territory. Whichever theory one supports, it is clear that the Jewish deportations which began in 1941 preempted those of the Gypsies.[2]

When King Carol II abdicated on 6th September 1940, he entrusted the country to the then military leader Ion Antonescu, who became the Head of State and President of the Council of Ministers. The King left behind a pro-German legacy which the new head of state was hard-pressed to escape. Given Romania's major loss of territory in 1939-40 to the Hungarians and the Soviets, coupled with the defeats of the western allies early in the war, Antonescu kept his country together by opting for what he considered the lesser of two evils – collaboration with the German Nazis rather than waiting for a possible invasion from the Soviet Communists. Romania joined the war on June 22nd 1941. Turned down by major opposition leaders in his attempts to form a coalition government, Antonescu formed a joint government with Horia Sima, leader of the Iron Guard. The Iron Guard, also known as the Legionnaire movement, was popularised in the late 1920's by Corneliu Codreanu and was heavily

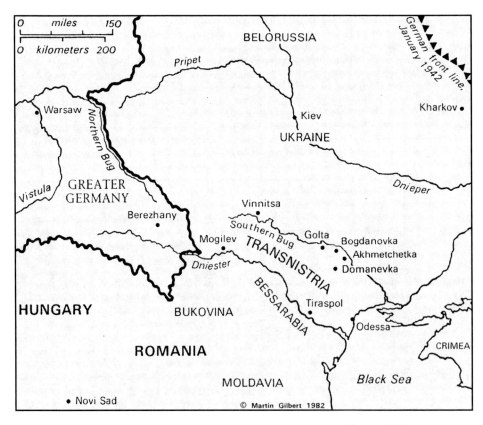

Map of Transnistria.

supported by Germany. The group's main principles were to fight against communism and return Romanian politics to a Christian Orthodox base. Among Guardists anti-Semitism was the norm, the motivation being religious and nationalistic. The Iron Guard not only advocated anti Semitic legislation, but also instigated violence against Jews. Antonescu broke up the coalition government in 1941, creating a military dictatorship which lasted until August 23rd 1944.[3]

Policy towards Gypsies

In turning to the question of the Gypsies, it appears that sociological factors prompted the deportation policy enacted under the Antonescu regime. Gypsies were an essential part of daily life for Romania's agricultural society. Gypsies, most of whom were illiterate and lived in rural areas, did not threaten Romanians economically or politically. Outside of a few marginalized racial publications and scientific reports, little evidence suggests that Romanian intellectuals, politicians, or the rest of society harboured anti-Gypsy sentiments. Those researchers who did call for close monitoring of the Gypsy population were as equally concerned with the Hungarian, Ukrainian, and Jewish populations, even though the Gypsies constituted one the largest minority groups in Romania.[4]

The examination of Marshal Antonescu's testimony at his war trial, his notes ordering the streets of Bucharest to be cleared of Gypsy vagabonds and nomads, and his opinion of them suggests he raised no objection to the deportation of certain types of Gypsies from Romania.[5] The Marshal testified at his war-trial that only Gypsies displaying criminal elements were sent to Transnistria, the territory acquired from the USSR between the rivers Dniester and Bug. The Marshal reveals his central motivation:

"The town populations were terrorised at night by bands or individuals, often armed who stole and sometimes even killed. The culprits were Gypsies. Everyone asked for them to be shot... Transnistria greatly needed workers. I decided that Gypsies with murder records or who had more than three [convictions] would be deported to Transnistria."[6]

But is this statement sufficient in summarising the policy of Gypsy deportation? Did Antonescu then devise an internal policy to deal with supposed Gypsy criminality or should his policy be interpreted in a larger sense relating to the deportation and extermination of Gypsies living in occupied and collaborating Nazi countries?

Background to the deportations

After the emancipation acts of the late nineteenth century, the majority of Gypsies in Romania were musicians, blacksmiths, craftsmen, sieve makers, silversmiths, pot washers, domestic workers, and unskilled labourers. A 1930 census (excluding nomadic Gypsies) indicated that 262,501 individuals declared themselves ethnically Gypsy in Romania.[7] By 1942, the figure had shrunk to 208,700 in Romanian-controlled regions due to loss of territory early in the war.

At the request of Antonescu, statisticians at the Central Institute for Statistics reported on the demographic information concerning the Gypsy population in 1942. The report is important because it breaks down the concentration of rural and urban Gypsies as compared to the majority population (see illustration.) Statisticians analysed the 208,700 Gypsy population figure and decided that it was too low. They concluded, however, that the exact number of Gypsies was unknown.[8] The difficulties in estimating the Gypsies were attributed to poor record keeping and increased assimilation of Gypsies with local populations. While no statistics were available for nomadic Gypsies due to their frequent movements, scientists estimated them to be considerably less numerous than their sedentary counterparts.

Additionally, the report transforms ethnographic data into nationalistic sentiment and warns the Romanian leader that action must be taken to prevent the further intrusion of Gypsies into Romanian society. The Institute cautioned Antonescu that because the Gypsies' "primitive crafts are indispensable to the agricultural activity of the peasant's social strata," it would bring Gypsies closer to ethnic Romanians, and result in "a lessened Romanian repulsion for this foreign population...leading in some places to a mixing of the population."[9] The authorities believed that determining contaminated regions was of paramount importance because Gypsies with half blood or less were numerous and despite low living standards, they adopted Romanian national characteristics and set aside their own. To rectify previous oversights and to retard integration, the Institute proposed an in-depth anthropological study to identify the descent of former slaves from noblemen, merchants, and monks.[10]

Whether Antonescu was directly influenced by the Institute in shaping Gypsy deportation policy is unknown. Other reports regarding the economic, political, and social conditions also crossed the Marshal's desk and provided the background material that presumably swayed his final decision to deport the Gypsies. Monthly reports compiled by the local constables in various regions, for instance, notified Bucharest of local living conditions, the overall mental state of the population, and concerns such as communist activity.[11] From these facts a picture emerged detailing a region's prosperity or poverty. Reports from Transnistria transmitted its deficiencies in cereals, petrol, and wood, alongside communicating the despondency of the local population who suffered from produce shortages.[12] Rumours of foreigners colonising the region frightened the local population as the region lacked arable land, reserves of corn and grain

98

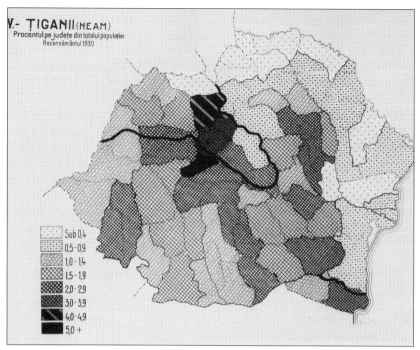

Percentage of Gypsies as compared to the total population in Romania by region from the 1930 census.

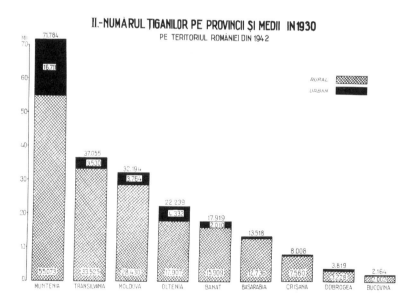

The number of Gypsies by province in rural and urban areas from the 1930 census for the Romanian territory in 1942.

for daily living, and work animals for the land available.[13] The constables' reports do not indicate that colonisation would be successful. Yet Antonescu chose Transnistria to place the Gypsies. Fully alert to the region's hardships and its people's fear of foreigners, his policy, we assume, was derived out of a desire to expel part of the Gypsy population.

For Antonescu, Transnistria was an appropriate location for deportation because he had no plans to annex the territory after the war, thus ridding him of the responsibility for those transferred there. The Marshal acquired the territory in August 1941 when Hitler petitioned him to accept Transnistria as a gift to celebrate their shared victory in the east.[14] And Transnistria had never before been under Romanian rule, Hitler's ill-disguised intention was to compensate Antonescu for Transylvanian land lost to Hungary. Antonescu agreed to a Romanian administration in exchange for economic exploitation of the region throughout the war, making it clear that Romania had no designs for permanent acquisition. The Romanians would administrate between the rivers Dniester and Bug, leaving the Germans to establish order from the Bug to the Dnieper.

At the onset of the acquisition, Hitler requested the deportation of Jews housed in work camps in Romania to Transnistria, a request which Antonescu refused, stating that military operations were still too unstable.[15] Through General Vasiliu at the General Inspectorate of the Constabulary, the police commanders prepared for Transnistria's takeover and stabilisation. Vasiliu wrote to Antonescu that colonisation in Transnistria was possible following agrarian reform. Although he did not specify for whom, Vasiliu assured the Marshal that territory would be reserved for colonisation.[16] Although colonisation was not new to Antonescu's administration – it had already resettled more than a half million Romanians displaced by the war from Dobrudja, Transylvania, Bucovina, and Bessarabia; in Transnistria the term would attempt to disguise the realities of the forced removal of the Gypsies and Jews.

In May 1941, the government reorganised the Under-secretariat of State for Romanianization, Colonisation and Supply, as well as the Office for Romanianization, which had been created the preceding year.[17] Originally designed to rectify the problem of Romanian ethnic refugees evacuated from their homes, it became a means of clearing the country of Jews and other foreigners by placing Romanians in their places. The Office for Romanianization's first concerns were "to reintegrate the Romanian element with all its legal rights, and resolve the Jewish problem."[18] A national law passed earlier that March turned over urban Jewish properties to the patrimony of the state, an action which was justified by its enforcement of national Christian ownership.[19] Antonescu claimed the seriousness of the Romanian refugee problem warranted seizing Jewish businesses and property, thus playing upon anti-Semitic fears artificially inflated through Legionnaire propaganda. It is also clear that the Marshal used the revamped office to forward another of the state's goals: the build up a reservoir of qualified Romanian workers. The legalisation of the state's patrimony over foreign owned properties established a precedent which a year later would permit the same Office for Romanianization to confiscate Gypsies' property.

The criteria used retroactively to sanction the Gypsy deportation were closely linked with a policy legalising Jewish removals from Romania. A royal decree issued on August 21st 1942 provided the guidelines for confiscating both Jewish and Gypsy properties and outlined categories of those to be deported. Concerning Gypsies, the decree specified that those failing to uphold morality standards were to be resettled in Transnistria as forced labourers to reconstruct bridges, roads, and buildings. The period of resettlement was unspecified.[20] Individuals not self-supporting, with questionable morals, criminal records, or unstable residences were defined as dangerous undesirables and they would be deported. The ambiguity of the text's definition of moral behaviour allowed it to encompass the majority of Romania's Gypsies – the poor, the marginalized, the criminals, the nomads.[21] Vague consolation was offered for Gypsies who could prove "good" moral status and had been sedentary during the prescribed ten year period from August 1st 1932 until August 1st 1942. Supposedly the authorities would permit them to remain in Romania, but in practice this exemption was not respected as many with prison sentences which had terminated before 1932 were evacuated. Men qualifying for the military were excluded, being drafted instead of deported. Exempted Gypsies would receive a "normalcy" identity card and authorities would permit them to remain in the country. For the rest of the Gypsies, the Royal Decree indicated settlement in Transnistria in groups of 1,200-1,600 would be their lot in Transnistria. The Romanian Railway would organise their transportation.

Evacuation of nomadic Gypsies: June 1st - August 9th 1942

For the nomadic Gypsies problems had begun even before the Property Laws or the Royal Decree were passed. In November 1940 the Ministry of Internal Affairs forbade the roaming of nomadic Gypsies during the winter upon the recommendation of the Ministry of Health, which feared that nomads and beggars would spread typhus.[22] It is unknown whether the health law affected Antonescu's decision to expel the nomadic Gypsies, however two years later they were marked first for deportation. In May 1942, Antonescu ordered a census of Gypsies meeting the retrospective criteria detailed in the Royal Decree.

The President's Council of Ministers ordered the General Inspectorate of Constabulary to supervise the deportation of nomadic Gypsies whose caravans would serve as transport into Transnistria.

The nomads

Nomadic Gypsies differed from the sedentary in their pattern of nomadising to seek work, travelling by caravan in extended family groups, their customs and dress, and sometimes language. Men were generally coppersmiths who sold their wares to settled populations in exchange for food, clothing, household goods, and money. In addition to coppersmithing, some nomads were horse traders, wood carvers, silversmiths, and blacksmiths. While the men's income supported the family, the women contributed substantially by their assistance with smaller tasks including pot making and wood working, raising children, and looking after the household. Economically women supplemented their husbands' income by telling fortunes to non-Gypsies using cards, tea leaves, and maize. Nomadic Gypsies were not only identifiable by their trades, but also by their appearance. Men's extended moustaches and long hair, often covered with a dark hat, were their trademarks. Women's' ankle-length, brightly coloured skirts and head kerchiefs along with their hair, braided in two plaits in front of their ears, showed them to be nomads. Frequently women wore part if not all of their families' fortune – gold coins – either woven in their braids, or worn as necklaces and earrings. Romani was the spoken language, although early on children learned Romanian, and sometimes Hungarian, Bulgarian, or Turkish depending on the region in which they travelled more regularly.

A group of semi-nomadic Gypsies dating from before the deportation.

A separate sub-category of Gypsies, semi-nomads, merits discussion alongside nomads since officials classified and deported them as nomads despite the distinctly different lifestyles of the two groups. Semi-nomads differed from nomads in their dress, hairstyle and customs. Travelling during the spring and summer months, semi-nomads settled during the rest of the year, accepting whatever work they found in autumn and winter. Like nomadic Gypsies, semi-nomads spoke Romani and often were multilingual. Some maintained stable residences and owned property.

For the Ministry of Internal Affairs, semi-nomads presented a classification problem as many were settled property owners. Although the official policy was deportation for nomads and semi-nomads, the General Inspector of Constabulary fluctuated in its application and thus the discretion of local authorities typically determined a family's fate. More often than not, police and constables expelled those conforming to the Ministry's definitions. The constables from the city of Craiova, for instance, reported discovering and deporting three families of spoon makers comprising seventy-five members who fited the criteria for expulsion:

"didn't have a stable residence, exercising the trade of spoon makers, wandering from town to town and when they found good working wood from different owners, they would settle there for one year, or two, living in earth houses until the wood supply terminated, after which they would leave for another area."[23]

Local constables were confused in the cases of property-owning nomads or semi-nomads. If nomadic Gypsies owned property, did it exclude them from deportation? When the local constables from Bacau discovered the Luca Moldovan family, who travelled by caravan, implying a 'nomadic' lifestyle, but owned property in Bucharest, they were unable to decide whether to deport them.[24] The Inspectorate of Constabulary resolved the dilemma. Ownership of land did not disqualify Gypsies leading a nomadic lifestyle from deportation. The Moldovans were to leave immediately for Transnistria.[25]

By the end of August 1942, officials estimated that approximately 13,000 Gypsies crossed over into Transnistria. Before the journey even commenced, the Ministry ordered that neither time to prepare for the departure nor information about the destination was to be given to the deportees. In a letter to Antonescu regarding the execution of these orders, Colonel Tobescu at the General Inspectorate of Constabulary asserted that warnings were unnecessary for nomads since they had few assets to liquidate and their habitual wandering was preparation enough.[26] Constables entering the camps of nomads or their stopping places in villages ordered the Gypsies to pack their wagons for the trip, without specifying the final destination. All members of a salas (extended family group) were forced to leave without exception. Women with spouses serving in the army, and parents and children of soldiers and deceased veterans, pleaded for exclusion, but they were ignored. To facilitate cooperation, some authorities invented scenarios in which Gypsies would receive houses, animals, and work guaranteed for their "voluntary" compliance in the resettlement campaign.

According to survivors, the authorities' lack of courtesy caused numerous, avoidable hardships during the one to three months' journey to Transnistria. For example, few had time to collect food for the trek as their consumption needs were met by regular trading. Incomes normally generated from the sales of their crafts and fortune-telling were halted with the daily transfers by constables thus reducing further the ability to provide for themselves.

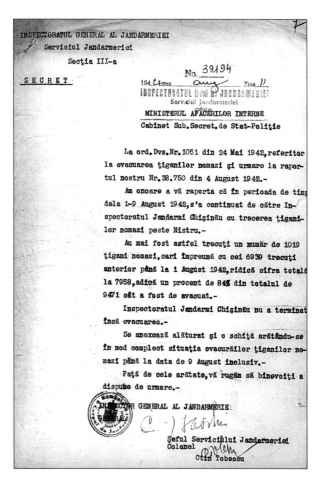

On August 11th 1942, the General Inspector of Constabulary sends a letter to the Ministry of Internal Affairs indicating that the deportation of nomadic Gypsies ordered the previous May is almost complete as 7,958 nomads, or 84% of the nomadic population, have crossed the Dniester River.

Once the Gypsies reached the boarder after crossing through Bessarabia, they were obliged to exchange their Romanian currency and gold for German marks at the Dniester, a process which sometimes lasted an entire day. Local commanders of constables waited for the Gypsies and assigned them to various localities mainly in the Golta, Balta, and Oceacov regions. The former Mayor of Oceacov wrote on April 15th 1945 his memories of the Gypsies' arrival:

"At the end of August 1942, the Gypsies began to arrive at Trihai [along the Bug, in the northeast of the Oceacov district.] They were welcomed by the commandant of the local constables with the firm order not to leave their assigned locations. The Gypsies were distributed among some farms according to norms established by myself at the Town Hall. During one week 15,000 Gypsies arrived. The commander of the constables reported to me verbally… that [the Gypsies] were in an incredible state of misery… there were a lot of old people, women, and children. In the wagons there were paralysed, older persons well over 70 years of age, blind and on the verge of death. The great majority of them were naked in rags. I spoke with them. They were protesting, they screamed, they cried, they ranted: why were we arrested and sent to Transnistria? Many showed me that they had children at the front, women whose husbands were at the front, there were some who had lost sons or spouses who died on the front. Some others had wounded relatives in hospitals."[27]

In the effort to sweep the country of nomads, mistakes were made. Parents, wives, and children of soldiers fighting or killed in the current war, and veterans of the first war or their widows and children were not supposed to have been deported. When errors surfaced later, the General Inspector of Constabulary backed local authorities' illegal actions by rationalising that individuals with relatives in the army could not survive economically without the salas, hence the complete expulsion.[28] Gypsy soldiers, outraged to learn their families were deported while they risked their lives on the front line, refused to accept their families' forced evacuations. Striving to calm the ranks, the Ministry of Internal Affairs ordered commanders with Gypsy soldiers to carefully explain the categories for those who were deported, and the appeal process for those believing their loved ones head been erroneously expelled. To rectify errors, the General Inspectorate of Constabulary proposed to the Ministry that while families of nomadic soldiers should not be repatriated to Romania, their living standard should be improved in Transnistria. Colonel Tobescu proposed preferential treatment and recommended furnishing soldiers' families with houses, land, goods and possibilities of employment.[29] He also suggested settling soldiers' families separately from other nomads.[30] However no record of these improved conditions has yet been found.

Evacuation of sedentary Gypsies: September 12th-19th 1942

On May 17th 1942 the Ministry of Internal Affairs ordered the police to conduct a census of the non-nomadic, or sedentary Gypsies.[31] Eight days later the police indicated that 31,438 sedentary Gypsies resided in urban and rural territories

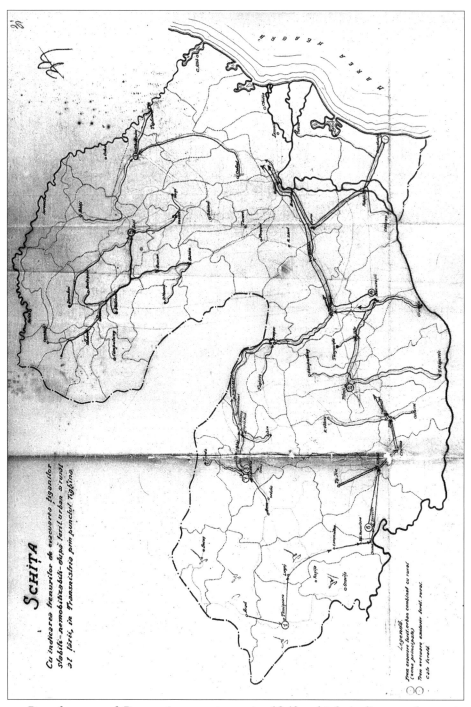

Rough map of Romanian territory in 1942 which indicates the train routes used for deporting 13,176 sedentary Gypsies to Transnistria from major Romanian cities.

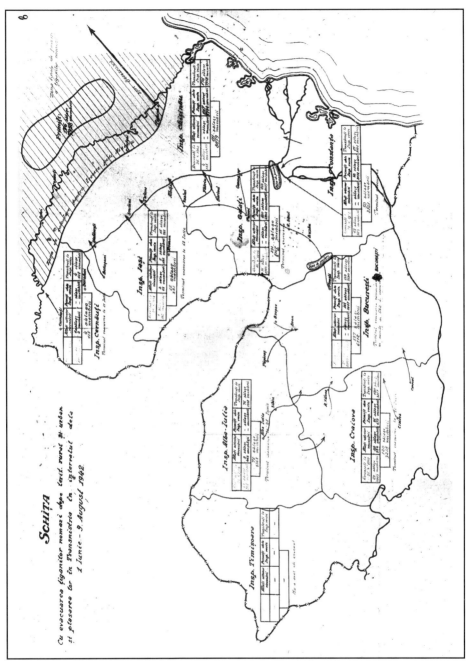

Rough map displaying the deportation plan for nomadic Gypsies by region conducted under the supervision of the General Inspectorate of Constabulary during the period of June 1st - August 9th 1942. For each region the number of salaşi, or family groups, is marked, along with the number of individuals.

```
SPECTORATUL GENERAL AL JANDARMERIEI
    Serviciul Jandarmeriei
         Secţia III-a                                              37.

                        S I T U A Ţ I A

      evacuărei evreilor şi ţiganilor cu indicarea trenurilor de evacuare şi
      transporturilor directe.


Denumirea   Distanţa pe care   Data şi ora
trenului    circulă            plecărei              Data şi ora sosirei
                                                     la Tighina

tren E.1    Timişoara-Tighina   8.IX.ora 9.00        10.IX.ora 13.28
  "  E.2    Iaşi    -Tiraspol   8.IX.ora22.55         9.IX.ora 10.07
  "  E.3    Bucureşti-Tighina  12.IX.ora 20.10       13.IX.ora 23.42
  "  E.4    Piteşti -Tighina   12.IX.ora 8.45        13.IX.ora 15.21
  "  E.5    Timişoara-Tighina  13.IX.ora 9.00        15.IX.ora 13.58
  "  E.6    Alba Iulia-Tighina 13.IX.ora 8.00        15.IX.ora 2.58
  "  E.7    Iaşi   -  Tighina  14.IX.ora 22.55       15.IX.ora 8.56
  "  E.8    Tr.Severin-Tighina 14.IX.ora 18.40       16.IX.ora 13.58
  "  E.9    Deva -  Tighina    15.IX.ora 21.00       17.IX.ora 20.34
     E.10   Constanţa-Tighina  15.IX.ora 10.00       16.IX.ora 12.31
  "  E.11   Chişinău-Tighina   16.IX.ora 10.00       16.IX.ora 12.38


                 SITUAŢIE   RECAPITULATIVĂ


Nr.     Denumirea
crt.    trenului         E v r e i          T i g a n i

1.-    Tren E.1..........1.474..............---
2.-    Tren E.2..........611...............---
3.-    Tren E.3..........---...............---
4.-    Tren E.4..........---...............1.922
5.-    Tren E.5..........---...............1.544
6.-    Tren E.6..........---...............1.624
7.-    Tren E.7..........---...............1.029
8.-    Tren E.8..........---...............1.559
9.-    Tren E.9..........---...............1.530
10.-   Tren E.10.........---...............1.352
11.-   Tren E.11.........---...............1.714
12.    Direct............---...............1.590
13.    Direct............25................---
14.    Direct............---...............33
15.    Direct............---...............96
                         ---...............130

          T O T A L   GENERAL  2.110
                                           12.497
```

The train schedule used to deport sedentary Gypsies and Jews from Romania in September 1942.

who matched the Ministry's criteria for deportation to Transnistria.[32] 12,497 of those who were considered the most dangerous, undesirable, and unfit for military service were destined for the first train transport.[33]

The Ministry placed the bulk of the responsibility for deportation on the constables, but the action also involved rural and urban police departments, mayors, the National Centre for Romanianization (CNR), the National Rail System (CFN), the Under-secretary of State for Supplies, the Under-secretary of State for Romanianization, Colonisation, and Property, as well as the Ministry of Finance.[34] The deportation of sedentary Gypsies differed from that of the nomads not only in the means of transportation used, but also in the more meticulous instructions sent by the General Inspector of Constabulary to avoid mistakes. As directed, constables contacted local police officials for assistance in rounding up the listed Gypsies and bringing them either to the train station

Summary of the 24,686 nomadic and sedentary Gypsies deported to Transnistria in 1942.
The list is divided into the two categories, and further broken down into men, women and children.

or to constables headquarters twenty-four hours ahead of the scheduled departure times organised by the National Rail System.[35] Trains would carry the Gypsies considered criminals – any sort of delinquent, pickpocket, train thief, highway robber, and anyone having tendencies to live by theft and who were considered dangerous – to Transnistria.[36] Wives and dependent children of such offenders were sent to Transnistria although adult male children of offenders living outside the home were assessed separately. No instructions were given concerning adult female children.[37] Orders issued to constables paralleled earlier instructions concerning nomads that sedentary Gypsies should not be warned in advance to prevent liquidation of their assets.[38]

Evacuations began on September 12th 1942. Accompanying each train was a commander, an officer of lower rank, a non-commissioned officer and private soldiers, based on the number of Gypsies aboard.[39] Guards had permission to shoot without warning if threatened. After loading the Gypsies on the cargo trains, the local constables cabled Bucharest to report the figures for urban and rural Gypsies, and to identify in which trains the Gypsies had departed. In all, nine trains were used to transport the Gypsies from various regions in Romania to Tighina.[40] The Ministry instructed the Under-secretary of State for Provisions to furnish daily bread rations for Gypsies during their five-day transport understanding that they were unable to provide food for themselves. The Gypsies were allowed to take only what could be carried in hand luggage.

Whatever was left behind – land, houses, farm animals, furniture, kitchenware, caravans and so on – reverted to the local office of the National Centre for Romanianization. Where no Romanianization office existed, the mayor's office or the public notary was responsible for making an inventory of confiscated property and goods.

Survivor Gheorghe Potcoava, who was 13 when constables forced them onto a cargo train in Giurgiu, describes his experience en route to Tighina:

"There were maybe over one hundred people [crowded] into the a car without seats. You stayed in groups with your family. It was hot, it was September. We slept one on top of another. [There were] no toilet facilities. You went to the WC when the train stopped. The windows had iron bars as thick as a finger so no one could escape. Where was there to go? Constables gave us bread and salami. The train stopped in every little station and sometimes stayed for a day. If you asked, one person from the family could go [into town] for an hour or two to get food. We gathered water in wooden bottles.

If some got sick, that's how they stayed. Many women had babies on the train. We made spaces for them. Gypsy women became midwives for each other. One would put her foot on a woman's back, another would cut the [umbilical] cord, another would wrap the baby up, and another would take a rag, and wipe the mess up and throw it out of the window.

When we got to the Bug, we went in a boat. Then we got in a little train that took us to Nikolaiovka. Constables waited for us in trucks and took us about four kilometres from Nikolaiovka. There we got out and they put us in this village."[41]

During the eight-day operation, 13,176 sedentary Gypsies, a slighter higher number than anticipated in the original plan, arrived in Transnistria.[42] On October 3rd 1942, the General Inspectorate of Constabulary reported to the Ministry of Internal Affairs that the Gypsies deported were turned over in Tighina to the Transnistrian government (established by Antonescu and led by former university professor Gheorghe Alexianu) for placement in cooperatives. In return for their labour, Gypsies were to be given housing and food. The 18,262 "less dangerous" Gypsies designated for a second transport were to arrive in the spring of 1943.[43] Their deportation was not carried out due to unexpected developments in the war and the terrible conditions faced by those already resettled.

TABEL NOMINAL

De ţiganii nenomazi – nemobilizabili – şi familiile lor, ca se evacuează în Transnistria conf. ord. Nr.40169 din 26 Aug.1942 al Inspectoratului General al Jandarmeriei.-

Nr. cor.	Numele şi Pronumele	Vâr-sta	Comuna	Ocupaţia	Faptele de care care se face vi-novat.	Observ.
1	Stoica Lazăr	73 B	Galaţi	F.ocup.	Cond.2 luni	C.fam.
2	Matei Tica	54 F	"	"	Cond.6 luni	Soţie
3	" Maria	27 c	"	"	–	Copil
4	" Mina	2 c				
5	Rupa Rosalim	35 B	"	"	Borfaş	Singur
6	Duca Sofron	64 B	"	"	Trăeşte din fur şi cer-şit.-	C.famil.
7	" Sofron	9 C	"	"	–	Copil
8	Rupa Teodor	54 B	"	"	Cond.2 ani	C.fam.
9	" Maria	36 F	"	"	Cond.6 luni	Soţie
10	" Eva	15 c	"	"	–	Copil.
11	" Gheorghe	10 c	"	"		"
12	" Olimpia	9 c	"	"	–	"
13	" Sofia	6 c	"	"	–	
14	Duţu Romul	28 B	Răuşor	Ziler	Trăeşte din fur-turi.	C.famil.
15	Stoica Ileana	22 F	"	"	–	Concub.
16	Duţu Maria	3 c	"	"	–	Copil
17	" Minerva	2 c	"			
18	" Maria	60 F	"	Zileră	Trăeşte din furturi.	Singură
19	Grancea Nicolae	62 B	Dejani	Ziler	Cond.6 luni	Singur
20	Căldărar Visalon	68 B	Lisa	"	Cond.15 zile	C.famil.
21	" Rozalia	62 F	"	"	–	Soţie
22	" Victor	20 c	"	"	–	Copil
23	" Const.	10 c	"	"	–	"
24	" Maria	18 c	"	"	–	"
25	Pavel Gheorghe	38 B	"	Fierar	Borfaş	C.famil.
26	" Marica	36 F	"	Casnică	–	Soţie
27	" Gheorghe	14 c	"		–	Copil
28	" Ioan	12 c	"		–	"
29	" Octav.	7 c	"		–	"
30	" Maria	4 c	"		c	"
31	" Eugenia	2 c	"		–	"
32	Lingurar Virgil	19 B	Comana de Sus	Ziler	Cond.3 ani	C.famila
33	Poşa Victoria	17 F	Idem	"	"	Concub.
34	Solomon Gheorghe	55 B	"	"	Trăeşte din furturi.	C.famil.
35	" Floarea	49 F	"	"	Idem	Soţie
36	" T.Floarea	19 c	"	"	–	Nepoată
37	Danciu Victor	29 B	Porumbacul de Jos	"	Borfaş	Singur
38	Căldărar Petre	33 B	Idem	"	Idem	Singur
39	Păcurar Petre	37 B	Rucăr	"	Cond.1 lună	C.famil.
40	Irina	39 F		"	–	Soţie
41	" Lina	50 F	"	"	Cond. 2 luni	Singură
42	Stoica Ioan	17 c	Toderiţa	F.ocup.	Trăeşte din furturi.	Singur

./.

Deportation list for sedentary Gypsies listed by the local constables in Alba Iulia for the Fagaraş region. The list indicates the names of each individual, their age, sex, village, occupation, family status, and the reason for deportation.

The immediate question plaguing Bucharest after the evacuation ended was: who were the 679 extra Gypsies? Had the constables not followed the correct procedure? Two issues were at work: under- and over-deportation. Enquiries were made to regional offices in an attempt to discover where errors had occurred. One train commander, Ioan Mihailescu, reported several reasons for the higher than expected number. Many of the excess Gypsies were children who had not been counted in the initial census, either because they were yet unborn, or simply were not around. On his train alone, three women gave birth en route.[44] Mihailescu also explained that relatives not on lists requested to be transported with their families. Other commanders filed similar statements, one adding that the Gypsies profited from a free train ride. And, as the General Inspector of Constabulary feared, some individuals were mistakenly evacuated, a problem that they would deal with over the next two years.

Timisoara was just one of the regional constabulary offices which was held accountable for sending insufficient numbers. Timisoaran constables declared that Major Ioan Peschie as the officer responsible. In a letter to his superiors, Peschie defended his actions stating that misinterpretation of the General Inspector's orders by officers under his command was just one reason behind the lower figure of Gypsies deported. Also listed was negligence on the part of several village commanders in verifying the draft status of Gypsy men. Peschie discovered several Gypsies eligible to fight and excluded them from transport. The Major also found discrepancies in reports of criminality among those destined for evacuation. If Gypsies accused of criminal behaviour produced documentation indicating good moral status, Peschie allowed them to remain at home. Additional errors arose concerning Gypsies serving jail sentences, as they were listed but were ineligible for transport until their prison terms ended. Economic self-sufficiency was also a factor in Peschie's decision whether to evacuate some families. If Gypsies supported themselves, despite poor living conditions, the Major did not deport them on the grounds that work ability must first be considered. This rationale saved one village's dog catcher. Also excluded from transport were parents of Gypsy soldiers.

Peschie was not alone in defending his actions. Bucharest forced other commanders to explain themselves as well. Constables in the villages of Baili Herculean, Caran Seges, Lugoj and Orsova blamed Bucharest for the insufficient number of deportees, arguing that it was the unclear instructions from headquarters that were at fault, not their units. Disappearances also accounted for reduced figures as some Gypsies went into hiding while others surveyed in the May census travelled during the summer for work and had already departed when the evacuation orders came. In Risitu, for instance, the constables put only thirty-one out of fifty-two Gypsies listed for deportation on the train.[45] In other towns, over-deporting was the issue and Bucharest cabled local authorities for explanations. In Arad, sixty-two Gypsies were evacuated instead of fifty-eight as registered.[46] Constables explained that fifteen Gypsies on the list disappeared, and nineteen were rounded up in their places, all of whom authorities claimed, had insisted on being deported.

Conditions in Transnistria

By mid-summer 1942 when nomads and semi-nomads crossed the Dniester River, their health had already deteriorated due to hardships of the long trek. The Transnistrian government, ill-prepared for the new arrivals, made no arrangements for housing or food, and placed the Gypsies mainly in large open fields unattended until a plan could be implemented. The government's lack of organisation, compounded by that of the Gypsies', gave way to a state of chaos by fall. Constables reported to Bucharest that controlling the 7,058 nomadic Gypsies already in the area was only possible by confiscating their caravans (to limit their movement) and putting the Gypsies at work sites:

"As Gypsies do not respect the police measures, moving from the locations in which they were placed, wandering aimlessly through villages, the government decided to take their wagons and horses, and to place the Gypsies in the fields to work. Nomadic Gypsies provoke numerous difficulties by their rebellious spirit and they don't work where they are put, contributing to the great state of misery in which they live."[47]

Although the confiscation of the caravans eased temporarily the authorities' control problem, it increased the Gypsies' already miserable living conditions. The wagons provided more than transportation, they were the Gypsies' homes. The loss of clothing, pillows, blankets, kitchenware, and daily living necessities was never replaced. In several areas after securing the caravans, authorities then transferred Gypsies by trucks or on foot to villages or agricultural cooperatives for placement either in evacuated Ukrainians' houses or in barracks that were devoid of basic furnishings. Survival thus depended on individuals' abilities to acquire food, heating supplies, water, and other goods. One survivor, Salica Tanase, confessed that theft from nearby crops, trade with local police, and ingenuity ensured his survival. Those unable to deal or sell their services ultimately perished.

The arrival of sedentary Gypsies exacerbated the disarray and by October 1942, the combined result of the two deportations was disaster. Reports back to Bucharest alerted officials that major systematic planning was required for those already installed in Transnistria before yet another group of sedentaries could be relocated. On October 17th, the Ministry of Internal Affairs suspended further deportation plans until the spring and attempted to reorganise the existing calamity.[48] A steady stream of accounts filed by constables in Transnistria would reveal over the next months the government's inability to cope with the situation. The December constable report from Oceacov informed headquarters of the overall regional situation – the ethnic Romanians' black market activities, the exchange rate of the mark, the unavailability of produce in the markets, and the miserable plight of the Gypsies. One commander reconstructed the depth of the Gypsies' distress:

"On November 29th 1942, the Gypsies in the Oceacov district were placed in three camps: in the villages of Covaliocva, Balsoi Karanika, and Alexandrudar in the zone near the constabulary post in Beicusul Mare. The first two camps are located in part of the respective villages, and [in the third camp Gypsies] were housed in some barracks on the edge of a riverbank, a distance of 8-10 kilometres from the city of Oceacov.

Since Gypsies are not given wood or other combustibles to heat food and houses, in the course of the two months that they have been housed in these barracks they have destroyed all the wooden parts of the buildings: doors, windows, roofs and interior walls, which they used for firewood. They blocked the windows with bricks.

Winter conditions made it impossible for the Gypsies to remain in these barracks. First, the roof which they damaged for its wood threatened to cave in on them; secondly they will die of cold because they are so poorly dressed that if you saw them it would bring tears to your eyes. The Mayor, together with the Commander of the Constabulary, reached the decision that the Gypsies from Alexandrudar would be housed in villages. Thus they evacuated about half the village, moving all the Ukrainians closer to the banks of the Bug river and they began to send 300 Gypsies with their wagons to Ancekrak to be distanced from the above mentioned villages. In this manner they will be removed and rehoused from Alexandrudar to the respective communities finishing by December 15th.

But the Gypsies are so thin and frozen that they die in their wagons. On the first day, 300 died on the road. During the time that they stayed in barracks in Alexandrudar, the Gypsies lived in an indescribable state of misery. They were insufficiently fed being given only 400 grams of bread for those capable of working and just 200 grams for the old people and children. They were given a few potatoes and very rarely salted fish was given in extremely small quantities.

Due to the poor quality of the food some Gypsies, and this constituted the majority, lost so much weight they shrank into mere skeletons. In recent days especially, as many as ten or fifteen have died daily. They were full of parasites. They received no medical treatment and had no medicine. They are naked, without any clothes, and clothing and heating materials are completely lacking. There are women with their inferior parts completely naked in the true sense of the word. They have not been given any soap and they have neither washed themselves nor their clothing, not a single shirt which they have. In general, the Gypsies' situation is terrible.

Because of the misery, many among them are reduced to mere shadows, and are almost wild. Their state is caused by the bad housing, food, and cold. Due to the hunger to which they were subjected, their thefts frightened the Ukrainians. Although in the villages [before in Romania] some Gypsies stole out of habit, there are [other] Gypsies who were honest back home and started to steal only when hunger brought them to this shameful state.

By November 25th, 309 Gypsies died as a result of neglect. Their bodies were found along the Oceacov-Alexandrudar highway. They died from hunger and cold."[49]

The image of naked, crazed Gypsies dying of exposure and starvation is striking. In particular constables noted shortages of food, adequate housing conditions, fuel and heating materials, medical supplies, and clothing. Constables in Balsaia Karanicain reiterated to Bucharest the haunting sights of the Gypsies' dire living conditions. The report implicates the Mayor directly for the deaths and suffering of the Gypsies, citing the administration's failure to ensure basic survival needs for Gypsies, motivated out of malice. The report implores that immediate action from the administration is necessary in order to prevent further agony and loss of life:

"I. HOUSING

1. 3,881 Gypsies are housed in the village of Balsaia Karanica in the Oceacov District; up to now they have destroyed 129 houses, a school, and 119 barns to take the wood for cooking

2. This group of Gypsies were brought to this location from different *colhozuri* (agricultural cooperatives) between October 20-25th 1942. From that date until now, 150 Gypsies died of hunger, but only eighty-five bodies could be identified as the rest were not claimed by their families, who most likely had run away.

3. The deaths of these 150 Gypsies was provoked by a lack of food, because they were each given only 200-400 grams of corn meal [daily], and as almost all the families lacked dishes and wood, they could not prepare food.

4. The residents do not have beds or sheets. The majority are almost naked, and some of them go completely undressed, being covered with sacks or rags.

II. FOOD

1. As the Gypsies are not organised in the respective village, and the Mayor of Varvarovca does not have sufficient personnel or even the good will to administer the villages, the distribution of food is somewhat insufficient (400 grams of corn meal per person per day, and occasionally only 200 grams [are given]). Between October 20th and 31st, when they were evacuated, [the Gypsies] received nothing. They haven't received potatoes in a month, and children under fourteen years of age only receive 200 grams of corn meal, resulting in the death of over 150 Gypsies.

2. If [the Mayor] does not take the necessary measures to organise these Gypsies, grouping them in families, by the villages and districts from which they were deported in order to distribute the necessary flour on time and to every Gypsy (because many get no flour at distribution time). If [the Gypsies] are not given the possibility of making *mamaliga* (corn-meal porridge) from the flour provided, they will all die or continue to steal from the neighbouring communities because [the Mayor] will not give them any kind of food other than flour and potatoes, not even salt.

IV. SOCIAL ASSISTANCE

1. The Karanica sector has allocated a doctor and the needed steriliser [for the tools]; however, he doesn't have personnel, instruments, or even the necessary medicines, so the Gypsies die worse than animals, and they are buried without a priest.

2. From December 12th to 18th 1942, while I was working in the community, sixteen Gypsies died, so four [sic] each day, and previously there were days when 8-10 died daily."[50]

115

Despite the details of the horrific deterioration of the Gypsies, almost nothing was done physically to relieve their sufferings. Death tolls rose with the onslaught of disease. Typhus destroyed thousands as it spread quickly among Gypsies housed in overcrowded schools, houses, barracks, and shacks. The former Mayor of Oceacov, Vasile Gorsky, wrote in 1945 of typhus-infected Gypsies. Upon discovering the prevalence of the disease, the Mayor took measures to prevent further spreading of the infection. However, the belated effort was not enough as thousands succumbed to fever, heart disease, fatigue, bronchial pneumonia, delirium, and damage to their nervous systems. Gorsky noted:

"The Gypsies were full of lice. An initial disinfecting was done at Tribak, upon their arrival but it was incomplete. They lacked wood and lamp oil. Soon after their arrival they started to die. The doctors realised only too late it was due to typhus. (The Gypsies' skin being darker, the red spots did not show.) After analyses were made in Odessa and Bucharest, we took the necessary measures. We were sent disinfecting sterilisers from the government, lamp oil, soap, and medicines. The disinfecting was done three or four times, but not completely. During the winter of 1942-43, between 3,000 and 4,000 Gypsies died."[51]

Survivors' accounts

Survivors' accounts transform the official reports of Transnistria into a reality. While reading their testimonies we learn of the severity of the deportation and its effect on individuals and families. Survivor Ion Neagu's description of typhus illustrates that the disease contributed not only to the body's destruction, but also the soul's. Already forced to existed in subhuman conditions, Ion recounts the effect of typhus on families housed with him in an abandoned school in Vladiovka:

"They put us in a big school with two or three floors. We were eating here, there was a toilet. From each Gypsy family, two or three [people] died. They didn't have wagons, money, they didn't have anything. I noticed that when only one person remained alive, out of a family composed of seven, he willed his own death. We were destroyed. I can't say how many Gypsies died, how many children died, how many mothers and fathers did not care about their children anymore. They were trying to get out alive. Here died my sister-in-law, my sister, and my little brother [from typhus]."[52]

Constantina Pitigoi, a semi-nomadic Gypsy woman, was infected with typhus and survived after receiving treatment upon her return to Romania. She remembers distinctly the horrendous living conditions in Transnistria and her struggle alone (her husband was fighting on the front) to obtain the bare necessities to keep herself and her four children alive. When constables confiscated their caravan and horse, they were robbed of their last material comforts, and Constantina fought to sustain her family's daily existence. In one conversation she stressed the difficulties women had contending with the children's cries of hunger which were never appeased, combating filth and disease, scrounging for daily sustenance, and battling to maintain Gypsy traditions:

"I stayed [in Transnistria] for ten months. After ten months my husband came to bring us from there. Everyone ate horse meat. In Vladiovka, Russians took our horses and wagons, our pillows – we had huge pillows – they ran away with them. What we could, we hid so as not to be broke. With the gold that we had, we made holes in the ground, and we hid it there, sleeping on top of it. We stayed on it until morning. When we moved, we had to take it because we were going to other places. We took it out and they [the Russians] saw it. The Russians took everything, even the wedding rings from our fingers.

It was harder for women than for men. The men left for work at the collective and the women stayed home all day with the children. The children cried for us to give them food. The women washed, thinking that they would all die. It was hard. A woman with five children told them: 'Don't cry, daddy will come and bring food.'The children watched the road. 'Mama, daddy is not coming.' 'He'll come, dear.' When he came, sometimes he had a little bread, sometimes he didn't bring anything. If he didn't bring anything, the woman made a little mamaliga, three potatoes, cabbage.

We made [food] at home. We shared with one another. If I had something, I gave it to small children. If there was more, I gave more. If there wasn't, I gave more to my children. [Constables] gave us five frozen potatoes a day and a kilo of corn meal. We said, 'We have a lot of children, give us more.' 'I can't do anything, that's the rule.' No meat, no cheese, no milk, no bread. This old man who died had one boy. The boy said: 'Father died?' and took two portions of mamaliga from the fire, eating and crying for his father.

At the customs in Tighina, I didn't change all the Romanian money, I changed only half and half remained so I could see what to do with it there. They gave us marks. When I could find milk and cheese, I took it, all with our money. Not with their money, which was more worthless than ours. [The Russians] thought we were Turks. [When] we went to buy, a blouse like ours [embroidered white cotton] would buy corn meal, potatoes, onions. We washed in holes made by bombs. I had soap from home. But I lost a piece of it on the road. Those that didn't have any said, 'Give me a bit to wash a little.' 'Here, take it.' We didn't drink from there. We walked kilometres looking for water. We found a spring and we took water from there, putting it in cans. Maybe it was a week before we washed [again].

A woman gave birth to a baby, leaving it to die because she didn't have anything to clothe it. We weren't stable there. [Constables] moved us from village to village. She left it there to die. One of the elders got up: 'Woman, you are sinning. We already have enough sins upon us. Leave it with me, leave it with me." The child lived three more days and died. The woman thanked God she got rid of it. Her hands were tied, there was nothing she could do."[53]

Constantina discussed how some Gypsies ate their horses and mules as meat. She did not elaborate further because for her there was no need: to consume the animal that sustains one's life illustrates destruction. The inconceivable

117

became conceivable. Their despair drove them to perhaps the most extreme measure against their culture – infanticide. Women abandoned newborn babies in the bitter winter's snow. Self-preservation overrode all. Constantina was not the first survivor to tell of women putting their children out to die – in their culture where children are always celebrated and cherished, and represent the family's happiness, luck, and survival. Constantina's body mended from the onslaught of disease, but her soul still cried nearly sixty years later for the tragedies she witnessed and suffered.

Another survivor, Vasile Ionita, was forty years old when the constables came to announce he must leave the village to relocate in Transnistria. A semi-nomadic coppersmith, he never believed the Gypsies would be subjected to the horrors they experienced in Transnistria. He watched his brother, his son, and countless others perish in the misery. During the interview, Vasile opened his tattered vest, displaying nearly twenty metal crosses of various designs pinned neatly inside. God carried him through life's ordeals, he insisted, especially that of Transnistria.

"A year before, articles started to appear in the press, talking about this deportation. I was in a pub and some Romanians reading a newspaper said: 'Listen here, man, it says that all Gypsies will be sent to Transnistria.' We didn't believe that it was going to happen. We didn't expect to be sent there. Before the deportation, it was perfect in the country. We lived in peace with the people. We accepted each other. We were taken by surprise, unprepared. People should have reacted then, many should have woke up. There were people who protested, some intelligent people with book learning, but without any effect.

I was a coppersmith, making objects for home use. My father taught me. It is a trade you learn which comes from the olden times. We learned it from the elders. A village constable I knew told me:'You will have to leave, like all the others, to Transnistria.' I said: 'Why send me? Look, I will give you some money.' I gave him 1000 lei. And a copper pot that I made. The constable told me: 'Okay, hide until this wave of fury and evil passes. I'll help you then.' But it seems that a Gypsy who had his family sent didn't like this, and he turned me in to the authorities. He told them where I was hiding, and then they came and took me and my family to Transnistria. The constable tried to keep his promise and help me. We left with a wagon and horses, my wife and four children. I had four brothers and a sister named Natalita who left. The police and constables accompanied me. I was sent from place to place to Transnistria.

On the road to Transnistria we were beaten, [but] beaten less by the Romanian constables. On the other hand, when we passed Bessarabia there everybody beat us. Antonescu hated the Gypsies. He was the one who hated and harmed us. When we arrived there, they made fun of us and put us to hard labour, working us like animals. They kept us there for two years without us being spared any suffering.

[In Transnistria] all of us were living in the open air, except for those who had wagons, and they could sleep in or under them. [It was] a place in a kind of field, which was very long and flat. It was an open field. It was hot because it was springtime or summer

118

and we could stay outside without needing a roof. We didn't have houses to stay in at that time. Maybe we were 10,000 families there. We were left free by ourselves. But when winter came, they took us from there and brought us to a big town. They put us in a sort of house, a barn where animals stayed. Hundreds of families were kept together. They did not allow us to live together with the [Ukrainian] people. They gave us an ear of corn and a potato per day. They gave us 200 grams of corn meal that we couldn't do anything with; it had sand in it. We were dying of hunger.

There were all kinds of Gypsies there. The first to be deported were the nomads and then the semi-nomads. But after this also those who didn't speak the language [Romani] were sent. However, we had an easier life compared to the nomadic Gypsies, who were sent outside [of the barn]. They made earth houses and had to live there. So terribly were those people living that they reached the point of eating their horses for which they cared so much. In those days horses were so sacred, especially for them as they were nomads. They had long hair, and different, more colourful clothing. For semi-nomads like us, it was much easier to live than for the nomads who were mistreated because they were seen as different.

The deportation of the Jews started a long time before [us]. The majority were killed. But before, they were selected by their trades-tailors, shoe makers, and others. They were sent to Germany [sic] to work. Those who did not correspond to the authorities' standards were shot. The Jews made large graves, they were put on the edge of the grave and shot with automatics. I know a case where one of the Jewish girls escaped. She was taken by a man whose daughter was killed. He waited until the army left and he took this girl and said she was his. And he gave her his deceased daughter's name and this saved the girl.

We were dying of hunger. Many tried to go and bring some corn from somewhere, to steal it, corn from the fields that were close to them. But they did not succeed because they were immediately shot. A nomadic Gypsy tried to get out of the community, the place where they had placed him to go and get some sunflower seeds.

Those who were guarding us immediately shot him. They shot him with an automatic. The sunflower field was like twenty or thirty meters from us. But when that person crossed [the line], he was shot. We couldn't escape. Because if we ran away, we were caught and killed. If they caught us on the train, they threw us off and killed us.

I did agricultural work, harvested wheat, dug the ground. I would have rather gone to war because my family would have remained at home and I wouldn't have had this daily fear. For me it would have been easier to be by myself than with my family that I had to look after. I couldn't bring anything for my children. I was watching them die of hunger, watching how they got sick.

Many people died of hunger. Where they were lying down on the earth, they died after a while of hunger, and remained where they lay. We didn't have cemeteries there. We made shallow graves with a little earth. My brother died of hunger, of misery, of sickness. When we buried him we didn't have the strength to make a deep grave. We made it on the surface. We covered him with a little earth and put plants over him.

119

God and my family [kept me alive]. I was thinking of the return and my oldest brother encouraged us all the time. He told us we had to live. We had to live so that we could come back. Many people died of hunger there. Three quarters. A quarter remained. We didn't argue anymore. Hunger was so great that the stronger one made life harder for the weaker one. It was a fight for survival. We didn't know what to do to escape. Our only hope when we saw how bad the situation became was in God. We didn't think of people anymore. We didn't think that they could help us."[54]

The government's solution

The Gypsies disintegrated from hunger, cold, and wretchedness. The government drew up a detailed work plan to alleviate the misery, however this effort would fail because the regions refused or could not comply with its conditions. Gypsies were expected to make their living either as tradesmen or agricultural workers. The decree stipulated that Gypsies living in Transnistria "will be settled in towns in groups of 150-350, according to the need for and the possibility of useful work, under the supervision of one of their number, with the obligation to work..."[55] The control of the Gypsies was delegated to local constables and local labour exchanges. All qualified Gypsy labourers were to be employed in existing workshops or new ones to be established. Unskilled Gypsies between the ages of twelve and sixty (without regard to sex) were to labour either in workshops cutting and shaping wood (fashioning crude wooden objects like spoons and brooms) or on collective farms. Unapproved absences from assigned residences or work places meant transfers to punishment camps.

By February 1943, the Governor of Transnistria, Alexianu, reported to the Ministry of Internal Affairs that 12,384 Gypsies brought to the Oceacov region were settled in the villages of Bogdanovca, Bulganovca, Crivoi Balca, Ilinscove, Marcovca, Novo Bogdanovca, Novogrigorevca, Petrovcoje and Vladimirovca.[56] Alexianu assured Bucharest that good houses and sufficient food were provided for the Gypsies. In response to criticisms of the decree, the Governor maintained that food distribution occurred properly every few days and attributed the Gypsies' suffering as self-inflicted with their immediate consumption of the rations. The Governor clung to the work decree as the means of improving Gypsies' living conditions and he wrote the harder they worked, the better housing and food distribution would become.

However much Alexianu believed his decree would ease the sufferings, Transnistria differed dramatically from its vision on paper. During the winter of 1942-43, the agricultural collectives were almost inactive, and the Ukrainians took what little work was available. As a person's workload determined their rations, the Gypsies' lack of employment accounted for their gross deprivation. Unwilling to wait for conventional methods of improving their lot, Gypsies stole corn, clothing, pots, and blankets from neighbouring Ukrainian villages for survival. Bands roved at night, stealing whatever they found.[57] As Ion Neagu explained, sometimes parents sent their children to steal food for the family.

They didn't always return. "I remember when three or four children left – seven, eight and ten years old – to get potatoes from the field. Only one of them came back. Shot. A bullet went through his back and came out of his chest."[58] Although the work decree punished theft by prison, often shootings or beatings replaced the officially prescribed deterrents.[59]

Returning to Romania: escape and repatriation

By 1943, Gypsies escaped from Transnistria by any means available. The horrendous living conditions, deaths of family members, and their own impending destruction forced their hand. Bribery, falsification of documents, and luck contributed to successful escapes. Wealthier Gypsies purchased illegal passage on trains by bribing train personnel for a prepaid sum. A few gold rings bought falsified repatriation certificates from local constabulary commanders which provided a family's passport back home. Sometimes Gypsy soldiers, whose relatives died before their arrival with the correct paperwork, sold or gave the documents to Gypsy acquaintances. Others hid on trains undetected or with the assistance of sympathetic guards.

Ana Carpaci, Elena Carpaci, and Maria Ciuraru from the village of Maciova refused to die in Transnistria and escaped twice. After their initial return to Romania, local authorities discovered and questioned the three. Ana Carpaci's verbal testimony to constables reveals the motivation and means of the first flight:

"My name is Ana, 20 years old, of the Orthodox faith, unmarried, having no savings, not able to read or write, living in the village of Maciova in the Gypsy colony. I was evacuated to Transnistria together with the other Gypsies and they brought us to Odessa [but from there to] where exactly I don't know. There were many of us there and no one worried about me and no one guarded us. About two days before Christmas many of us left from there, around sixty men and women, because the Captain who shared food with us said that if we could escape, we should go where we would not die of hunger.

I left, together with my companions Elena and Maria, for Odessa, arriving on December 24th. From there we got on a passenger train and left for home. On this train nobody asked me for tickets until we arrived in Tighina. There a conductor asked us for tickets and where we were going. We answered that we didn't have tickets, and we were going home from Transnistria because we were dying there. He let us stay on the train. When we got to Bucharest, we changed trains and asked people which train we should take. After that we got on a train again. On this train they asked us for tickets but seeing our poor, miserable state, they left us in peace and other travellers even gave us bread. This is how we arrived at the railway station of Cavovau on December 28th1942. From there we walked home.

I declare that in Transnistria many of us stayed in a place and [constables] gave us very little food. Every day 8-10 people died. More of us could have left as nobody

121

watched us but we waited until Christmas because we knew the train would be emptier, making it easier for us to get back."[60]

Ana's companions recounted similar events, telling of their individual experiences. Elena Carpaci, 60 years old, was deported with her husband who, according to Elena, died from neglect in Transnistria. In her plight she risked fleeing rather than dying. Maria Ciuraru, 17, left Romania voluntarily with her boy-friend Romulus Ciuraru, who officials deported as a thief.[61] She stressed the horrible living conditions forced her to run away. Ana, Elena, and Maria petitioned the authorities to remain in Maciova.

But these women were not alone in their attempts to flee from the Transnistrian horrors. Records from the General Inspectorate of Constabulary indicate that 795 Gypsies returned to Romania at the end of 1943.[62] The returnees caused difficulties for local officials, who under orders from Bucharest, re-deported them to Transnistria. Most city officials, like those in Maciova, reported cases of returned Gypsies seeking the right to remain to the Regional Constabulary

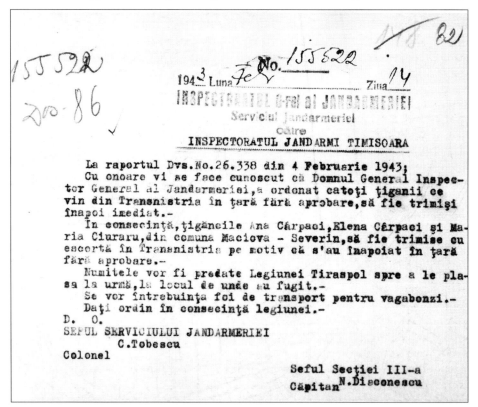

On February 14th 1943, Tobescu at the General Inspectorate of Constabulary orders that Ana Carpaci, Elena Carpaci, and Maria Ciuraru from the village of Maciova are to be sent back to Transnistria because they returned to Romania without permission.

offices. Local constables or police indicated the circumstances of the original deportations and gave their opinion concerning repatriation. The Regional constable office added their input and forwarded the paperwork to Colonel Tobescu, Chief of Security and Order, at the General Inspector of Constabulary in Bucharest. The file travelled next to General C.Z. Vasiliu, Undersecretary of State at the Ministry of Internal Affairs. Either Vasiliu or Tobescu determined a case's final outcome; however Vasiliu's decision outweighed Tobescu's in a dispute. If Vasiliu or Tobescu decided a case warranted further investigation, the file spiralled down the chain of command and up again when the information was completed. Detailed descriptions of the reason for each Gypsy's deportation were required by Bucharest to rule out possible errors on the part of the constables or the police. Once Tobescu and Vasiliu resolved a case, the file was channelled backward and the local officials were ordered either to redeport Gypsies or permit them to stay in Romania.

For Ana Carpaci, Elena Carpaci, and Maria Ciuraru, the process dragged on for months. The first round of paper work called for their redeportation.[63] However, when the Mayor learned of the women's dilemma, he petitioned the central authorities to let them remain in Maciova, stating that they disturbed no one. The regional constables in Severin shared the Mayor's opinion.[64] They wrote because of Elena's age (60) and her husband's death (she was deported because of him), she should be allow to stay in Maciova. The constables also requested that Ana and Maria remain in Romania. Bucharest reviewed the first communication without any knowledge of the more recent report, and Tobescu ordered the women to be re-deported. This motion reached the Maciova constables, who stalled in executing the orders, and waited for more positive instructions. When none came, Ana, Maria, and Elena were put on trains back to Transnistria. A few days after their departure, the letter granting the women repatriation arrived.[65]

In the majority of cases reviewed, Bucharest ordered the Gypsies' relocation to Transnistria, even if local authorities lobbied for their repatriation. However, a few like Romulus Ciuraru, Maria Ciuraru's ex-boyfriend, were allowed to remain in Romania.[66] Romulus had escaped with the women and returned to Maciova to support his six-member family. The local constables discovered him and wrote in their report that Romulus should be re-evacuated because he had been deported as a thief. The village mayor countered the constables' opinion with his support. He wrote that the constables deported Romulus because he was poor, not because he was a thief. The mayor added that since Romulus' return to the community, he supported his family in the absence of male family members who fought on the fronts. Romulus accepted a deal. He would join the army in the spring and authorities would let him stay in Romania.[67]

Soldiers' families

Not all Gypsies were forced to run away from Transnistria for repatriation. Soldiers' families had the best chance of legally returning to Romania. Despite the constables' orders that families of soldiers were not be evacuated, local authorities did not always adhere to regulations as several Gypsy soldiers discovered when returning home on sick-leave, only to find their families gone. Fearing a rebellion of Gypsy soldiers, the Ministry of Internal Affairs ordered commanding officers to read to the Gypsies in their units the criteria used for deportation, stressing that if their families did not fall into criminal categories, they need not worry.[68] The Ministry needed to rectify the mistakes or risk desertion from their Gypsy soldiers.

In a letter to the Governor of Transnistria, General Vasiliu detailed which sedentary Gypsies could appeal for repatriation. This response was prompted by a report about Gypsies settled in the Oceacov villages of Katurga, Karanika, and Kovalievka. Vasiliu also recognised that placing 13,000 Gypsies in Oceacov caused a desperate situation.[69] While he admitted no responsibility for the Gypsies' plight, Vasiliu proposed separation and dispersion of the Gypsies in smaller groups of 100-200 families. Theoretically, this would render the Gypsies easier to control, ease the overcrowding, and allot proper, sustainable working conditions as provided for in the work decree. Like Governor Alexianu, Vasiliu believed that his plan would better the Gypsies' situation.[70]

Thirteen categories of sedentary Gypsies were listed which might merit repatriation. These included: invalids and those who took part in the First World War; widows of the First World War with or without pensions; wives, parents, and children of those killed in the current war; families of those drafted in the current war; parents of those who took part in the 1941-42 war; those who took part in the current war and had been released from duty; families of officers and non-commissioned officers fighting on the front; Romanians deported in error as Gypsies; Gypsies mistakenly deported; and anyone else taken by mistake.[71] Although this policy granted relief to some soldiers' families, it by no means guaranteed it. General Vasiliu warned that only the aforementioned categories of Gypsies would be investigated and that criminality or other dubious circumstances would nullify one's right to return to Romania. One such "dubious" situation was marriage. Frequently Gypsies married outside of civil or church ceremonies, a practice condemned as immoral by some local authorities who blocked the return of soldiers' common-law wives.[72] The Ministry of Internal Affairs fluctuated in their decisions to repatriate these women if marriage certificates were not presented.

Army commanders explained to Gypsy soldiers the appeal procedure. If a soldier believed his family had been wrongfully expelled, he was to write directly to the Ministry of Internal Affairs. Accompanying this letter often was another written by a soldier's commander which described the respective man's conduct in battle and his bravery with the intent to lend credence to the case.

Once received at the General Inspectorate of Constabulary, local authorities were asked to identify the reasons for a family's deportation. If the investigation revealed that city officials considered a family in good moral standing and no known criminal records existed, repatriation was approved. The soldier was then temporarily released from duty to retrieve his family at his expense.

The Mayor of Oceacov remembered well the crowds of wounded Gypsy soldiers descending on his district to reclaim loved ones:

"From Romania to the Oceacov area there came a lot of Gypsies in uniform, either from the front or from hospitals, and even invalids from this war without a leg or hand came to look for their wives, children, and parents. Their justified anger was terrific. During the winter they left Oltenia [and] Transylvania in order to come to Oceacov to find their loved ones. Some came with approval on the part of the Ministry of Internal Affairs and the Government [of Transnistria] for their return, some others coming only with a few papers, a little proof and they had to go back again to Odessa and Bucharest to obtain permission. I remember one who told me that he had to go three times to Bucharest for approval. They asked him [each time] for new papers."[73]

Rupita Gheorghe's father was one soldier who had to return twice before claiming his family. Rupita was a young boy when his father traded his pot-maker's tools for a gun, leaving their small village to serve his term of military service. When the war broke out the army reassigned his father to the front. He did not know that while he defended the country, constables entered his village forcing his family to pack up their wagon and relocate to Transnistria. Rupita's mother managed to send a letter to his father's unit which alerted him to their whereabouts. Desperate to locate his family, Rupita's father went to Transnistria without the proper papers and had to return to Bucharest to began the long appeal process. By the time repatriation was granted, this soldier's mother and wife were dead.

According to Rupita, the remaining family members endured an exhausting two-month trek home in winter, motivating themselves with thoughts of Romania. "When the night caught us, when we couldn't walk anymore, we would lay our heads down on the earth. Rain or snow, we stayed there to rest because the next day we would arrive in Romania."[74] Heavy allied bombings of the railways made travel by train dangerous. Sometimes treading through knee-deep snow, Rupita's family were at the point of death when they reached their village. The generosity of his countrymen with their gifts of food, clothing and household supplies saved his life. Later their kindness impressed Rupita as it contrasted with the government's sterile attention to the soldiers' families, motivated not of concern for the Gypsies' welfare but out of fear that returnees would start a typhus epidemic. During the two months that Rupita recovered in Bucharest at the Military Hospital, he remembered trouble in readjusting to food, beds and cleanliness.

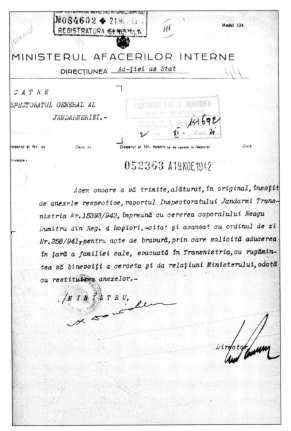

*On November 19th 1942, the Ministry of Internal Affairs approved the
repatriation of soldier Dumitru Neagu's family from Transnistria.*

Another soldier, Dumitru Neagu, counted himself lucky to retrieve most of his
family from Transnistria. When Dumitru returned home on injury-leave and
learned of his family's forced departure, he enlisted his superior's assistance to
request repatriation. Dumitru's commander convincingly appealed on his behalf
in a letter to the Ministry.[75] An investigation revealed that village authorities
had categorised and deported the Neagus as nomads because Dumitru's father
travelled as a horse trader. The Neagu family had owned property in the village
of Vidra since the late 1890s.[76] Dumitru produced the deeds to the house and
land, and successfully refuted the charge of nomadism. Five months after the
Neagu family's expulsion, Bucharest sanctioned their return to Romania.
Dumitru arrived in Transnistria only to learn that the mistaken evacuation had
killed his wife, sister and brother.

Dumitru's surviving brother Ion, just thirteen when their wagons departed for
Transnistria, told of their tribulations on arriving back in Romania in January 1943:

"We came back on the train in cattle trucks. When we got off the train, they beat us,
killed some of us, and I thank God that some of us got out of there alive. The

Romanians were laughing at us, saying, "From three or four thousand crows, only two flowers came back." [From three or four thousand miserable Gypsies, only two children came back.] When we came back to Romania, we had no house. We had nobody. The Romanians [in our village] gave us corn meal, bread, something to eat. We came' with only a blanket on our shoulders. We lost our work, horses, wagons, gold coins, fortunes, and dead children."[77]

The survivors of the Neagu family returned home malnourished, ill, half-naked, financially ruined, and grieving for deceased relatives. Neighbours' generosity eased their transition, but it was years until the family reestablished its material losses. Dumitru was called back to the front, risking his life to fight for the government which shattered his world. No reparations were ever given to compensate for the undue deaths, destruction, and sufferings Dumitru's family endured.

Massive returns and the long trek home

By the end of 1943, Antonescu knew Germany would not win the war. As the situation worsened along the Eastern front, increasingly Gypsies crossed the border into Romania to seek food, shelter and work from adjacent regions. After more than 300 Gypsies fled Golta in November 1943, Bucharest demanded explanations.[78] The Golta constables outlined faulty policy, overcrowding, and under-staffing as the reasons for the illegal departures. Constables explained the Transnistrian government's poor planning to their headquarters:

"[1]. The organisation of work shops and the procuring of machinery did not develop as needed to give deported Gypsies possibilities for earning their living.
[2]. Gypsies between the ages of twelve and sixty were not given the work which was planned for them in the [work] Decree.
[3]. Children under twelve years and persons older than sixty remained without the means to feed and clothe themselves since food is given only to those who are employed at a job. Some receive a payment which can only provide for a small quantity of food."[79]

Constables also commented on logistical problems. The number of Gypsies assigned to five cities in Golta was 8,893, which far surpassed the recommended figure of 150-300 persons for each community.[80] The large groups caused control difficulties for constables who were inadequately equipped to guard such numbers. Despite these handicaps, the Golta constables had already caught and sent back 2,000 Gypsies attempting to escape, most of whom fled at night when areas were not patrolled.[81] In an effort to lessen the disorganisation and to improve the Gypsies' living conditions, constables transferred 475 Gypsies to a former Jewish camp which offered easier control by guards and improved facilities.[82] The solution however offered only temporary respite as the camp's limited capacity reduced its ability to feed all the Gypsies.

Unable to cope with the influx of Gypsies crossing the border, local Romanian authorities cabled the General Inspectorate of Constabulary for instructions. In line with previous policy, Tobescu ordered illegally returning Gypsies to be sent back to Transnistria. On January 18th 1944, the policy changed. Tobescu replied to an enquiry from the authorities in Alexandria that escaped Gypsies were to remain wherever they were apprehended.[83] What provoked the policy shift? It is probable that failures on the front lines and increased reports of an Allied invasion had influenced Bucharest's decision. As early as January 1944, Romania began debating abandoning Germany to join the Allies.[84] Through neutral connections, Marshal Antonescu sent a message that he would not resist an Allied entry into the Balkans.[85]

While the policy change suited Romania's political needs, it was anything but convenient for city officials who over the next few months dealt with housing, feeding, and placing the Gypsies in workplaces. On April 23rd 1944 Bucharest clarified the instructions for returned nomadic Gypsies in a circular order to local constables.[86] Interestingly, the General Inspector of Constabulary's orders from here on refer only to "nomadic" Gypsies, which is likely to have been a clerical oversight in considering all Gypsies as nomads, regardless of their original classifications.[87] Bucharest believed the Gypsies threatened "the wealth and even the lives of the citizens" as they had resorted to petty theft to survive.[88] In cooperation with regional Mayors and Chambers of Agriculture, every village was given orders: to stop and detain Gypsies from further movement into Romania; to provide them with a provisional residence to remove their threat to public health; to place Gypsies for work at grain mills which had sanitary facilities approved by the above mentioned offices; to provide strictly the necessary amount of food and clothes to prevent Gypsies from stealing; to forbid fortune telling. Punishment was to be strictly enforced for not respecting the hygiene rules, unexcused absences from work or laziness, travelling into the village or between villages, and fighting among themselves.[89] The suggested punishment for not adhering to the above-mentioned conditions was a public whipping of twenty-five lashes.

Though these measures were intended to control the Gypsies' movement further into Romania and to protect the local populations, many officials resented the impractical orders. In the examination of these reports, once again the government's inability to manage the situation becomes evident. Authorities angrily articulated to Bucharest the inapplicability of the General Inspectorate's work instructions since the Gypsies' poor health and age – too young or too old – rendered many of those fleeing unfit or ineligible for employment.[90] One of the most critical accounts of the discrepancies comes from the Galati region's constabulary Inspector's office which commented that the Gypsies' situation was just as precarious as ever because the refusal of local employers to hire them and the decline in demand for their traditional trades left Gypsies without sufficient income.[91] The regional commander Colonel Sarbulescu wrote in a cable to Bucharest that the Gypsies were dying of hunger. He suggested two solutions: the settlement of the Gypsies in work camps where in exchange for their labour they would receive food, or the transport of the Gypsies back to their villages where their skills would be more welcome as they would be known by the locals.[92] Five days later on June 9th 1944, the Colonel received this response: "The General Inspectorate of Constabulary cannot ask the government to feed lazy people. Whoever wants to work, will live; whoever does not, should remain in Transnistria under the care of the administration."[93] The reply illustrates not only Bucharest's lack of compassion, but also its deliberate refusal to resolve the life-threatening situation facing the Gypsies.

Conclusion

Massive Allied air strikes in April 1944 and the advancing Russian troops alerted Antonescu that his army was unable to continue the war without massive German assistance.[94] Nonetheless, the Marshal maintained his agreement with Germany while continuing negotiations for an armistice with the Soviets. In the meanwhile another armistice was negotiated independently by the opposition parties, joined by King Michael.[95] On August 23rd 1944, the King announced the dissolution of the Antonescu government and proclaimed an armistice with the Soviet Union, Great Britain and the United States.[96] Antonescu was arrested and two days later Romania declared war on Germany.

The archival records concerning the release of the Gypsies from Transnistria are few, possibly due to the confusion of the change in government. Survivors' recollections reconstruct more accurately the events precipitating their return. Many learned of the end of the War from Romanian constables who abandoned their posts to escape before Russian troops took over the area. Some Gypsies said that the guards told them to flee while others recalled how constables abandoned them without any information. Afraid to strike out one their own, many Gypsies waited a few days before leaving. But liberation did not halt the hardships. Weakened by almost two years exile in terrible conditions, abandoned by the government which had forcibly ejected them, denied practical means of ensuring daily survival and their passage home, some Gypsies were forced to leave behind family members who physically could not make the journey unassisted – namely the young and old. Survivors today told of placing small children alongside Ukrainian houses and disabled grandmothers near villages in the hope that the Ukrainians who treated the Gypsies with kindness during the worst of times would once again take pity, offering their relatives water and food.[97] Not all who began the journey home completed it. Daytime travel was hazardous for Gypsies because they risked encountering German soldiers in retreat who would shoot them on sight.[98] Night time brought another danger as bombings continued over the region. Vasile Gheorghe preferred risking night travel using roadside ditches as his shelter.[99] Some Gypsies died and others lost their strength to continue and had to be left behind, hidden in trees or shrubs to shelter them from retreating Germans. For those Gypsies who trekked home, death was not yet beaten. Untreated illnesses, such as typhus, claimed the lives of many after their return. Some came home to discover nothing left of the goods which remained behind. They attributed their survival to God and the generosity of their neighbours who provided whatever could be spared.

On September 13th 1944, one day after Romania signed the official armistice in Moscow, the Ministry of Internal Affairs issued an order which granted Gypsies freedom to practice their respective trades.[100] Presumably Gypsies were allowed to return after that to their original communities, however no paperwork was found to indicate this. Lists of survivors compiled by constables show that approximately 6,000 out of the 25,000 Gypsies deported to Transnistria returned to Romania.[101] The rest succumbed to misery, disease, hunger, cold, and maltreatment. Marshal Ion Antonescu and C.Z. Vasiliu were tried and found guilty of war crimes in May 1946.[102] One charge that neither man disputed was deportation of the Gypsies to Transnistria. On June 1st 1946, both men were executed.[103]

VI. The Soviet Union and the Baltic States 1941-44: the massacre of the Gypsies

Michael Zimmermann

Historians investigating the policies of the National Socialists towards Gypsies are generally in agreement that it was the Second World War – set in motion by the regime on September 1st 1939 with its attack on Poland – that led to an immense increase in oppression and that ended persecution ending in genocide.

The Task Forces

The extermination of the Romanies in the territory of the Soviet Union began soon after the German attack of June 22nd 1941 and quickly acquired the character of genocide. Together with Jews, officials of the Soviet Communist Party, partisans and other 'undesirable elements' they were victims of the Task Forces who followed behind the advancing German army and carried out murders behind the front line.

Four such Task Forces (*Einsatzgruppen*) – mobile killing units of the SS – each a battalion in strength, were created for the German attack on the USSR that had from the start the character of a racist war of conquest and extermination. They received their detailed instructions from the National Security Headquarters (RSHA). For administrative purposes they were under the army who supplied them with fuel, food, quarters and, if necessary, with communications. Task Force A was attached to the Northern Army Group that marched towards Leningrad, Task Force B to the Middle Army Group that aimed to capture Moscow and Task Force C to the Southern Army Group, that was to bring the Ukraine into the area governed by the Germans. Task Force D followed the 11th Army that advanced into the far south of the Soviet Union.

The Task Forces were each divided into from four to six operational units in company strength that were called Special Units (*Einsatzkommando* or *Sonderkommando*). In all, the four Task Forces comprised some 3,000 men. They were to kill over a million people. They were formed from members of the Security Police, the Armed SS and the Security Constabulary, together with German, Estonian, Latvian, Lithuanian and Ukrainian auxiliaries.[1]

Einsatzgruppe A	*Einsatzgruppe C*
- Sonderkommando 1a	- Einsatzkommando 4a
- Sonderkommando 1b	- Einsatzkommando 4b
- Einsatzkommando 2	- Einsatzkommando 5
- Einsatzkommando 3	- Einsatzkommando 6
Einsatzgruppe B	*Einsatzgruppe D*
- Sonderkommando 7a	- Sonderkommando 10a
- Sonderkommando 7b	- Sonderkommando 10b
- Sonderkommando 7c	- Einsatzkommando 11a
- Einsatzkommando 8	- Einsatzkommando 11b
- Einsatzkommando 9	
- Vorkommando Moskau	

The organisation of the Task Forces (Einsatzgruppen) and the Special Units.

In theory the *Einsatzkommandos* were to operate behind the lines and the *Sonderkommandos* on the front – in practice they were deployed according to geographical sectors and the distinction disappeared. In the English text both are referred to as Special Units.

Before the attack on the Soviet Union Heydrich, Himmler's Deputy and the Security Headquarters, in conjunction with the leaders of the army, had given the Task Forces the role of destroying the framework of the USSR. The primary targets were those designated as "Jewish Bolshevik" and the elimination of the servants of this framework. That meant the murder of the Jewish members of the Soviet state and party apparatus, the Jewish intelligentsia and finally those Jews who were considered as potential resistance fighters. Already in the first month of the war against the Soviet Union, the Task Forces went further and chose as hostages primarily Jewish citizens of military service age, whom they later killed in reprisal for real or imagined acts of resistance by the population. When the Nazi leadership believed, at the beginning of August 1941, that the collapse of the USSR was imminent, they strengthened their orders to the Task Forces in accordance with their idea of a Final Solution to the "Jewish Problem". They were to murder as completely as possible the whole Jewish population of the Soviet Union. Himmler announced this decision during his visit to Special Unit 8 in Minsk on August 14th and 15th 1941.[2] At the same time the order to kill was evidently extended to the Gypsies. It was followed by the first murder of Soviet Romanies by the Task Forces in the second half of August.[3]

The statement of Otto Ohlendorf, the leader of Task Force D, at the Nuremberg Trial after the war, gives some idea of the grounds upon which the murder of the Gypsies was to be legitimized. Ohlendorf's line of defence in 1947-48 was to claim the necessity of obeying orders and also that a Special Order for the Task Forces to kill had been announced shortly before the attack on the USSR. While this explanation is difficult to sustain in the light of historical investigation, the remarks of Ohlendorf regarding the murder of Gypsies are of great historical relevance. During the Nuremberg Trial of the Task Forces he declared, in October 1948, that it was their role "to keep the rear of the troops free by killing Jews, Gypsies, Communist Party officials, active Communists and all persons who could endanger security". Thus Ohlendorf sought to justify the murder of Jews and Gypsies with the motive of the security of the German troops. The structure of his argument makes the racist nature of the murder of Jews and Gypsies clear. For the Task Forces – by the middle of August 1941 at the latest – their mere existence, whether man, woman or child, was considered a threat to security.

With regard to the Gypsies, Ohlendorf added particularly that the same rules applied as against Jews.[4] Gypsy children "had to be killed, along with their parents, as the killing was not intended to be temporary solution, but was to lead to a permanent solution. As children of parents who had been killed they represented no less a danger for the Germans than the parents themselves." Further, Ohlendorf motivated the killings with the cliché accusation that both Jews and Gypsies were spies. Just like the Jew – he said – Gypsies had carried out the role of spying in all wars as "they were not sedentary people and were intrinsically willing... to change their standpoint."[5]

Once it had been given, the 1941 Special Order of the Task Forces took on a life of its own. The rationalisation that developed within the mobile operational units for the killing of Gypsies corresponded to the anti-Gypsy stereotypes of the time. Alongside the clichés of spying and helping the partisans, there was also the stigma of being antisocial, well-known for thieving and a foreign element, culminating in the general claim that the Gypsies were a burden in every way.[6]

A message from Task Force C from October 1941 illustrates the attraction of such reasoning:

"On the journey from Vyrva to Dederev the Special Unit detained a Gypsy band of thirty-two persons. On searching through their caravans, German armaments were found. As this band was without papers and gave no information about the items they had with them, they were executed."[7]

When, in spring 1942 near Vitebsk, Special Unit 9 was going to shoot a group of twenty Romanies, an old woman asked to be spared. The commander refused with the justification that if she was allowed to escape she would report the execution.[8] Thus, even murder itself was used to justify further murder. If, during the shootings, there were open or hidden criticisms the killers took refuge in their last bastion of defence – they were only carrying out orders. Members of Special Unit 4a who, on a spring day in 1942, shot some 300 Jews and Gypsies in Klintsy reacted to the expressions of disapproval from the circle of watching soldiers with this statement – that they were carrying out orders.[9]

All four Task Forces murdered Gypsies.

- Special Unit 3 of Task Force A announced on August 22nd 1941 the execution of three Gypsies, a Gypsy woman and a child. Further announcements of killings by Task Force A date from January 2nd, March 16th and April 24th 1942. In these reports they announced the liquidation of ninety-three people "including a Gypsy band that had carried out their terror in the neighbourhood of Siverski" and that in Keknya thirty-eight Jews and one Gypsy had been shot as well as seventy-one Gypsies executed near Leningrad.[10]

- In the area covered by Task Force B, Lepel, the local military commander, handed over to Special Unit 8 in the second half of September 1941 thirteen male and ten female Gypsies. They received Special Treatment – they were killed – as "they were terrorising the local population and carrying out many thefts".

Special Unit 7a killed forty-five Gypsies in March 1942. The rearguard of Special Unit 7a shot a further fifty Gypsies in Klintsy in the second week of April 1942. For the second half of August 1942 Special Unit 7a reported the capture of thirty Gypsies while Special Unit 7b captured fourty-eight. Many more Gypsies were shot or buried alive by members of Task Force B in the neighbourhood of Smolensk.[11]

Special Unit 8 (also of Task Force B) registered for March 1942 thirty-three persons receiving Special Treatment and for the last two weeks of August 1942 sixty-three arrested Gypsies. Special Unit 9 killed at least twenty Gypsies at the end of March or the beginning of April 1942 and in August that year

134

murdered fifty-three more people whom they classified as "Gypsies and antisocials"

- The officers of Task Force C "eliminated" six antisocial elements (Gypsies) during the first weeks of September near Novoukrainka.[12]

- Thirty-two Gypsies were arrested and executed by Special Unit 4a – part of Task Force C – between Vyrva and Dederev, as described above.[13]

- Gypsies were also murdered at Taganrog near Rostov. Taganrog had been the headquarters of Special Unit 10 of Task Force D since the second half of October 1941.[14]

The Chief of Police in Kaunas reports on the execution of a Gypsy band. July 13th 1942.

The Task Forces used broad guidelines to select the targets for their killings. Precise definitions did not interest them. Task Force A calculated the number of its victims up to February 1st 1942 at 240,410. Together with 218,000 Jews shot and another 5,500 killed in pogroms, they listed categories of dead as "Lithuanians crossing the border, Communists, partisans, mentally ill and others". The composition of the 311 "others" was not detailed.[15] Gypsies may have been classified among the "partisans " and "others".

Task Force B announced on October 25th 1941 the Special Treatment of 812 persons whom they labelled, without further details, as "completely racially and mentally unworthy elements". On December 19th 1941 the same Task Force mentions operations in the outer streets of Mogilev. There they had captured 1,356 people mostly Jews. The Jews had not carried the prescribed identification signs, the other non-Jewish persons were "nomadising (or) did not have the required papers on them." 127 of the arrested 135 were shot. In the second half of February 1942 Task Force B reported on their activity in White Russia: eleven more mass executions carried out including forty Jews and eleven women.[16]

Task Force C named the following selected groups that they had executed: political officials, looters, saboteurs, active Communists and political activists, Jews who had managed to escape from the prison camp by giving false information, agents and informers for the Soviet Secret Police (NKVD), people who, through false statements and influencing witnesses, had taken part in some measure in the deportation of ethnic Germans, Jewish sadists and revenge seekers, undesirable elements, antisocials, partisans, political commissars, spreaders of epidemics and infection, members of Russian bands, snipers...those helping Russian bands with food, agitators and troublemakers, rootless young people, Jews in general.[17] In individual reports Task Force C used to classify the victims of their executions as political officials, Jews, the incurable mentally ill and the residual category of saboteurs and looters.[18]

Even more imprecise were the reports of the Leader of the SS and police in South Russia whose units in late summer 1941 killed alongside Task Force C. In August 1941 alone they "shot 44,125 persons, mostly Jews"[19]

It is likely that Romanies were sometimes to be found also amongst those murder victims who had been labelled as antisocial, saboteurs, looters, agents, partisans, racially and mentally unworthy or undesirable elements, as nomads and "others". On the other hand, it is unclear whether any non-Romanies were shot under the classification of "Gypsy". A member of the Criminal Police said, after an execution in Klintsy in which he took part as a guard, that, apart from Jews, "a kind of Gypsy" had been shot.[20]

Task Forces A, B and C did not systematically look for Gypsies as part of their "enforcement action" (the term is that of Task Force C).[21] The Gypsies were generally handed over to them by the Army, reported to them by the

Russian population, seized during a check on prisons, killed during general checks of the civil population in areas near the front or picked up when a Unit was en route to its next station.[22]

There is an important difference here in comparison with the killing of Jews. When the speed of the military advance and the density of Jewish settlement permitted it, the Jewish population centres were systematically cordoned off, searched and destroyed by the Special Units. Similar large Romany settlements did not exist. The Romanies lived together with their families and not in a large social grouping like the Jewish districts, which were based on the need for a minyan, the quorum of men for prayer. As a result of the cultural barrier between Romanies and non-Romanies, the former had a more mistrustful view of the Germans than did the Jews, who had a positive memory of the Germans from the First World War, valued German culture and had not picked up any news of the anti-Semitism of the National Socialists from the Soviet media. Having adopted the general urban and social conventions, the Jews were deceived by the announcements and posters that told them to assemble for the purpose of "resettlement"[23] The Task Forces never thought of employing similar measures against the Gypsies, as they imagined them stereotypically as completely nomadic and therefore continually travelling, an idea which did not stop them from also shooting settled Gypsies.[24]

The instructions given to the Task Forces set out a hierarchical picture of the enemy.[25] At the top stood the Communists and Jews with their imaginary link in a Jewish Bolshevik world conspiracy.[26] In this picture of the world the Gypsies played a lesser, although not unimportant role. They figured as racially unworthy, generally antisocial, partisans, spies and agents of the imaginary world enemy – the Jewish Bolsheviks. Considered by the Task Forces to be carriers of this Jewish Bolshevism, the Gypsies were the victims of murder whenever the mobile death squads became aware of their existence. Being merely helpers of the World Enemy they were not seen by the murderers as a priority to be found and shot. The Task Forces killed all the Gypsies that came into their grip but – except for Task Force D – they did not search for them with the same intensity as they did for the Jews and Communists.

The Crimea

The situation of Task Force D was different. Their units 10b, 11a and 11b met in November 1941 in the Crimean peninsular on the Black Sea and remained there until April 1942. That enabled their killing units to intensify the murders or – as Ohlendorf put it euphemistically to the Allied Nuremberg Tribunal – "to carry out a very thorough political supervision of the population there."[27]

Between November 16th and December 15th 1941 the units of Task Force D had already killed 17,645 Jews, 2,503 Krimchaks, 212 Communists and partisans and 824 Gypsies. The Krimchaks followed the Jewish religion but were not ethnically Jewish. These total figures included the victims of death squads 10a and 12 who killed outside the Crimea.[28]

After an interruption in the murders at the end of 1941 and the beginning of 1942 because of weather conditions,[29] Task Force D killed ninety-one persons labelled as looters, saboteurs and antisocials between January 15th and February 15th 1942, and in the second half of February 421 Gypsies, antisocials and saboteurs. Then, in the first two weeks of March, a further 810 antisocials, Gypsies, mentally ill and saboteurs were also killed and by the end of March a further 261 antisocials, including Gypsies.[30]

In all the units of Task Force D killed over 31,000 people between November 1941 and March 1942, the majority being Jews. According to the estimate of the General Staff of Task Force D there were, with the exception of small groups in the north of the Crimea, no Jews, Krimchaks or Gypsies to be found. All the towns on the peninsular had been "combed through at least twice". Local militia as well as informants and the associated information system had helped to achieve this "success". In the town of Simferopol the Special Units required the evidence of two members of the native population to identify a Gypsy. The Romanies in the peninsular were Muslims like the Tatar population. They also spoke the Tatar language and could not be differentiated by looks from the indigenous population. In order to avoid ill will through the possible murder of non-Romanies, the killers took the advice of Tatars who knew the locality.[31]

The town of Simferopol had a Romany quarter. The people living there were registered by name in November and December 1941. On one December day they were brought out of their houses under the guard of armed police belonging to Special Units 10a and 11b. Their names were read out and they were loaded in groups of twenty-five onto lorries that drove off at short intervals. It seems that there were about twenty-five lorries made available by the German army.[32] As the site of execution the Special Units had chosen a place near the road from Simferopol to Karasubasar. The area was cordoned off by members of the Field Police and Special Unit 11b. Traffic was diverted to a distant road. The army lorries stopped at a pre-arranged point. There the victims were forced out of the vehicles by armed members of Task Force D (members of the Gestapo, the Security Police, the Constabulary and the SS). The Gypsies were uneasy. They could hear the shots of the firing squad. Their coats, furs, gold and valuables were taken from them.

The Task Forces used to distribute the clothes among the local population,[33] while the valuables were given to the Quartermaster of the General Staff of Task Force D after the shootings. He put them in a parcel which was sent to Berlin.

The Gypsies were led in groups to the edge of a two metre deep trench. Such trenches were prepared with explosives by an army engineer for the Task Forces. The Gypsies were ordered to face the trench. However, some turned round and looked at the firing squad who from a distance of five to six metres directed their weapons at the head of the victims. Several platoons, each led by an officer, took turns to make up the firing squads. There was no military doctor present to ascertain that the victims were really dead. For this reason, as has been reported with other executions of Jews and Gypsies, "the pile of bodies heaped up in the trench moved up and down for a long time"[34] After the Simferopol executions the firing squads filled the trenches with earth. The road blocks were removed. The soldiers went back to the town. Adjutant Schubert passed a report to the leader of Task Force D, Ohlendorf, who was "satisfied". Schubert recalled in 1948 that there had been no protests. Afterwards no more was said about the matter.[35]

The support that the units of the army gave the Task Forces in the shooting of Gypsies corresponded to the part played by the army in the murdering of Jews.[36] The military passed numerous victims to the death squads, often themselves suggested shooting and, as in Simferopol, gave varied logistic and organisational help to the executions.

We may note that the General in Command of Rear Army Area North in late autumn 1941 issued a Special Order concerning the Gypsies. According to this, "settled Gypsies who for two years had lived in their place of residence and had no political or criminal record" should be left there. On the other hand "wandering Gypsies" were to be handed over to the nearest Special Unit of the Security Police.[37] The loose formulation of the order against settled Gypsies could cover each and every one denounced to the Task Forces while the order against the wandering Gypsies who, because of the spy stereotype, were particularly suspected by the military, showed that the army did not just quietly tolerate the murder of the nomads but was actively involved.

Army units themselves killed Gypsies. In the area of the 281st Security Division in Rear Army Area North the District Commander at Novorshev permitted the shooting of 128 Gypsies. This murder was carried out by a unit of the army's own Secret Field Police. They had proposed "rendering the Gypsies harmless" for reasons of security and espionage. The Commander in Novorshev also relied upon Order 822 of May 12th 1942 from the Army Field Commander which said that "Gypsies should always be treated as partisans". In fact, no partisan activity or support for partisans was proved against the Gypsies. To rationalise the murder it was said that the Gypsies had not registered, had no regular work, earned their living begging from place to place and had no fixed dwellings. These trumped-up anti-Gypsy clichés served the Secret Police in creating a stereotype of spying Gypsies:

"The experience, found in countries other than Russia, that Gypsies, through their wandering life style, are particularly suited to be secret agents and are almost always ready to carry out such duties has also been noticed in Russia. (As) there is always suspicion of partisan activities where Gypsies are concerned, it can be assumed in this case." So, "immediate ruthless action on the spot" was deemed necessary.

The 281st Security Division and other military units claimed later the collaboration of military units in the liquidation of Gypsies and Jews had not to take place. Nevertheless, the Division insisted to the Commander of Army Area North that "in spite of the absence of formal proof" the murder of the 128 Gypsies in Novorshev was correct. The deaths were legitimised with the partisan stereotype. Since the carrying out of the shootings – it was claimed – there had been no more attacks in Novorshev.[38]

Behind the front line

In the autumn of 1941 a new and even more brutal stage of the German mass murders in the Soviet Union began. Behind the front line the position of the SS was secured together with a civil administration that worked under the newly created Ministry for the Occupied Eastern Areas in the State Commissariats of Ostland and the Ukraine. The State Commissariat for Ostland in its turn was divided into the General Districts of Estonia, Latvia, Lithuania and White Russia; the State Commissariat for the Ukraine was divided into the General Districts of Kiev, Podolia, Zhitomir and Volhynia.[39]

The SS and the police acted independently alongside the officials of the Ministry for the East. At the top of the police apparatus stood the Senior SS and police Chiefs North and South for Ostland and the Ukraine. SS and police leaders in the districts were responsible to them. The Senior SS and police Chiefs co-ordinated the actions of both the Security Police as well as the Security Constabulary, who, for their part, also took orders from the National Security Headquarters or the Headquarters of the Security Constabulary in Berlin.[40] The Task Forces were absorbed into the Security Police.

The total numbers, so far as the Security Police were concerned, remained unchanged compared with the strength of the Task Forces of summer 1941. Nevertheless, the Heads of the SS and police, because of their control of the Security Constabulary, had larger forces at their disposal than the Task Forces had in summer 1941. The German Rural Constabulary and Municipal Police were also expanded with security units composed of local auxiliaries of Balts, White Russians and Ukrainians.[41] These auxiliary troops outnumbered the German police personnel. In Ostland there were 31,804 local recruits alongside 4,428 German rural constables and municipal police. The equivalent figures for the Ukraine were 68,957 and 9,463.[42]

The orders to kill which had been given to the Task Forces applied also to the units under the Heads of the SS and police, without their bouts of killing having to depend upon the tempo and rhythm of German military movements.[43] Because they were permanently stationed in one place the murder squads, enlarged by the Rural Constabulary and the Municipal Police, could prepare themselves much more systematically, especially as they could rely upon the contacts, local knowledge and languages of the auxiliaries.

140

Ostsee

Tallinn

Leningrad

Riga

Reichskommissariat
Ostland

Reich

Kaunas

Moskau

Vazma

Smolensk

Minsk

Bialystok

Warschau

Brest-Litowsk

Lublin

Generalgouvernement

Gomel

Militärgebiet

Rowno

Kiew

Lemberg

Charkow

Reichskommissariat
Ukraine

Transnistrien

Cernauti

Ungarn

Dnjepropetrowsk

Chisinau

Odessa

Nikolajew

Melitopol

Rostow

Asowsches
Meer

Rumänien

Militär

gebiet

Simferopol

Bukarest

Schwarzes Meer

- - -   Frontline, Autumn 1942
· · · · ·   Borders of the administrative zones
- · - · -   Borderlines

0   100 200 300 400 500 600 km

The civil and military administrations in the occupied USSR.

The Constabulary took part in the killings mainly by arresting the victims and then handing them over to the Security Police for shooting. This way of dividing the work of murder was made clear in the letters which Constabulary Captain Fritz Jacob sent in May and June 1942 from Kamenets-Podolsk in the Ukrainian district of Podolia to the SS Lieutenant General Rudolf Querner. In the area which Jacob had to "look after," with twenty-three German constables and 500 Ukrainian auxiliaries, he was, as Section Leader of the police, at one and the same time prosecutor, judge and executioner.[44]

"We don't sleep here, [he wrote]. Each week 3-4 actions. Sometimes Gypsies and sometimes Jews, partisans and such rubbish". Where the action required immediate punishment, the Constabulary arranged the link with the Security Police and "the correct verdict was passed immediately". Jacob meant the shooting of whole families. "If we had followed the principle of normal justice it would not have been possible to eliminate a whole family when only the father was the guilty one." [45]

The indigenous auxiliaries often arrested Jews, communists, Gypsies and other "undesirable elements" and passed them on to the German constables who, in their turn, handed them over to the nearest unit of the Security Police for shooting.[46] Regarding the shooting of Gypsies this practice has been documented for the Ukrainian district of Zhitomir.[47] In other cases the auxiliaries themselves shot Gypsies under the direct orders of officers of the German Security Police.[48] It is reported from the Ukrainian district of Mosyr that members of the Auxiliary Force also killed Gypsies of their own accord. There were some Gypsy families who had hidden in the woods during the warm periods of the year and who looked for winter quarters in the areas of Khvoyniki, Vorotets and Strelichev. Some were discovered by local units of the auxiliaries, others were betrayed by villagers. They were forced by the Ukrainian police to play music and dance and then were shot.[49]

The Baltic States

In the Baltic States the systematic murder of Romanies started on December 5th 1941 with the shooting of some one hundred Gypsies from Libau in Latvia. The perpetrators were members of the German Municipal Police division in that town.[50] This murder was the reason for an initiative of the Commander of the Security Constabulary in Ostland, Georg Jedicke.[51] He arranged for the State Commissioner Hinrich Lohse, who, as leader of the civil administration, had in no way any authority over the police, to write a letter that signalled his agreement to the murder of Gypsies. The letter was written late December but was ante-dated to December 4th, i.e. before the execution. In a rationalisation of the racially motivated killing, Lohse described the Gypsies wandering around in the country as acting as carriers of infectious illnesses especially typhus, in addition to being unreliable elements who would neither obey the orders of the German authorities, nor be willing to carry out useful work. Further, he claimed, there was well-founded suspicion that they were harming the German cause through passing on information.

A b s c h r i f t

Abt.II Gesundheit u.
Volkspflege
II e Az. I. F

4. Dezember 1941

An den

Höheren ∕∕ - und Polizeiführer

in   R i g a

Die im Lande umherirrenden Zigeuner bilden eine Gefahr in
doppelter Hinsicht:

1.) als Überträger von ansteckenden Krnakheiten,
    insbesondere von Fleckfieber,

2.) als unzuverlässige Elemente, die sich weder den
    Vorschriften der deutschen Behörden beugen, noch
    gewillt sind, eine nutzbringende Arbeit zu
    verrichten.

Es besteht begründeteter Verdacht, dass sie durch Nachrichten-
übermittlungen im feindlichen Sinne der deutschen Sache schaden.
Ich bestimme daher, dass sie in der Behandlung den Juden gleich-
gestellt werden.

gez. Lohse

Hinricks Lohse's letter of December 1941.

Abschrift von Abschrift.

Der Höhere ℋ-und Polizeiführer   Riga, den 12.Januar 1942.
  für das Ostland
  Az. Ia

Betr.: Zigeunerfrage.

Auf meine Anregung hat der Herr Reichskommissar entschieden,
daß die im Lande umherirrenden Zigeuner, da sie als Übertrager
ansteckender Krankheiten, insbesondere des Fleckfiebers und als
unzuverlässige Elemente, die weder die Anordnungen der Deutschen
Behörden befolgen, noch gewillt sind, nutzbringende Arbeit zu
verrichten, in der Behandlung den Juden gleichzustellen sind.

Ich ersuche in jedem Falle das Erforderliche zu veranlassen.

       In Vertretung
        J e d i c k e
      Generalleutnant der Polizei
      und ℋ- Gruppenführer.

Verteiler: pp.
F.d.R.d.A.
gez. Unterschrift
Hauptw.d.Sch.

     —.—.—.—.—.—.—.—.—.—

Der Befehlshaber der Ordnungspolizei Riga, den 13.1.1942.
    für das Ostland
Kdo. Abt. Ia 40.00 350/42

An die
ℋ-und Polizeiführer
- Kommandeure der Ordnungspolizei -
Litauen   in K a u e n.

   pp.
    Abschrift zur Kenntnis.

       Für den Befehlshaber der Ordnungspol.
        Der Chef des Stabes:
         I. A.
        gez. Unterschrift
      Oberstleutnant der Schutzpolizei.

Wachtm.d.Sch.d.Res.

Jedicke's letter of January 1942 (see p.49).

Labelled in this way as spies, antisocials and a menace to the people's health the Gypsies were presented by Lohse as fit for slaughter. "I declare that they should be treated in the same way as Jews."[52]

Jedicke, the Commander of the Security Constabulary, gave Lohse's text to his superiors on January 12th 1942.[53] His explanatory statement – "I try in every case to carry out what is required" – was put into the concrete instruction "to deliver Gypsies to prison". The Constabulary was restricted to the task of arresting the victims and delivering them to the Security Police for shooting. Constables and auxiliaries therefore played an important role in the division of labour of the killing process but, except for the action in Libau, they were not confronted with the actual killing.[54]

The shooting was left to the local offices of the Security Police for whom, as successors to the Task Forces, murder had become routine.

Lohse's circular of December 4th 1941 had neither defined how a person should be classified as a Gypsy nor whether the phrase "Gypsies wandering around in the country" meant also sedentary Gypsies. The German Security Police in Latvia interpreted the statement of the State Governor in the sense that "settled Gypsies who have regular work and who were not a danger to society in a political or criminal sense" should be exempted from arrest and shooting.[55] On the other hand, their counterparts in the Security Constabulary who arrested Gypsies and handed them over to the Security Police took the phrase "Gypsies wandering around in the country" to mean all Gypsies.[56] Therefore, in Latvia, the Baltic state with the largest Gypsy population,[57] both nomadic and settled Gypsies were handed over for shooting to the Security Police in the first months of 1942.[58]

Because of this, the settled Romanies in Kurlandish Shlock were completely massacred. In the east Latvian districts of Rezekne, Ludza and Vilani all the Gypsies were murdered. Many had already died in prisons or, as in Ludza, in a synagogue which was declared as a place of arrest by the German police and then set on fire. The rest were shot in the woods. The protest to the German authorities made by Vanya Kochanowski, a Latvian Romany, then a student in Riga against this murder had no effect.[59] In Kurlandish Talsen, however, the shooting of settled Gypsies was halted.[60]

The lack of clarity that prevailed between the Security Police and the Constabulary about the definition of the murder victims led Karl Friedrich Knecht, the Commander of the Constabulary for Latvia, to issue an explanatory circular in March and again in the beginning of April 1942. According to this, it had been decided, after discussion with the Commander of the Security Police in Latvia, that in future "only wandering Gypsies" should be arrested and handed over to the Security Police.[61] During 1942 and 1943, throughout Latvia, Gypsies lost their lives as a result of this vague circular which created no exact boundary between "wandering" and settled Gypsies and thus gave the police a free hand in the following months in the selection of the victims.

145

- In Valmiyera about fifty Gypsies were shot in April 1942
- Fifteen were shot in Valmiyera October/November the same year
- In the Ayzpute district nineteen Gypsies were shot on May 21st 1942
- About 280 were killed near the town of Yelgava on May 27th - 28th 1942
- 130 were killed at Yelgava in June/July 1942
- In March 1943 another 400 were murdered at Yelgava
- In Bauska in May 1942 some 250 were murdered
- By the Valgum Lake near Tukum in July 1942 more than 200 Gypsies were murdered.[62]

Further murders have been recorded for Riga and Valka.[63] If we add these figures to the earlier murders by the Task Force and the shooting of the Gypsies in Libau in December 1941, an estimated half of the some 3,800 Gypsies in Latvia were killed.[64]

Those settled Gypsies in Latvia who were not shot[65] received the order not to leave their place of residence.[66] In January 1942 the granting of the right to residence for a Gypsy woman in Libau was linked to a demand for her to be sterilised.[67]

In Talsen there were restrictions on Gypsy children attending school.[68] Many Romanies lost their chance to earn a living through the forced residence. Eleven men from Saldus (Frauenburg), who had worked as cart drivers in the forestry industry in the area and whose horses had been confiscated,[69] petitioned the Governor on March 12th 1942:

"We are ready to carry out any suitable work that is within our ability and we earnestly ask his Honour the State Governor to give us the possibility to work in Frauenburg and the surroundings. In Frauenburg we are known as Gypsies with no criminal record, in Frauenburg we have houses and our children go to the primary and secondary schools. And if we are not allowed to work as carters to earn our daily bread, we would like to work on a farm or as day labourers so that we can support our children at school and not get into financial difficulty as the income from [renting out] the flats in our houses is very low."[70]

The Estonian Gypsies were confined in the prison of Harku which was designated as a concentration camp as early as autumn 1941. After about a year in prison they were shot.[71] Lohse's order to kill, issued at the end of 1941, was also directed to the police in Lithuania,[72] however details of the murder of the Lithuanian Gypsies are not known.[73]

A new policy

In early summer 1942, as the Ministry for the Occupied Eastern Territories and the senior officials of the State Administration for Ukraine and Ostland began to consider Gypsy policies, arrests and mass shootings by the German Security

Police and Constabulary were already in full swing. Nevertheless, the head of the Department for General Policies within the Ministry did no more than request, on June 11th 1942, a report from the State Administration for Ostland on the treatment of Gypsies. He wanted it made clear to what extent the Gypsies living there were settled or not, what occupations they had, if the number of Gypsies of mixed race was high and in particular if "the Gypsies are to be placed in the same position as Jews with regard to their treatment"[74]

In the State Administration for Ostland an answer was drafted for the Minister.[75] In pejorative terms it picked out the Latvian Kurland as the area in the Eastern Territories most favoured by Gypsies and labelled the nomads (more so than the settled Gypsies) as specialists in horse stealing. The report justified the mass shootings by the police: "Today the removal of the Gypsies is irrevocably linked to police measures against typhus." So, the author of the report came out – in barely concealed terms – in favour of the murder of the settled Gypsies, too.

At the beginning of July 1942 this report, in which the civil administration wished to go further than the SS, was sent to the Minister for the Occupied Eastern Territories. There, the following draft circular *The Treatment of the Gypsies in the Occupied Eastern Territories* was discussed:

"Gypsies who have their residence or regular stopping place in the Occupied Eastern Territories are to be treated as Jews, unless they possess foreign nationality. No distinction is to be made between settled and nomadic Gypsies. Gypsies of mixed race are as a rule to be treated as Jews, particularly when they live in a Gypsy fashion or are not socially integrated."[76]

Who should be considered a Gypsy for the purpose of these regulations was, as a rule, to be decided on the basis of direct knowledge of the person concerned or that of another member of the family regarding their being a Gypsy, the way of life and social conditions. In some circumstances information about the genealogy should be sought. The outward appearance of the person concerned and his relatives could also be of importance.[77]

A vague definition of this sort met the desire to extend the group of victims to include the sedentary Gypsies. The killings had furthermore to be legitimised in such a way that they could not be hindered by any legal objection.

The discussion about the proposed circular, *Treatment of the Gypsies in the Occupied Eastern Territories*, continued in the Ministry for the East until early 1943. In contrast to their thoughts in summer 1942 the Ministry now turned against the placing of Gypsies in the same category as Jews[78] and against making a distinction between nomads and sedentaries. Instead, the Ministry proposed that all Gypsies should be brought together and put under guard in special camps and settlements, the nature of which was not defined.

Himmler, as Leader of the SS, together with officials of the National Security Headquarters rejected the Ministry for the East's proposal. Now they were of the opinion that settled Gypsies and part-Gypsies should be treated as the other inhabitants and all wandering Gypsies and part-Gypsies should be placed under the same regulations as Jews. While in 1942 those labelled as "wandering" had been shot, now, in 1943, it was proposed that they should be brought into concentration camps.[79] This was, once more in concealed language, an instruction to concentrate the nomadic Gypsies and Gypsies of mixed race in Auschwitz-Birkenau where the SS had set up the special Gypsy Section in early 1943. Himmler was able to put forward this concept of murder against the views of the Minister for the Occupied Eastern Territories because the latter had little influence within the National Socialist hierarchy. In early 1944 an unknown number of Romanies were, in fact, deported to Auschwitz from Brest-Litovsk, which belonged to the General Administration of White Russia, and from Lithuania.[80] For the Baltic countries and the occupied Soviet Union this deportation would have meant the last phase of the genocide of the Gypsies. However, by the end of 1944 the German Army had been forced out of most of its conquests in the east.

Conclusion

It is hardly possible to calculate precisely the total number of murders committed by the Task Forces together with military and occupying forces in the Soviet Union. The estimates of 30,000 by Donald Kenrick and Grattan Puxon for the whole USSR and that of Jerzy Ficowski of 3,000-4,000 Volhynia alone need further historical investigation.[81] For the Crimea and the Baltic States relatively exact figures can be given. In the Crimea 2,000-2,400 Gypsies were shot by Task Force D. In Latvia the mobile Task Force and static police units killed at least 1,500 of the 3,800 Romanies living there. In Estonia and Lithuania nearly the whole Romany population, numbering in each case some 1,000, was massacred.

VII. Bohemia and Moravia – two internment camps for the Gypsies in the Czech lands

Ctibor Necas

Introduction

Before 1938 Czechoslovakia was not only inhabited by Czechs and Slovaks but also by various large national minorities. One of these was the Romany and Sinti minority. Their exact number was not entered in the official statistics, for their ethnic identity was not established by any of the population censuses between the two world wars. According to a reliable estimate there were more than 100,000 Sinti and Romanies in the regions of Bohemia, Moravia, Silesia, Slovakia and Carpatho-Russia on the eve of the fall of the united country. The Czech Romanies lived in Bohemia and especially south Moravia, the Sinti in the north and west border regions of Bohemia, in the surroundings of Prague and also in the north and south border regions of Moravia, while the nomadic Lovari and Kalderash travelled throughout Czechoslovakia.

Towards the end of the 1930s boundary changes were forced on the country and the territorial integrity of Czechoslovakia was broken through diplomatic presssure, the force of irridentism and finally through open military attacks, as a result of which the Gypsies found themselves spread through several states. In October and November 1938 the greater part of the Czech border lands were annexed by force by Germany. After the Munich Agreement the Gypsies from these lands found themselves in Nazi Germany, in the newly formed Sudeten and Ostmark regions. In March 1939 what remained of Czechoslovakia ceased to exist as an independent state. Slovakia was set up as an independent republic while through the occupation of Bohemia and Moravia the Sinti and Romanies who lived there found themselves in a theoretically autonomous Protectorate.

In the new state created in this way a terrible fate awaited the Gypsies – the German occupation was to have fatal consequences. The brutal solution of the so-called Gypsy question in Nazi Germany was to be applied to them also. The Protectorate of Bohemia and Moravia was the final result of the German armed invasion. It was set up illegally in accordance with Hitler's orders on March 16th 1939. It was not an independent state even if it had its own citizenship, practised sovereign jurisdiction and had a President who enjoyed the trappings of authority. In the territory of the Protectorate lived three groups of inhabitants. First, there were the existing Bohemian Germans and the Germans who came with the occupying army. This group was the favoured group in the Protectorate who, in accordance with the Nuremberg Decrees, were German citizens. The Czechs held citizenship of the Protectorate and thus were in an inferior position compared to the German citizens. The Protectorate nationals were a population group strong in numbers but without full rights. The inhabitants of so-called non-Aryan groups not only had their human rights and freedom taken away but were also deprived of legal protection. Alongside the Jews the Romanies and Sinti waited for the final solution of their problem.

While in Germany the terms Gypsy and part-Gypsy had already been defined from a racial point of view in the circular concerning the operation of the German Citizenship Law of November 14th 1935, a similar definition for the Protectorate did not come for a long time. Those persons classed as Gypsies were those who, in accordance with the (Czechoslovak) Law No.117 of 1927 had a so-called Gypsy identity document or were recorded in the Criminal Headquarters in Prague. According to Law No.89 of 1942 it was not decided which citizenship they had or if they were stateless. It was only on May 3rd 1943 that the Government Decree on the *Removal of Social Benefits* divided them into full-blooded and part-Gypsy. Conformity with German practice did not happen, therefore, until a time when the question of the Gypsies in the Protectorate was – as we shall see – already reaching its final stage.

The first Order against them was issued by the Protectorate Government on March 31st 1939. The authorities were to devote special attention to the life and behaviour of the Gypsies and above all made sure that they did not live or camp in groups which were larger than the extended family. In the new border zone nomadising was forbidden by the order of the German Ministry for Internal Affairs and the nomadic families were deported to the interior.

The presence on Czech territory of Sinti and Romanies who had fled as individuals or as families from Germany and occupied Austria into Czechoslovakia, as well as from the Sudetenland and the territories occupied by the Germans after the Munich Agreement, led to an increase in the numbers in Bohemia and Moravia. This circumstance which was deliberately exaggerated by the official press gave the Protectorate Government the excuse for taking its first measures.

In the Decree of November 30th 1939 the Minister of the Interior ordered that the Gypsies should be permanently settled within two months and should no longer nomadise. This Decree was followed by a circular from the same Ministry on February 13th 1940, in accordance with which the district officials and police were to strive with the greatest of energy for the definite and permanent settlement of the nomads and report regularly on progress in this matter.

Anyone who did not respect the decree forbidding nomadism was to be sent to the work camps which had been set up according to the Government Decrees of March 2nd and April 28th 1939 for persons over eighteen who were not working and who could not show that they earned their living in a respectable manner. The camps were in Bohemia in Lety parish and in Moravia in Hodonin parish. The administration of the Protectorate which could not or was unwilling to solve the problems which arose from the decreed settlement of the nomadic families took advantage of this opportunity and began to lock up the Sinti and Romanies in work camps. Gypsies represented 10-25% of the internees.

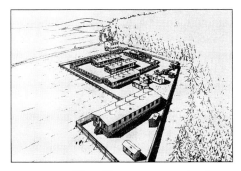 

The Gypsy camp in Lety.   *The Gypsy camp in Hodonin.*

Open discrimination against sedentary Gypsies began with the Government Decree on the Preventive Fight against Criminality of May 9th 1942, which was a word-for-word copy of the equivalent decree in Germany. Organized police control was to be applied to criminals as well as persons who had been released from prison. Preventive imprisonment was available for those persons who were a danger to society through their asocial behaviour. Under the term

151

asocial "Gypsies and persons wandering in Gypsy fashion" were specifically included and they were forbidden to leave the places to which the authorities had assigned them.

Preventive police imprisonment in camps was thus introduced in the Protectorate. In this respect internment camps were established. The original hard labour camps in Lety and Hodonin and the work camps in Prague-Ruzyne, Pardubice and Brno were turned into internment camps. Outside the territory of the Protectorate preventive imprisonment was established in the main concentration camp in Auschwitz I to which in the period between April 29th 1942 and February 24th 1944 a total of fourteen transports were sent from the Czech lands. In the first two of these transports there were only men; later both men and women were sent. With the exception of the transports of December 7th 1942 and January 28th 1943 Sinti and Romanies were a comparatively small percentage of the deportees.

Following the German model the General Commander of the civil police in the Protectorate on July 10th 1942 issued an order for the *Elimination of the Gypsy Menace*. Following this, the persecution of the Romanies and Sinti proceeded faster in the Protectorate than in Germany.

The Registration Day for Gypsies was fixed for as early as August 2nd 1942 when all those concerned were forbidden to leave their permanent accommodation. At the same time they were ordered to present themselves at the relevant police or local police station where detailed documentation was set up for every family from which it was decided provisionally wether, in each case, a person was a Gypsy, part-Gypsy or person wandering in a Gypsy manner.

The final evaluation of the material was carried out gradually so that by the end of the first three months of 1943 the security authorities had registered 11,886 persons of whom they listed 5,830 as Gypsies and part-Gypsies. There were 948 persons separately registered who lived without a fixed address or were in hospitals, prisons or other institutions. The registered Gypsy population was then divided into two sections. This division was very hastily carried out and it was not possible to avoid errors. Correcting this took half a year.

In the minority were placed Sinti and Romanies for whom preventive imprisonment was recommended or suggested. These persons, together with their families were placed together in the so-called Gypsy camps which had been set up by a further change in the status of the internment camps at Lety and Hodonin.

The Lety Gypsy camp

The camp originally consisted of one large and forty-two small wooden huts which could hold 300 prisoners. Later, extensions were built and the capacity was increased to 600 men, women and children. The accommodation included a kitchen, sick-bay, workshops and several smaller buildings, washroom, toilets, a delousing unit, laundry, warehouse, a shed, garage and stables. The camp compound was surrounded by a wooden fence with four sentry boxes. The commander's quarters were located in a single storey building outside the perimeter fence, as were houses for the personnel employed in the camp who, with the exception later of a Jewish doctor, consisted mostly of Czechs.

The first camp commander was Josef Janovsky but he was found to be not up to the task of running the camp and he was dismissed. He was temporarily replaced by the commander of the Hodonin camp and then, permanently, by Frantisek Havelka. There was an administrative staff consisting of two accountants and two secretaries. Guard duties were carried out by thirty wardens whose number was later increased to fifty-six. These uniformed and armed personnel were recruited from the ranks of the Czech constabulary.

Medical service in the camp was undertaken by Dr Kopecky, Dr Neuwirth and Dr Stejskal. They were general practitioners in neighbouring villages who visited sick prisoners and checked their health once a week. After an outbreak

The barracks in Lety.

of typhoid fever an additional Jewish doctor, Dr Michael Bohin, began helping in the camp, aided by a disinfection specialist and, for a short time, three nurses.

After arrival at the camp, all deportees were subjected to a perfunctory medical examination and had their hair cut. All the men, together with any women or children found to be infested with lice, were shaved clean, while the remaining women and children's hair was cut very short. This was supposed to be followed by a wash in a washroom where the showers did not work or, collectively, in the nearby Lipeze lake. When the washing was over the prisoners had to relinquish their personal documents (identity cards, Gypsy identity cards, nomad's licences) and all their meagre possessions (cash, savings books and valuables) to the camp authorities.

Prisoners.

From the money collected, 100,000 crowns were lodged in the local Credit Union in Mirovice and the rest was deposited in the camp safe. This cash was used to repay the deposits of any prisoners released and by August 8th 1943 there remained 81,367 crowns. Thirty-nine savings books were confiscated which held, with some exceptions, very small sums belonging to individual savers. The valuables taken from the prisoners included two gold rings, three gold earrings, three silver pocket watches and one chrome-plated wristwatch.

Each prisoner was meant to get the uniform of a cap, a jacket, trousers and two shirts, in addition to a pair of stockings and two pairs of underpants and shoes. However, full kits were scarce in the camp warehouse as well as central government stores. Because of this, much of the kit was replaced by other items or supplied only in part. To the extent that there was a camp uniform, it consisted of previously worn army clothes, dyed black, and was issued only to men and those women who were sent to work outside the camp. The rest of the women and all the children wore the clothes and shoes in which they had arrived but these were often worn-out and many of the children had no shoes. When winter arrived the women were provided with clogs and a kind of slipper was made for the children in the camp workshops from old rags and felt. Clothes and underwear for the youngest children were also made in the tailor's shop, either from the strictly rationed textiles or from second-hand clothes.

When the prisoners had thus been at least partly clothed, they were divided into three groups according to their age and sent to their separate dormitories. In huts 1-16 men and boys were lodged, the children were quartered in huts 17-20 and the larger building, while the girls and women were in huts 21-42. Each small building was 2.5 x 3 metres and from four to six adults could be fitted into one of them. This capacity was soon filled.

Living conditions

All the prisoners ate together and their food consisted of three basic meals. For breakfast adults were given ersatz coffee, with or without milk, while the younger children received milk. Lunch was usually either soup and goulash or meat with a portion of vegetables. Sometimes, however, the internees were served only potatoes – on their own or with fried vegetables. For dinner there was just a thick soup – often reheated from lunchtime. Children received half portions while the youngest children had only semolina pudding to eat. From December 1942 onwards children suffering from malnutrition were given two extra snacks daily – soup and bread in the morning and white coffee with bread in the afternoon. The amount spent on each adult prisoner per day decreased from seven crowns in August 1942 to four crowns in January 1943, and then increased slightly to 4.5 crowns and finally to almost five crowns in March and April 1943. The small rise was made necessary by the appalling insanitary conditions and the debility of the prisoners in the first three months of 1943 but it did not match the decreasing purchasing power of the Protectorate currency. The food was cooked in the camp kitchen from where it was distributed by kitchen hands to the individual barracks. There it was given to prisoners who had been placed in responsible positions – the Barackalteste (Senior prisoner) in each of the small huts and the Aufseherin (Supervisor) for the children. They had wooden boards indicating the number of the dormitory and the total of prisoners it held, and they were then issued with the corresponding number of portions.

The official reason for concentrating the nomadic Romanies into internment camps was to teach them discipline at work. Their day started with a wake-up call at 5.0 a.m. in the summer and 6.0 a.m. in the winter. They then had to get up quickly, wash and tidy up their bunk beds. The working brigades were given breakfast first to enable them to start work on time. The men were employed to finish the construction of a road between the villages of Lety and Stare Sedlo, or felling trees and clearing the nearby forests. Inside the camp they were employed in making craft items in the workshops or in maintaining the barracks and camp buildings. The women harvested potatoes and occasionally gave other help to farms in the neighbourhood. In the camp they worked in the kitchen and laundry or looked after children and patients in the camp hospital. Teenagers worked alongside the women and also did cleaning. Younger children were given simple jobs and had lessons in reading and writing under supervision.

The working day lasted from eight to ten hours, according to the season, and, if targets were not met, it was lengthened. The work done was paid for at a fixed rate and this money was sent to the Ministry of the Interior by the camp commander. It was used to cover the cost of running the camp. In 1942 the sum of 505,047 crowns was paid into this account. After their return from work, the prisoners cleaned their work clothes and shoes and supper was handed out, including a portion of bread for the following day. In their spare time the internees were not allowed to play any games or amuse themselves in any way which the guards thought might cause quarrels or fights. Smoking and drinking were also banned but this rule was never applied as neither alcohol or cigarettes ever got into the camp. With the commander's permission they could send and receive, once a month, two letters or one parcel. All mail was subject to censorship and was destroyed if anything untoward had been discovered. Under the camp rules, the prisoners were under the direct control of uniformed guards and had to carry out their orders rapidly. They had to take off their hats and stand to attention when greeting them and to address them with the title Herr plus their rank. The official language in the camp was German and use of the Romani language was forbidden. After the curfew (9.00 p.m. in the summer and 8.00 p.m. in the winter) all prisoners had to lie down in their bunk beds, the fire in the stove was put out, oil lamps were extinguished and silence enveloped the camp.

Prisoners.

Health

The level of health in the camp was precarious. The youngest suffered from physical weakness and malnutrition. The few old men suffered the illnesses common to their age group. The conditions of internment helped these illnesses to spread and quickly worsen. The cause was partly the decrepit wooden dormitories, already damaged by previous use. The walls did not reach ground level and there were no cellars which meant they were plagued by dampness and mould. The huts, which were designed for summer use only, were difficult to heat, while the rooms in the large building, in which the majority of the children were housed, often got cold because orders were for the fires to be put out at night. The bunkbeds, which were the only furniture in the dormitories, were infested with bedbugs and other insects. There was only one well which was insufficient to supply the whole camp. Extra water was brought into the camp but not enough to alleviate the chronic shortage. Personal hygiene and washing clothes became impossible.

Strong proof of this can be found in the notes which the camp doctor repeatedly wrote in his patients' records when fighting scabies in October 1942:

"October 10th. Has to wash, said not to have any water, they don't want to give [them] water.
October 12th. Too much dirt found.
October 21st. Too much dirt found again."

The state of health of the prisoners was directly caused and exacerbated by overcrowding in insect-ridden dormitories, the shortage of water for washing themselves, their clothes and bedlinen, the small amounts of poor quality food and the continual trauma of the armed police regime. All this produced a breeding ground for many common and rarer infectious diseases.

The first sick detainees were already in need of medical care on August 3rd, the day after the camp opened. One suffered from catarrh of the trachea, another had a fever and the third was a mother who could not breast feed and needed extra milk for her child. In the space of three weeks the doctor examined fifty patients. Most of them suffered from bronchitis and inflammation of the bone but there were instances of diphtheria and trachoma and the invalids had to be transferred to Pisek hospital. The following weeks saw the spread of measles, mumps and other children's diseases. By December the level of illness reached a critical stage, as – according to the monthly reports – from the total of 966 prisoners half had gone down with colds, 200 with influenza, 156 with tonsillitis and ninety-eight with pneumonia. On December 13th 1942 typhoid was diagnosed, followed by typhus on January 23rd 1943. The disease spread quickly and became an epidemic. It was this that caused the supreme commander of the plain clothes Protectorate Police to announce, on February 17th 1943, that the whole camp area was under strict quarantine.

Children in the camp.

Death claimed five prisoners in August 1942, seventeen in September, sixteen in October, twenty-three in November and sixty-seven in December. A further 136 died in January the following year, forty-six in February, eleven in March and five in April. The dead were at first buried in the Catholic graveyard in Mirovice and then, from January 16th 1943, in a temporary camp graveyard. There were more children than adults among the dead and there was an unusually high mortality rate among very young children and new-born babies. Altogether 326 prisoners died, of whom thirty-three were men and boys, fifty-two women and girls, together with 241 children.

Statistics

In August 1942 dozens of prisoners were sent to this camp in quick succession. There was a transport of sixty-six persons on August 2nd, 207 on August 3rd, 265 and 151 on the following two days, 144 on August 6th and 166 on August 7th. In the following weeks the avalanche of arrivals died down and finally stopped completely but even this could not alleviate the terrible overcrowding of the camp. This lasted until January 1943 when two more huts and another large barracks were built and the accommodation at last began to approximate to the number of people interned.

The first registration numbers were issued to Joseph Paffner and his family. He was followed by the brothers Josef and Oskar Hais, and then the extended family of Josef Slehofr. Josef Paffner was soon transferred to a forest work camp. His son, Antonin, died shortly afterards in the camp and his wife, Anna, was deported to the main Auschwitz concentration camp. Members of the Slehofr family were released after a confinement of ten days while the Hais brothers had to suffer in the camp and did not regain their freedom until its liquidation. In a way, the fate of these early prisoners are typical of the ordeal of all the men, women and children who were to follow them into the camp.

Of the 1,220 registered prisoners, the vast majority were taken to the camp during the first weeks of August:

August 1942	1,100
September	20
October	7
November	20
December	16
January 1943	2

Children born in the cruel conditions of the camp became prisoners too. The first baby born there was Hypolit Janecek on August 12th 1942. Together with his mother Frantiska, he was sent to a hospital in Pisek when he was two weeks old but died soon after his return to the camp. A similar fate awaited most of the other thirty-five babies (twelve boys and twenty-three girls).

In all, 1,256 prisoners suffered internment in the camp, of whom 30% were released or escaped, 26% died in the camp and 43% were transferred to the extermination camp of Auschwitz.

Some release orders were issued by the Criminal Police Centre in Prague immediately after the opening of the camp. Thirty-two prisoners regained their freedom on August 10th, nineteen on August 22nd, one on August 27th, nine on September 1st, three on September 4th eleven on September 9th and five on September 26th. Rumours began circulating in the camp about the release orders, implying that they were issued only to those who gave large bribes to the relevant authorities. The speed with which the rumour spread reveals the depth of despair of prisoners who found themselves in a strange and terrifying environment and were willing to believe anything which would fuel their hopes of freedom. Another wave of releases came on the eve of the liquidation of the camp in May 1943, after the departure of a mass transport to the Gypsy Family Section in Auschwitz-Birkenau. 198 prisoners remained interned in Lety, of which fourteen were transferred to police cells elsewhere, fifteen detailed for cleaning work, one woman prisoner was sent to Pisek hospital and the last 168 prisoners were released on May 27th 1943. The reasons given for their release was that they were "non-Gypsies".

The barracks.

Escape was another – illegal – way of leaving the camp. The first to try this were two boys, Ladislav Stockinger and Josef Vrba, who escaped as early as August 15th 1942. However, they were caught fourteen days later and sent back to the camp. Josef longed for freedom so much that he repeated his attempt on September 24th but he was caught again after three weeks and re-interned. Not only individuals but groups and families also fled. The first group escape was on September 14th 1942 when Maria Blumova fled with her one-year old son, Alfons, together with Alzbeta Bernhardova and her three sons – three year old Josef, six year old Alfred and eight year old Karel Petr. We believe that the escape of the two mothers with their children was successful.

Prisoners were fleeing the camp throughout its existence. The number of escapes reported was nineteen in August 1942, sixteen in September, fourteen in October, twenty-three in November and eleven in December. In the following year there were a further five in January, ten in February, three in March and one in April. More than half of all these break-outs ended in failure and the prisoners' hopes were dashed. The commander ordered captured male escapees to be put in the camp prison and some were handed over to the Criminal Police in Prague for deportation to the main Auschwitz concentration camp.

Closure of the camp

For most prisoners, their forced stay in the camp ended when they were transported to "a new location in the General Government" of Poland. The first transport consisted of sixteen men and seventy-seven women – ninety-three in all – who arrived at the main concentration camp in Auschwitz on December 3rd 1942, labelled as: "anti-social elements". All probably died very soon after their arrival. On March 11th 1943 twenty prisoners from Lety were amongst a mass transport of Gypsies from Bohemia who were deported to the newly opened Gypsy Family Section in Auschwitz-Birkenau. Their names were added to the transport list after their return to health and discharge from the Strakonice and Pisek district hospitals, where they had been because of typhoid. The remaining 420 prisoners from the Lety camp – 215 men and 205 women – were destined for the same camp with further mass transports of Gypsies from Bohemia and Moravia.

A general view of Hodonin.

The Hodonin Gypsy camp

Hodonin camp consisted of seven barracks of which the three larger ones were designed to hold 100 prisoners each and the smaller ones used for administrative, hospital, kitchen and control purposes. Overcrowding at the start and the difficulties in running the camp that arose from this led to certain building improvements, after which up to 800 prisoners could be housed in the camp. A fence was erected around the buildings and beyond it were further buildings for the administration and guards and a second kitchen, in addition to one large and three smaller buildings. The camp commander, Stefan Blahynka, was temporarily ordered to Lety and his deputy, Jan Sokl, took over responsibility. Four people were employed in the camp administration and the camp was guarded by a body of men whose number rose from thirty-two to forty-two. The commander, as well as the administration workers and guards were armed and wore constabulary uniform. The doctor contracted to work in the camp was Dr Habanec, who practised in a small town nearby, and it was from here that he regularly commuted to Hodonin to examine the prisoners, However, when the sickness rate began to increase, Jewish doctors were additionally allocated to the camp, first Dr Alfred Milek and after he left, Dr Michal Bohin, who was transferred from the closed Lety camp. The civilian workers included two cooks – a man and a woman – for the kitchens, a disinfection specialist in the delousing unit and a tailor as head of the camp workshops.

Prisoners.

Reception procedures, as well as the other hard aspects of the internees' daily life, were the same as in Lety. After their forced transfer to the camp, the new arrivals washed themselves in the barracks' washrooms, which had a trough with cold running water, while their outer clothes and underwear were disinfected by a specialist team brought in from Brno for this purpose. Those who suffered from fleas were shaved completely by barbers and had paraffin spread over their head. Then the prisoners were made to hand over their cash, which amounted to 72,138 crowns and their savings books, in which 2,187 crowns had been deposited. Confiscated valuables, according to the records, consisted of four gold and two silver rings, a pair of gold earrings, a necklace with a gold pendant and two small silver chains.

In a similar procedure to that at Lety, the men received camp clothes while the women and children kept the clothes and shoes with which they had arrived at the camp. A few women and children were later given camp clothes. After that, each group of prisoners was housed in one of the three wooden barracks, in each of which there were – in the sleeping area – a hundred bunk beds arranged in three rows, two along the length of the building and one across the width of one side. The supply of bunk beds was quickly exhausted when the seven prisoners left behind from the former labour camp were joined by twenty-two persons on August 2nd 1942, 117 on August 3rd and 239 on August 4th. Later arrivals had to be housed in confiscated caravans of which there were a total of nineteen placed inside the fence at the edge of the camp area and, after that, in tents.

The first person to be registered was Karel Vrba with seven members of his family, followed by a flood of men, women and, especially, children. Those from nearby were marched in on foot or came in their caravans but those who came from more distant parts of Moravia were rounded up and held first in a forced labour camp in Brno. From there they were transported by rail to Nedvedice or Skalice nad Svitavou and thence by any available means of transport, or again on foot, to their final destination at Hodonin. On their journey they should have been helped by aides positioned along the transport routes by the constabulary but, because of a lack of manpower, the never-ending convoys were not given any help en route but merely guarded by mobile constabulary patrols.

Living conditions

An idea of life inside the camp can be gleaned from the records of the prisoners' work and food. According to the monthly reports the cost of food for an adult prisoner ranged between four and six crowns a day.

November 1942	4.20
December	4.40
January 1943	4.30
February	4.20
March	4.40
April	4.80
May	5.00
June	5.20
July	5.20
August	6.15

The decrease in the allowance in early 1943 reflects badly on the management, for at that time the purchasing power of the crown was falling and there was a worsening of the overall state of health in the camp. On the other hand, the rate began to increase again from the moment when the German Criminal Police reiterated their demand for the deportation of prisoners from Hodonin to Auschwitz – and the mass transport was to contain only healthy persons or, at least, those who looked healthy.

Just over 200 prisoners could not withstand the extreme insanitary conditions. According to the Cernovice register of deaths, which contains records of the decease of about 194 prisoners, the most common causes of death recorded were pneumonia, tuberculosis of the lungs and typhoid fever. Death certificates from Brno, containing the records of thirteen patients from Hodonin who died in the Brno County and Children's Hospitals, show that they died from the same causes. Of the 194 prisoners who died in the camp itself, seventy-three were buried in the Catholic cemetery in Cernovice and 121 in an adhoc camp cemetery.

Work

Brigades of men, women and older children worked on road construction between Stepanov and Rozsec, breaking stones and digging. Other work included maintaining rail embankments and fields, clearing grass out of ditches, laying down drainage pipes and draining fields. All these tasks were seasonal and they were suspended betweeen February and May 1943. The total wages for the roadworks which amounted to 558,818 crowns were, as in Lety camp, transferred to the account of the Ministry of Internal Affairs. Men also worked in quarries near the camp and also employed inside the camp, together with women and children, in building new wooden barracks, constructing water and electricity supply systems and digging cellars for the storage of food reserves. A few dozen prisoners worked in the kitchen, tailor's shop, shoemaker's workshop or in the sickbay and quarantine barracks. Some had to cultivate the rented camp lands – meadows and fields planted with potatoes and other vegetables. They also tended the cattle, the horses in the camp stables and a few pigs which were kept in a sty.

Prisoners in Hodonin.

Health

The prisoners' suffering is proved by their medical records. Any sickness had to be reported at the wake-up call in the morning and the number of sick grew day by day. These reports were met with indifference at the start. The first signs of anxiety appeared at the end of September and the beginning of October 1942 when the doctor diagnosed patients with typhoid fever. A survey of health in the camp was ordered immediately and it was found that, apart from the typhoid cases sent to hospitals in Brno, 195 prisoners were suffering from trachoma, nineteen from syphilis, fourteen from tuberculosis of the lung and three from gonorrhoea. Of the children 160 had measles, five whooping cough and three smallpox. Apart from this, the medical examinations revealed fifty-four men dying of old age, twenty-five women in an advanced state of pregnancy, eighteen invalids and nine persons who were blind. As measles did not have to be reported and it was not considered necessary to isolate the cases, most attention turned towards the massive spread of trachoma. All the victims were examined twice and treated individually without, however, any visible improvement. On December 18th more prisoners showed symptoms of typhoid fever; the disease began to spread at epidemic level. Following their bad experiences in Lety, the commander general of the plain clothes Protectorate Police ordered the area of Hodonin camp to be closed off on the same day as was Lety. A desperate health report was prepared stating that one fifth of the internees were suffering from trachoma and an equal number from scurvy, more than a half from scabies and nearly all from diarrhoea. This probably contributed to the closure. As the report stated: "All the Gypsies interned in the camp should be regarded as probably having typhoid fever."

166

Children in the camp.

Statistics

During August 1942 1,229 prisoners were forcibly transported to the camp, of whom 176 were soon released. The total number of interned changed from day to day. There were 29 persons on August 2nd, 206 on August 3rd, 384 a day later, 1,168 on August 5th and a peak figure of 1,173 was reached by August 12th-13th. The numbers then fluctuated:

August 14-16th	1,106
August 17th	1,110
August 18th	1,104
August 19th-20th	1,106
August 21st-26th	1,078
August 27th	1,117
August 28th	1,055
August 29th-31st	1,053

(Internees in Hodonin camp).

The majority of the internees were relatively young and mostly female. The largest influx of prisoners into the camp came immediately after it was opened, in the first weeks of August. During the following weeks this stream gradually slowed down and had nearly stopped by the beginning of November. Transports built up again between May and July 1943 when small groups of prisoners were transferred to Hodonin from the defunct camp in Lety.

Altogether a total of 1,355 new prisoners were registered in the camp, in addition to the seven original inmates:

August	1,236
September	13
October	28
November	8
December	5
January 1943	-
February	2
March	1
April	6
May	13
June	26
July	14
August	3

(Registrations in Hodonin camp).

Interned Romany women also gave birth to thirty-four children in the camp – fifteen boys and nineteen girls. The first baby born was Antonin Kloc, born to his mother, Bohuslava, as early as August 3rd 1942 – a day after his mother's internment in the camp. Like the vast majority of the births in the camp, he was conceived while his mother was still free. The sole exception was Libuse Malikova, whose mother, Magdalena, gave birth to her on May 18th 1943.

There were thus 1,396 persons who underwent internment in Hodonin, including the newly born children. Of this total 19% were released, 3% escaped, 15% died and 62% were to be transported to the extermination camps at Auschwitz.

Most of those let out gained their freedom at the start of the internment period. Then, release warrants were given to members of the more integrated families who were able to return to their homes. The numbers discharged were:

August 14th	73
August 20th	28
August 28th	61
September 1st	24
September 18th	40

Eight individual inmates were released in the period between December 1942 and April 1943 and a last group when the camp was liquidated.

An unknown number of prisoners attempted to leave the camp by escaping and forty-seven of the attempts were successful. The first to escape was Ann Ruzickova with her daughter, Barbara, and grandson, Jan, on August 16th 1942. The escapees lived in the forests and lived on fruit and what they could gather from the field until they were found two weeks later and returned to the camp.

On the other hand, Frantiska Danielova and Antonie Barvinska managed to escape successfully on August 27th 1942 and disappear without trace. Most remarkable were the escapes of Jan Jundrich and Gabriel Daniel who escaped on June 23rd 1943 from the sickbay wearing only shirts. They were, however, found and re-interned six days later. All three then made a second attempt to escape but a guard noticed them and started shooting. Gabriel let himself be captured while Jan and Jindrich successfully disappeared into the forest, even though one of them was wounded.

Closure

The tragic climax of the internment was the closure of the camp and the deportation of the surviving prisoners – in three separate transports – to the main camp and Gypsy Family Section in Auschwitz.

There had been seventy-five prisoners in a transport on December 7th 1942 to the main camp at Auschwitz. There were forty-five men and thirty women. Of the male prisoners, almost a fifth were elderly and the same applied to over half of the women. They were brought to the concentration camp to work – as they were told – but in fact they were killed very quickly. According to surviving documents 54% of those transported died in the first month of their detention in Auschwitz, 17% in the second month and a further 6% in the third month.The murderous mission of the transport was completed in a relatively short time.

On August 21st a second larger transport departed – this time for the Gypsy Family Section at Auschwitz-Birkenau, leaving sixty-two persons still interned in Hodonin. This consisted of 748 prisoners – 164 men and boys, 290 women and girls and 157 young children. The youngest among the transported were the babies, Jan Didi and Vera Danielova, who had been born in the Hodonin camp during 1943.

A seventy-two year old woman died shortly afterwards and an eight-year old girl was adopted by a non-Romany family in nearby Olesnice. Twelve healthy prisoners were assigned to clean up the camp and twenty-six were released as "persons with predominantly Aryan ancestry".

Of the remaining prisoners, twenty-two sick persons were temporarily transferred to a forced labour camp in Brno. After their return to health more Romanies joined this group and on January 28th 1944 all of them – twenty-six adults and five children – were transported via Brno to the Gypsy Family Section in Auschwitz-Birkenau where they joined their fellows.

The Gypsy camps in Lety and Hodonin had interned by force those nomadic Romanies who were considerd as anti-social and causing problems. These "Gypsies, Gypsy half-castes and Gypsy-like nomads" were isolated in this way from the rest of society and forced into hard labour. Lety and Hodonin were not extermination camps. Nevertheless, as a result of the inhuman conditions, a large number of the internees perished. A quick demise also awaited the majority of the remainder who were transferred to Auschwitz. So the short history of the Gypsy camps in the Protectorate of Bohemia and Moravia was very much a tragedy with a catastrophic climax.

Epilogue

The majority of the Sinti and Romanies in the Protectorate who could show they had a regular dwelling and regular work remained temporarily free following the registration of August 2nd 1942. The identity cards of all the adults had been taken away on "race biological" grounds and replaced by so-called Gypsy documents. From March 1943 onwards they were ordered to report to assembly centres at which they were interned for a short time while a final selection was made and put on the list to be transported to the Gypsy Family Section at Auschwitz-Birkenau. It has not yet been established how this selection was organized. In some cases the mayors intervened on behalf of their citizens, personal friendship was sometimes helpful and, in a few cases, bribery. It was intended that the deportations should take place as quickly as possible but the German Criminal Police did not manage this and the whole action went very slowly. In the first stage most of the Sinti and Romanies from Moravia were deported on March 7th, those from Bohemia on March 11th and a transport from both territories on March 19th. In the second stage, on May 7th prisoners from the wound-up Gypsy Camp in Lety were deported together with those Moravian Romanies who should have been deported in March but had been left in freedom and then on August 22nd those from the wound-up camp in Hodonin. Finally in the final stage Sinti and Romanies from Bohemia and Moravia were transported in small groups on October 19th and January 28th 1944 or as individuals. In some cases it was a question of people who had previously been in prison or hospital as well as those who were discovered later or captured trying to escape to Slovakia.

The camp files for the Gypsy Family Section at Auschwitz-Birkenau record 4,493 Gypsies from the Czech Protectorate, in addition to those who had earlier been deported to the main camp of Auschwitz I.

VIII. A synoptic chronology of the persecution of the Gypsies under National Socialism (1933-45)

Reimar Gilsenbach

Introduction

I have chosen only a limited selection of events for both columns. I have also — at the request of the editor — confined myself to the Gypsies as victims. For a fuller presentation of the story of the Romanies and Sinti in these years, see the fourth volume of my *Weltchronik der Zigeuner* published by Peter Lang in 1998. Both there and in the book *Russlands Zigeuner* (Berlin 1994) I have also entered events where the Romanies are culturally or politically active. The dates in the chronicle below represent about a quarter of those in the *Weltchronik der Zigeuner*.

The country is given only when it is not part of Germany. In all the countries which fell under the control of the National Socialists there was persecution of the Gypsies. This synoptic chronicle is intended to give an overview of how this persecution evolved in time and space and how it was linked to the history of the Second World War.

The suffering of the Romanies

The Violent World

1933

1933-34: The painter Otto Pankok establishes his most important work *The Passion*. This cycle of sixty charcoal studies of the Passion of Jesus is Pankok's answer to Hitler taking power. The Gypsy pictures that he had created in 1931-33 in the camp in Heinefeld, Düsseldorf are one of the sources for *The Passion*.

22.3.1933: The State Cultural Chamber Act. This law means, for practical purposes, the forbidding of the exercise of the profession of music by Sinti and Romanies.

June 1933: The Sinto boxer Johan "Truckelle" Trollmann is stripped of his title as Light-heavyweight Champion of Germany for "racial reasons".

14.7.1933: *Act for the Prevention of Hereditarily ill Offspring*, also known as the *Sterilization Act*. Many Sinti and Romanies will be compulsorily sterilized as racially inferior.

18-25.9.1933: In a so-called Beggars' Week, the Police and auxiliary police, made up of SS and SA members, arrest 10,000 alleged beggars and vagrants, including many Sinti and Romanies.

1933

30.1.1933: President von Hindenburg names Adolf Hitler as Chancellor. The National Socialist Party takes power. The German provinces are integrated. Hitler prophesies in the Parliament that a future world war will lead to the destruction of the Jewish race in Europe.

27.2.1933: Burning of the German Parliament Building, the Reichstag. Arrest of about 10,000 communists and anti-fascists.

28.2.1933: Hindenburg's *Decree for the Protection of the People and the State*. Removal of civil rights.

March 1933: The first concentration camp of Hitler's Germany is built in Dachau in Bavaria.

23.3.1933: A majority vote by the centre and right wing parties in the Parliament passes the *Enabling Law* which gives Hitler full powers as a dictator.

31.3.1933: Unification of Germany incorporating the provinces.

1.4.1933: Boycott of all Jewish businesses in Germany, the first open discrimination against Jews.

26.4.1933: The Gestapo (Secret Police) formed in Prussia.

14.7.1933: After Hitler bans all other parties, the National Socialist Party is the only legal party in Germany.

19.10.1933: Germany leaves the League of Nations.

1934

23.3.1934: Expulsion legislation threatens with expulsion Gypsies who cannot prove their German nationality.

1934

20.4.1934: Himmler named Inspector of the Gestapo. Heydrich, Chief of the Security Service, becomes his deputy.

24.4.1934: The Peoples' Court is set up.

30.6.1934: The so-called Röhm Affair. Hitler orders the killing of his rivals in the SA. The SS becomes the instrument of terror. On July 20th Himmler is named National Head of the SS.

SA. (*Sturmabteilung* — "Storm Troopers") A uniformed organisation working for the Nazi party.
SS. (*Schutzstaffel* — Protection Squad) An elite organisation, founded in 1923, as Hitler's bodyguard. Later under Himmler it was to expand and become the main instrument of terror and mass murder.

2.8.1934: Hindenburg dies. Hitler merges the office of President with that of Chancellor. As Leader (*Führer*) and Chancellor he rules absolutely.

1935

1934-38: Councils and the Criminal Police compel Sinti and Romanies to stop on the outskirts of towns in Gypsy camps, often fenced and guarded.

12.2.1935: Dr Robert Ritter seeks funding for a bursary to carry out his work on the genealogies of Gypsy bastards.

June 1935: At the 9th Congress of the International Criminal Police Commission in Copenhagen, Karl Siegfried Bader, representing the Ministry of the Interior of Baden province, informs the Congress that the Baden Gypsy Information Centre in Karlsruhe has already filed 5,000 dossiers on Gypsies with police records.

26.8-1.9.1935: At the International Congress for Population Questions in Berlin, Dr Ritter for the first time announces his concept of genocide for Sinti and Romanies. The few "racially pure Gypsies" must only mate with each other, the continued procreation of the

1935

13.1.1935: Referendum in Saarland. 90% vote to join Germany.

6.3.1935: *Law for Building the Armed Forces* introduces compulsory military service in Germany.

28.3.1935: The first showing of the Nazi Party Day film *Triumph of the Will*, directed by Leni Riefenstahl.

21.6.1935: First International Writers' Congress for the Defence of Culture in Paris.

15.9.1935: During the Nuremberg Day of the National Socialist Party Göring announces the *Citizenship Law* and the *Law for the Protection of German Blood and Honour*. As "members of a non-European race" Gypsies, in addition to Jews, cannot be German citizens.

several thousand "Gypsy bastards" is to be ruled out.

14.11.1935: In accordance with the First Order for the carrying out of the *Blood Protection Act*, a marriage "can no longer take place which might result in offspring who could endanger the purity of German blood". This also applies to "Gypsies and Gypsy half-breeds".

1936

1936: Protestant Church archivists and vicars compile a card index of baptisms of foreign races in Berlin in which they separate out in the first instance Jews, Gypsies and Blacks. Duplicates of the card index are supplied to the State Centre for Genealogical Research.

15.3.1936: A decree of the Minister for the Interior removes the right to vote from Gypsies and Gypsy half-breeds.

22.5.1936: Hundreds of Sinti are deported from Berlin with their caravans by the police and settled on a caravan site at Marzahn.

5.6.1936: The International Central Office for Fighting the Gypsy Menace starts work in the Vienna office of Interpol.

Interior, publishes a *General Decree for Fighting the Gypsy Plague*.

20.9.1936: The Prussian State Criminal Police in Berlin becomes the Central Criminal Police Office (RKPA) into which, in 1938, the National Centre for the Fight Against the Gypsy Menace will be incorporated.

6.6.1936: Frick, the Minister of the November 1936: The Racial Hygiene and Population Biological Research Centre of the Health Office in the Ministry of the Interior begins its work. Under the leadership of Dr Robert Ritter it will carry out an "investigation of the nomadic population, that means, above all, the Gypsies and Gypsy bastards".

3.10.1935: Italy invades Ethiopia and occupies it by May 9th 1936. The League of Nations brands Italy as the aggressor.

1936

7.3.1936: The German army invades the Rheinland.

17.6.1936: Hitler names Himmler as Chief of the German Police.

12.7.1936: The construction of Sachsenhausen concentration camp commences. It is completed in August.

1.8.1936: Hitler opens the Olympic Games in Berlin.

8-14.9.36: At the Nazi Party conference in Nuremberg Hitler announces his Four Year Plan, the industrial programme of preparation for war.

25.10.1936: Germany's pact with Italy, known as the Berlin-Rome Axis.

25.11.1936: Germany and Japan sign the Anti-comintern Pact.

26.11.1936: The War Minister orders that pure Gypsies and people with a conspicuous amount of Gypsy blood should not be taken into active military service. This order is not fully carried out until much later.

1937

1937: Dr Ritter gives a paper at the 1st International Congress for Population Sciences in Paris on the "genealogical-historical investigations" which are the first steps in the recording of Sinti and Romanies in Germany.

March 1937: Otto Finger gains a medical doctorate for his thesis *Studies on two antisocial Gypsy half-breed tribes*.

July 1937: Dr Gunther, the Mayor of Berleburg, demands "drastic measures" to stop the growth of the Gypsy population. Since the 18th century some small Sinti settlements have existed on the edge of the town. By the end of the Nazi period they will have been wiped out.

19.7.1937: Opening of the national socialist propaganda exhibition *Degenerate Art*. Amongst the works on display is Otto Pankok's lithography *Hoto II*, the portrait of a Sinti girl.

17.8.1937: Adolf Würth, a worker in the Race Hygiene Research Unit recommends in a lecture to the German Society for Racial Research that "just as the National Socialist state has solved the Jewish problem, so, on the whole, the Gypsy question should be solved ".

14.9.1937: Arthur Nebe, Chief of the National Criminal Police repeats an earlier request for police stations to send in the reports of any prosecutions against Gypsies where their customs have played a part in the offence.

1938

1938: In his article "Gypsies and Vagabonds", Dr Ritter claims that "there are no longer any completely racially pure Gypsies". Ritter proposes the internment of gupsy half-breeds in closed settlements or their sterilization.

1937

Summer 1937: Opening of Buchenwald concentration camp.

6.11.1937: Italy joins the Anti-comintern Pact.

14.12.1937: Minister of the Interior Frick signs the *Decree for the Preventive Police Campaign against Crime*. Anyone classed as antisocial by the Nazi authorities could be taken into a concentration camp without trial.

1938

12/13.3.1938: The German army invades Austria. Austria is annexed to Germany as Ostmark.

4.4.1938: The circular on the *Decree on the Preventative Fight against Crime* state clearly that everyone should be treated as antisocial who "does not wish to conform to the self-evident rules of the National Socialist state, for example.... vagrants (Gypsies)."

21-30.4.1938: Himmler orders the Gestapo to arrest several thousand fit "work-shy" persons to be available as forced labour for the building of concentration camps. Amongst the arrested persons are Gypsies.

16.5.1938: Himmler orders the Gypsy Police Unit in the Police Headquarters in Munich to be made part of the National Criminal Police Office in Berlin with effect from 1.10.1938. It will be called the National Centre for the Fight against the Gypsy Menace. All district criminal police stations will have an office for Gypsy questions.

1.6.1938: Heydrich (Himmler's deputy) orders every district criminal police station to arrest "at least 200 fit male persons (antisocials)". Amongst the victims of a wave of arrests in the period June 13-18 are hundreds of Sinti and Romanies.

August 1938: The veteran Nazi Dr Tobias Portschy, Governor of the Burgenland recommends that Gypsies should be brought to extinction by the separate internment of men and women in forced labour camps.

22.8.1938: A new order from the Aliens Police threatens with expulsion Gypsies who cannot prove their German citizenship.

September 1938: The number of Sinti and Romanies in the Marzahn Gypsy camp reaches 852.

Autumn 1938: The Racial Hygiene Research Centre begins to set up an archive of Gypsy genealogies. Their experts, specially trained in race biology, seek out the German Sinti and Romanies in order to "question them firmly".

8.12.1938: In his order *The Fight against the Gypsy Menace* Himmler announces

5.8.1938: Italy: The first edition of *La difesa della razza* appears - a fortnightly racist and anti-semitic journal.

20.8.1938: Eichmann sets up a Central Office for Jewish Emigration in Vienna.

1.9.1938: Italy: The first Fascist laws against Jews are introduced.

30.9.1938: The Munich Agreement, signed between France, Germany and Great Britain permits Hitler to annex Sudetenland, the border area of Czechoslovakia.

1.10.1938. Czechoslovakia: The German army invades Sudetenland.

9/10.11.1938: *Crystal Night*. Pogrom against the Jews in Germany.

10.11.1938. Italy: New laws against Jews are untroduced.

that the "Gypsy question is to be solved from the concept of race".

1939

February 1939: Dr Ritter announces that investigations into thousands of Gypsies are being undertaken.

1.3.1939: Heydrich signs the National Criminal Police Office's instructions for carrying out the *General Gypsy Decree* which lay down guidelines for the registration of Gypsies, Gypsy half-breeds and people nomadizing in Gypsy fashion.

17.5.1939: For the National Census everyone has to fill in a detailed form which asks about origin.

5.6.1939: The National Criminal Police Office (RKPA) sends a secret order to the Criminal Police Headquarters in Vienna - *Preventative measures for fighting the Gypsy Plague in Burgenland*. It orders that 2,000 more men are to be sent to Dachau and 1,000 women to Ravensbrück concentration camps.

29.6.1939: A transport of 440 Romany women and children from the Burgenland arrives at Ravensbrück camp.

21.9.39: Heydrich has a conference with top SS chiefs and leaders of the Task Forces in Poland. The subject is the deportation of the Jews from Greater Germany into the German-occupied part of Poland. The 30,000 Gypsies will also be deported.

27.9.1939: The National Security Headquarters (RSHA) is set up under Heydrich, incorporating the National Criminal Police Office. The National Centre for the Fight against the Gypsy menace becomes part of the new Headquarters.

16.10.1939: From Vienna, Eichmann suggests to Nebe, Director of the Criminal Police, in a telegram: "the easiest method is to add some trucks of Gypsies to each transport (of Jews)" being deported.

1939

30.1.1939: Hitler informs Parliament of the destruction of the Jewish race in the coming war.

14.3.1939: Czechoslovakia: At the instigation of Hitler Slovakia declares itself a separate state.

14-16.3.1939. Czechoslovakia: The German army occupies the Czech lands. Hitler declares this area the Protectorate of Bohemia and Moravia.

22.3.1939: Germany annexes the Lithuanian border area of Memel.

28.3.1939: Spain: Franco's troops capture Madrid.

6.4.1939. Italy: Italy invades and annexes Albania.

May 1939: Opening of the women's concentration camp Ravensbrück.

23.8.1939: Non-aggression pact signed between Germany and the Soviet Union.(The Hitler-Stalin Treaty).

3.9.1939: Britain and France declare war on Germany in accordance with their treaty with Poland.

17.9.1939: Poland: As agreed in the Hitler-Stalin Treaty, the Soviet army occupied east Poland up to the so-called Curzon line.

21.9.1939: Beginning of euthanasia Action T4 in Germany. The killing of 200,000 mentally ill including many Romanies and Sinti.

27.9.1939: The Central Security Head-quarters (RSHA) is founded and Heydrich is named its chief.

28.9.1939. Poland: Fall of Warsaw.

6.10.1939. Poland: End of the last resistance by the Polish army.

17.10.1939: On Himmler's command, through a secret express letter signed by Heydrich, known as the *Settlement Decree*, the National Security Headquarters orders all Gypsies and Gypsy half-breeds in Germany not to leave their place of residence or current stopping-place

26.10.1939. Poland: The General Governor orders Jews and Gypsies to have special identity cards. Romanies get a yellow card with a black Z printed on it.

20.11.1939: A decree from the National Security Headquarters orders all Gypsy women who are suspected of fortune telling to be taken into a concentration camp as antisocials.

30.11.1939. Bohemia and Moravia: The Ministry of the Interior of the Protectorate tells its subordinate departments to forbid the Gypsies to nomadize.

1940

20.1.1940: Dr Ritter in a report on his work for the German Research Society says that more than 90% of German Gypsies are of mixed race and should be interned in work camps.

24.1.1940: Chief Medical Officer Dr Leonardo Conti demands the sterilization of all Gypsies and Gypsy half-breeds as a special measure.

30.1.1940: Heydrich holds a conference with senior SS leaders on the subject of Hitler's order for the resettlement by force of Poles, Jews and Gypsies.

6.4.1940. France: The French government forbids nomads to travel for the duration of the war. Several thousand nomadic Gypsies are made to settle in fixed places by the local police.

27.4.1940: Himmler orders the resettlement of Gypsies in the General Government of Poland. Some 2,500 Sinti and Romanies from the western and northwestern border areas of Germany will be deported with the first transport in the middle of May.

7.10.1939: Hitler names Himmler as National Commissioner for the Strengthening of the German People and gives him the task of eliminating the dangerous influence of foreign elements in the population.

12.10.1939. Poland: Hitler annexes Danzig and the western border areas of Poland into Greater Germany. He orders the setting up of the so-called General Government in the rest of German-occupied Poland with Cracow as the capital.

End of October 1939: Hitler, with his *Euthanasia Decree*, allows the mass murder of the hereditarily ill. The Decree is backdated to September 1st.

21.12.1939: Eichmann becomes Head of the Jewish Section in the Central Security Headquarters.

1940

5.5.1940. Poland: Rudolf Höss is ordered by Himmler to build the Auschwitz concentration camp.

10.5.1940: The German army attacks Belgium, Holland and Luxembourg.

12.5.1940: Invasion of France by the German army.

10.6.1940: Italy joins the war as Germany's ally.

14.6.1940. France: The German army enters Paris.

22.6.1940: The French army capitulates. Marshal Petain takes power and signs an armistice treaty with Germany. France is divided into occupied north and unoccupied south (Vichy France).

10.7.40. France: The National Assembly gives full powers to Marshal Petain.

3-6.8.1940: The Soviet Union annexes Estonia, Lithuania and Latvia.

27.9.1940. France: The German occupiers announce an anti-Jewish decree.

Mid May 1940: The deportation of whole families of German Sinti and Romanies in accordance with Himmler's Settlement Decree takes place. It is organized by section IV D 4 (Jewish section) of the National Security Headquarters under the leadership of Eichmann. In the General Government of Poland most of the deportees are placed in work camps or Jewish ghettos

18.6.1940: The Central Security Headquarters rules that certain categories of concentration camp prisoners, including Gypsies, may not be let out of custody.

August 1940. Austria: In Maxglan, a suburb of Salzburg, Sinti and Romanies have to work expanding an existing internment camp to take 300-400 prisoners.

10.8.1940. Bohemia and Moravia: Two labour camps for the unemployed and the homeless are set up. One for Bohemia in Lety and one for Moravia in Hodonin.

14.8.1940. France: Jews, foreigners and nomads are expelled from the coastal zone.

September 1940: In his article *Primitivity and Criminality* Dr Ritter demands that Gypsies should be interned in work camps or guarded settlements and that their procreation should be stopped by the separation of the sexes or sterilisation.

11.9.1940. Italy: The first provisions are announced for the internment of Italian Gypsies.

04.10.1940. France: The German military commander orders the internment of all nomadic Gypsies in the occupied zone.

October 1940. France: Nomadic Gypsies are interned in camps at Plénée-Jugon and Mérignac.

31.10.1940. Austria: In an express letter from the Minister of the Interior further measures against the Romanies in the Burgenland are decreed. They should be brought together in Gypsy settlements under police guard.

2.10.1940. Poland: The Warsaw ghetto is set up for Jews.

3.10.1940. France: The cabinet of ministers in the Unoccupied Zone exludes Jews from public life.

16.11.1940. France: 70,000 French citizens expelled from part of Lorraine annexed to Germany.

20.11.1940: Hungary joins the Axis Three Power Treaty, followed by Romania (24.11), Slovakia (24.11), Bulgaria (1.3.1941) Yugoslavia (25.3.1941) and Croatia (15.6.1941).

November 1940. Romania: The Ministry of Internal Affairs forbids Gypsies to nomadize during the winter.

22.11.1940. France: A German order forbids the practising of nomadic occupations in twenty-one departments of the west of France.

23.11.1940. Austria: An internment camp for Gypsies is set up in Lackenbach (Burgenland). It is under the Criminal Police Headquarters in Vienna.

1941

22.3 and 11.11.1941: The Minister for Science and Education demands the exclusion of Sinti and Romany children from the state school system.

20.4.1941. Slovakia: Decree of the Ministry of the Interior on *The organization of the living conditions of the Gypsies*. They must establish their homes separately from those of the majority population.

27.4.1941. Italy: The Ministry of the Interior sends out a further letter concerning the internment of Gypsies.

30.5.1941. Serbia: The German Military Commander in Serbia publishes a bilingual order affecting Jews and Gypsies. In Paragraph 18 it says Gypsies will be treated the same as Jews.

From 22.6.1941. USSR: Just behind the front line the Task Forces move into the occupied areas of the Soviet Union. They will systematically kill Jews and Romanies, captured political commissars and partisans. Amongst the some 2 million victims of the Task Forces are several thousand Romanies.

22.7.1941: An order of the National Security Headquarters orders all the Gypsies in East Prussia to be interned in communal Gypsy camps. From there those able to work are sent to forced labour.

31.7.1941: Göring gives Heydrich the task of the Final Solution of the Jewish question. Heydrich brings the Gypsies into the Final Solution.

1941

6-7.4.1941: Sudden attack by the Axis powers against Yugoslavia. Germany and its allies (Bulgaria, Hungary, Italy) crush the country and divide it into spheres of influence.

6-27.4.1941: The German army occupies Greece.

16.4.1941. Croatia: A clerical fascist puppet government takes power in Croatia (including Bosnia-Herzegovina). The Ustasha – a militia similar to the SS – sets up concentration camps and kills with unheard of brutality.

13.5.1941: Hitler issues a secret decree concerning the state of emergency in the Barbarossa region (the USSR). Actions which army personnel take against enemy civilians will not be subject to legal proceedings.

6.6.1941: Hitler issues the secret *Commissar Order*. Captured Soviet political commissars are to be executed immediately.

22.6.1941: Germany breaks the Non-aggression Pact with the Soviet Union. Under the code name Barbarossa the troops of Germany and its allies attack the Soviet Union.

22.6.1941: Romania enters the war on the side of the Axis

29.6.1941. USSR: The Communist Party of the Soviet Union calls for a great war for the motherland.

180

7.8.1941: A circular from Himmler decrees the utilisation of the race biological records of Gypsy people. The National Centre for the Fight against the Gypsy Menace in the Central Criminal Police Headquarters (RKPA) will decide who is a Gypsy or Gypsy half-breed. The expert decisions of the Racial Hygiene Research Centre are final.

14-15.8.1941: Himmler visits Minsk and during this visit probably orders the killing of all Gypsies.

22.8.1941. USSR: Task Force A executes three Gypsies (a man, a woman and a child).

28 and 30.9.1941 USSR: Task Forces carry out mass executions of Jews in the Baby Yar valley on the outskirts of Kiev. Amongst the 30,000 dead there are also many Romanies.

9.10.1941. Yugoslavia: Task Force C reported that as a reprisal for twenty-one German soldiers shot a few days ago by partisans near Topola, 2,100 Jews and Gypsies have been executed. The execution was carried out by the German army.

25.10.1941: During a conference on the final solution of the Jewish question Heydrich decides that the Gypsies from the Protectorate of Bohemia and Moravia are to be sent to a concentration camp.

November 1941. France: The German authorities order the replacement of the small internment camps by large ones.

3.11.1941. Serbia: The German military command orders the immediate arrest of all Jews and Gypsies to be held as hostages. Thousands of hostages will be executed as reprisals for German soldiers killed by partisans.

5-9.11.1941. Poland: On Himmler's orders a Gypsy camp had been set up in the Jewish ghetto of Lodz. During the first days four transports arrived, each with 1,000 persons from Austria and on the fifth day 1,007 more. Amongst the deportees were 2,868 children. Within a short time an epidemic of typhus broke out. 613 inmates died by January 1st 1942.

13.7.1941. Yugoslavia: Armed resistance begins.

19.8.1941. Romania: Hitler supports the annexation by Romania of Moldavia and the area between the Dniestr and the Bug (Transnistria).

29.8.1941. France: First execution of hostages as a reprisal.

1.9.1941: A police decree makes the wearing of a yellow Star of David compulsory for Jews in Germany.

September 1941: In the occupied eastern parts of the USSR two zones are set up and placed under German civilian control.

14.10.1941: Beginning of the mass deportation of German Jews to the General Government of Poland.

11.12.1941: Germany and Italy declare war on the United States.

December 1941-July 1942: The German Central Security Headquarters set up several extermination camps in the General Government of Poland; Chelmno (December 1941), Belzec (March 1942), Sobibor (May 1942) and Treblinka (July 1942).

21.12.1941: Establishment of the Criminal Biological Institute of the Security Police in the Central Criminal Police Office. Dr Robert Ritter is engaged as as director.

8.11.1941. France: The internment camp of Montreuil is opened. It will hold over 1,000 inmates at its peak.

16.11-15.12.1941. USSR: During the massacres in Simferopol and its surroundings by Task Force C, 824 Romanies were murdered. An announcement on January 9th 1942 said: The Gypsy problem in Simferopol has been cleared up.

5.12.1941. Latvia: All the Gypsies in the town of Libau, 101 in all, were executed.

December 1941. Baltic States: State Commissioner Lohse ordered that Gypsies should be given the same treatment as Jews.

1942

The beginning of January 1942 Poland: All the surviving Sinti and Romanies from the Lodz ghetto are loaded on to lorries and transported to the extermination camp of Chelmno and killed there in gassing vans.

19.1.1942. Bulgaria: Forced baptism of Muslim Romanies in Sofia.

13.3.1942: The German Minister of Labour orders that all special restrictions for Jews in the field of welfare rights should also apply to Gypsies.

Spring 1942 to the end of 1944. Poland: SS, Security Police and the army begin to systematically kill Gypsies in the General Government of Poland. Sedentary Gypsies are counted amongst the victims as well as nomads.

26.3.1942: A special Social Equality Tax for Gypsies is introduced on the lines of one that had been levied on Jews and Poles since 1940.

22.4.1942-January 1943. Poland: Many groups of Romanies are brought into the Warsaw ghetto. Some are kept in the prison in Gesia Street. In January 1943 they will be transferred to the extermination camp at Treblinka.

29.4.1942. Czech lands: The first Romanies are deported to the main camp at Auschwitz from Brno.

1942

20.1.1942: Heydrich announces to the State Secretaries and the senior SS leaders at the Wannsee conference that all Jews are to be killed.

1.2.1942: Establishment of the Commercial Administrative Headquarters of the SS. It converts the concentration camps into commercial enterprises for the SS and forces the camp prisoners to perform slave labour.

27.3.1942. France: First deportations on racial grounds.

April 1942: Action T4 is continued with the killing of concentration camp prisoners who are considered unfit for work.

12.6.1942: The General Plan for the East envisages that all east Europe will be Germanized.

16.6.1942. France: (La Relève). French citizens are invited to go to work in Germany in exchange for the release of prisoners of war.

14.9.1942: Goebbels coins the phrase "annihilation through work" in a conversation with the Minister of Justice, Thierack. The systematic killing of concentration camp prisoners through slave labour for the armaments industry begins.

182

May 1942. Bulgaria: A decree is issued ordering compulsory employment for Gypsies

17.5.1942. Romania: The Ministry of Internal Affairs orders a census of sedentary Gypsies.

19.5.1942. Croatia: The government and the Ustasha issue an order to arrest all Gypsies and deport them to the concentration camp in Jasenovac. In this camp Ustasha militia kill thousands of Romanies between the end of May and the beginning of July.

28.5.1942. Poland: The District Chief of the Warsaw Rural District orders that all the Gypsies should be transferred to Jewish ghettos.

June to August 1942. Romania: Several thousand nomadic Gypsies are deported to Transnistria.

24.6.1942: Göring publishes an order concerning the work contribution Gypsies and Gypsy half-breeds must make.

July 1942. Poland: Amongst the victims of the Treblinka forced labour and extermination camp are many hundreds of Polish Romanies. They are shot with their wives and children by the army and the SS in a nearby wood and buried in a mass grave.

10.7.1942: A decree of the General Staff of the Army orders that on race political grounds Gypsies and Gypsy half-breeds are not to be taken for active military service.

August 1942: Czech lands: Some 2,500 Gypsies sent to Lety and Hodonin camps.

21.8.1942. Romania: Royal decree on the deportation of Gypsies to Transdnistria.

25.8.1942. USSR: In a situation report from the Director of the Nazi Field Police he says: "The appearance of Gypsy bands is a serious threat to the pacification of the field of operations...Therefore it is necessary to wipe out these bands without mercy."

11.11.1942. France: German army occupies the south of France.

183

28.8.1942. Yugoslavia: Minister Dr Turner informs General Löhr of the South-east Army Region that in "Serbia the Gypsy question as well as the Jewish one has been fully liquidated."

12-19.9.1942. Romania: Deportation of 13,000 sedentary Romanies to Transnistria.

18.9.1942: Himmler agrees with Justice Minister Thierack that "antisocial elements", including Gypsies, who are serving prison sentences should be delivered to the Head of the SS (Himmler) for destruction through work i.e. to concentration camps.

13.10.1942: In a circular from the Central Security Headquarters (RSHA) it is announced: The Head of the SS envisages giving the pure Sinti Gypsies a certain freedom of movement. Himmler appoints nine Gypsy chiefs or "speakers" to set up lists of these families.

17.10.1942. Romania: Deportations to Transdnistria suspended.

3.12.1942: Martin Bormann, Head of the Chancellery of the Leader of the National Socialist Party (Hitler) in a letter to Himmler opposes this plan of giving back a certain freedom to the pure Sinti Gypsies.

16.12.1942: The Head of the SS (Himmler) issues the order to deport the majority of the Gypsies in Greater Germany to the concentration camp of Auschwitz-Birkenau.

1943

13.1.1943. France: Seventy male Gypsies are transferred from Poitiers to Compiègne and from there all, except four, to Sachsenhausen concentration camp.

29.1.1943: The Central Security Headquarters issues details for the carrying out of Himmler's order for the "internment of Gypsy half-breeds, Romany Gypsies and Balkan Gypsies in families into Auschwitz-Birkenau." The Auschwitz Action is scheduled to begin on March 1st.

1943

16.2.1943. France: The Forced Labour Service (STO) set up.

19.4.-16.5.1943. Poland: The Warsaw ghetto uprising. The SS and the army liquidate the Jewish ghetto.

7.6.1943: The gynaecologist Dr Clauberg, an SS officer, informs Hitler that he has worked out a method by which through one injection in the uterus one thousand women could be sterilized each day.

26.2.1943: The first transports of Sinti and Romanies from Germany are delivered to the Gypsy Section in Auschwitz-Birkenau. A series of numbers with the prefix Z is tattooed on the left arm of each inmate.

1.3.1943: Police with dogs surround the Gypsy internment camp in Magdeburg. All the Sinti and Romanies are arrested and deported to Auschwitz. The Auschwitz Action was started punctually here and in other German towns. The Criminal Police take little or no notice of the exceptions which Himmler's Auschwitz Order had foreseen.

6-31.3.1943: In this period twenty-three transports with 11,339 people (5,570 men and 5,769 women) are delivered to the Gypsy Family Section in the Auschwitz-Birkenau concentration camp.

23.3.1943: In the Gypsy Section of Auschwitz-Birkenau the SS gas some 1,700 men, women and children, suspected of having typhus.

Spring 1943. Austria: For two weeks the linguist Johann Knobloch visited the internment camp in Lackenbach in order to carry out Gypsy studies for his thesis.

24.3.1943: During the deportations of the Romanies and Sinti to the concentration camp of Auschwitz-Birkenau Eva Justin, one of the intellectuals responsible for the crime, has her oral examination for her doctorate at Berlin University. Her thesis has the title *The fate of Gypsy children who have been brought up by strangers and their offspring*. The author recommends the sterilization of the majority of Gypsies.

April 1943: Transfer of the Criminal Biological Institute of the Security Police, the Racial Hygiene Research Centre and the National Centre for the Fight against the Gypsy Menace into the building of the Security Police College of the Central Security Headquarters near Ravensbrück concentration camp.

9.7.1943: Italy: British and US troops land in Sicily.

25.7.1943. Italy: Fall of Mussolini. Marshal Badoglio is nominated head of the government.

8.9.1943. Italy: Armistice with the Allies.

23.9.1943. Italy: Mussolini sets up a new government at Salo.

13.10.1943: The Italian government under Marshal Badoglio changes sides and declares war on Germany.

16.10.1943. Italy: The German occupiers of north Italy liquidate the Rome ghetto. More than 1,000 Jews are deported to concentration camps.

6.4.1943: The Riefenstahl Film Company in Berlin makes a list of the payments to the sixty-eight Gypsies from Marzahn internment camp who appeared as extras in Leni Riefenstahl's film *Tiefland* from April 1942. By the time the accounts have been prepared these Gypsies are already in Auschwitz-Birkenau.

25.4.1943: Paragraph 4 of the 12th revision of the Citizenship Law states that Jews and Gypsies cannot be German citizens, nor can they even obtain the status of protected persons.

3.5.1943. Czech lands: Ninety-four Gypsies are deported from Lety camp to Auschwitz-Birkenau. Other transports follow from both Lety and Hodonin as those camps are wound down.

25.5.1943: A curfew is ordered in the Gypsy Camp in Auschwitz. SS staff seize 1,035 Romanies and Sinti who came on May 13 with transports from Bialystok and Austria. They are suspected of having typhus and are killed in the gas chambers.

30.5.1943: SS Major Dr Josef Mengele - assistant to Professor Otmar von Verschuer, the Director of the Kaiser Wilhelm Institute for Anthropology, Human Genetics and Eugenics in Berlin-Dahlem - is transferred at his own request to Auschwitz-Birkenau concentration camp.

June 1943. France: twenty-five male Gypsies are transferred from Poitiers to Compiègne. Three days later twenty-three of them are deported to Buchenwald.

July 1943 (?): SS Head Himmler visits the Gypsy Section in Auschwitz. Höss, Commander of the concentration camp at the time, wrote in his autobiography after the war: "He gave us the order to destroy them after we had selected those able to work, as for the Jews."

7.9.1943: Professor Ernst Ferdinand Sauerbruch, a famous surgeon, approves, as trustee of the German Research Institute, the project on specific protein and eye colour which Professor Verschuer has submitted. Mengele carries out both experimental projects in the Gypsy Section at Auschwitz.

24.9.1943: The Mittelwerk Company is listed in the Company Register at the court in Berlin-Charlottenburg. It transfers the production of the Wonder Weapons – the V1 rocket and V2 unmanned bomber – from Peenemunde to the Dora-Mittelbau concentration camp. With great haste, underground production is set up in the Kohnstein hills. Thousands of concentration camp prisoners are employed as slave labour, amongst them hundreds of Romanies and Sinti.

October 1943. France, Belgium: Beginning of round-up of Gypsies in the north of France and Belgium.

15.11.1943. USSR: Rosenberg, the Minister for the Occupied Eastern Territories, issues instructions for the treatment of Gypsies. "All wandering Gypsies and Gypsy half-breeds in the occupied eastern territories are to betreated in the same way as Jews and be placed in concentration camps." i.e. they should in due course to be killed. The sedentary Gypsies "are to be treated as local inhabitants". i.e. if they came under suspicion they could also be executed.

1944

15.1.1944. Belgium: A transport of 351 Romanies and Sinti of different nationalities leave Belgium for the Auschwitz-Birkenau concentration camp.

14.2.1944-13.11.1944: SS Lieutenant Galling from the SS Economic and Administration Head Office indicates that typhus experiments on prisoners in Buchenwald concentration camp should be restricted to Gypsies.

6.3.1944: In a letter to the President of the National Research Council, Ritter informs him that the number of catalogued Gypsies and half-breeds has reached 23,922 during the year. According to this, his staff have investigated some 2,500 more Romanies and Sinti since the Auschwitz Decree and facilitated their deportation.

1944

19.3.1944: The German army occupies Hungary and takes power. Eichmann arranges the deportation of 400,000 Jews in a few months.

6.6.1944. France: Landing of the allied forces in Normandy. Opening of the Second Front.

22.6.1944. USSR: Beginning of the great offensive of the Soviet army. It leads to the collapse of the German eastern front.

20.7.1944: An attempt on Hitler's life by Stauffenberg fails.

23.8.1944. Romania: Marshal Antonescu dismissed by the King and arrested.

25.8.1944: Romania declares war on Germany.

187

12.5.1944: Thirty-nine children from the St Josefspflege Catholic Children's Home in Mulfingen arrive in the Gypsy Camp at Auschwitz. These are among the children whom Eva Justin used as research material for her thesis (see entry for 23.4.1943 above).

19.5.1944. Holland: A transport of 245 Romanies and Sinti is sent to Auschwitz-Birkenau concentration camp.

21.7.1944: The last prisoners are registered at the Gypsy Section in Auschwitz. The register for female prisoners ends with the number Z-10,894 and the male register with Z-10,094, although a few inmates were tattooed with higher numbers.

August-September 1944: With a contract with the Air Force, Professor Wilhelm Beiglböck, Senior Doctor at the First Medical University Clinic in Vienna, together with Dr Hermann Becker-Freyseng, specialist for air force medicine, conduct salt water experiments on forty-four Romanies and Sinti in Dachau concentration camp.

2.8.1944: 1,404 Gypsy prisoners are taken by a goods train to Buchenwald concentration camp. After the train departs SS men drive the 2,897 surviving Romanies and Sinti to the gas chamber attached to Crematorium V.

3.8.1944: The transport with Romanies and Sinti reaches Buchenwald. Amongst the males are 105 children. The majority of the men are transferred to Dora-Mittelbau camp. There they are to construct the underground galleries for the V2 rockets under inhuman conditions.

August 1944-March 1945. Hungary: During the German occupation many thousands of Romanies are deported of whom only 3,000 return.

29.8. to 27.10.1944. Slovakia: Romanies join the fight of partisans in the Slovak National Uprising.

10.10.1944: 800 Gypsy children from Buchenwald arrive at Auschwitz-Birkenau. They include many of the 105 children who had been in the Gypsy

September-October 1944: Advance of the Soviet army to free Bulgaria, Hungary, Slovakia and Yugoslavia.

9.9.1944. Bulgaria: The Bulgarian government joins the Allies and declares war on Germany.

11.9.1944: Units of the American army reach the western frontier of Germany.

29.10.1944: The armanents complex Dora-Mittelbau is designated an independent concentration camp. Thousands of prisoners suffer under the fatal conditions. End of October 1944: Last gassings in Auschwitz.

Section before. They are killed in the gas chambers on arrival.

December 1944-March 1945: In Ravensbrück the gynaecologist Dr Carl Clauberg continues the sterilisation experiments on women prisoners that he had already begun in Auschwitz. He chooses mainly Gypsy women as victims.

1945

15-16.1.1945. France: The internment camp at Montreuil-Bellay is closed. 172 nomads are freed, 352 transferred to other camps.

27.1.1945: At 3.00 p.m. the first Soviet soldiers reach Auschwitz camp. Among the 4,800 sick prisoners who have been abandoned in the main camp there is just one Romany.

17.4.1945: The first British armoured units reach Bergen-Belsen concentration camp. Only a few thousand inmates have survived until their liberation.

May 1945: The number of Romanies and Sinti who have fallen victim to the Nazi holocaust is unknown. Estimates are as high as 500,000

1945

End of January-Middle of April 1945: Soviet offensive advances towards the Oder.

13.12.1945. Hungary: Budapest is freed by the Soviet army.

4.4.1945: The German army is driven out of Hungary.

9.4.1945: The German front in north Italy is smashed.

16.4.-2.5.1945: Offensive by the Soviet army towards Berlin.

25.4-28.4.1945. Italy: General insurrection. Mussolini captured by partisans and executed.

30.4.1945: Hitler commits suicide in his cabinet office.

1.5.1945: All Italy is free.

8.5.1945: Unconditional surender of the German army. Europe, with the aid of the United States, has freed itself from Hitler's regime.

20.11.1945-1.10.1946: Nuremberg Trial of the principal war criminals. Death penalty imposed on twelve defendants.

Postscript

The story which has unfolded in the preceding pages has been one of almost unremitting horror. A few acts of bravery have shone out and others could have been told, such as those of Dutch and Serbian farmers who hid Romany children throughout the war at the risk of death for themselves and their family if the Nazis discovered them.

After the liberation little was revealed about the persecution of the Gypsies. Most of the victims were unwilling or unable to tell their stories. Some writers, largely Jewish such as the late Miriam Novitch, then began to draw the attention of the world to this 'forgotten genocide'. In recent years some of the survivors have put pen to paper or had their story recorded. There have also been historians who have tried to minimise the slaughter. Some claimed that the persecution of the Romanies was a measure of social policy and not racial. We think that the evolution of Nazi policy as outlined in the other volume (*Interface Collection* volume 12) and killing of house-dwelling Romanies in eastern Europe (described in this volume) disprove this.

Other writers have been setting very high numbers for those killed. I do not wish to enter here into the mathematics of the genocide. It would have been crime enough if only one child had been put in a sack and thrown into a river – as happened in Croatia – merely because he was of a different race to the killer. A country by country survey however suggests a total recorded figure for deaths of around a quarter of a million which may rise as high as half a million as more information comes in from eastern Europe.

There has also been a controversy – in particular outside Europe – as to whether the Nazi policy towards Gypsies was milder or harsher than that towards Jews. Again I do not propose to carry out a detailed comparison here. The picture that comes over from the literature and the articles in this volume – including the chronology – is that, had Nazi Germany not lost the war, the Romanies were destined to follow European Jewry into oblivion and that probably the Slavs were the next on the list for a programme of slave labour, sterilisation and genocide.

These two volumes were planned as part of the 50th anniversary remembrance of the liberation and material is being collected for a third and a possibly fourth volume.

They give an in-depth picture of some aspects of the genocide of the Romanies – a genocide carried out not just by Germans but also by many from other ethnic groups who shared the fascist mentality. The reader will probably not need to be reminded that racism was not and is not just a phenomenon of Nazi Germany. The editors and authors of these volumes hope that what we have written will not only be a tribute to the victims but also a warning that we should be on our guard against any resurgence of the idea of designating a particular group as inferior. This can easily lead to excesses such as those described in this work.

Donald Kenrick

Notes

Editor's note: Archive references have been left in the original language to assist researchers. Place names occurring in the Oxford Gazetteer are spelt accordingly.

I. Gypsies in Italy during the Fascist dictatorship and the Second World War
Giovanna Boursier

1. Giuntella, Vittorio. - *Il Nazismo e i lager.* - Rome, 1979.
2. Narciso, Loredana. - *La maschera e il pregiudizio.* - Rome, 1990.
3. Karpati, Mirella (ed.). - *Zingari ieri e oggi.* - Rome, 1990.
4. Masserini, Annamaria. - *Storia dei nomadi.* - Padua, 1990.
5. On October 17th/18th 1988, on the fiftieth anniversary of Italy's anti-semitic legislation, an international conference was held in Rome the papers of which have been published as: Camera dei Deputati. - *Legislazione antisemita in Italia e in Europa.* - Rome, 1989. See also a useful book by Regione Emilia Romagna.- *La menzogna della Razza.* - Bologna, 1994; Sarfatti, Michele. - *Mussolini contro gli Ebrei.* - Turin, 1994.
6. The Gran Consiglio, created in 1922, was one of the main organs of the Fascist regime. It had a consultative and debating role, as well as the function of choosing ministers and making laws. It was composed of the topmost men in the Fascist Party and presided over by Mussolini.
7. It was October 28th 1922 when 50,000 Blackshirts marched to Rome and occupied it by force. The following day the King entrusted Mussolini with the leadership of the government. For the first time in Italian history the head of a minority party obtained, without any parliamentary vote and under mass pressure, the presidency of the country. On November 16th Parliament entrusted Mussolini with this post, thus offering the Fascists a legal position in accordance with the constitution.
8. De Felice, Renzo. - *Storia degli ebrei sotto il Fascismo.* - Turin, 1961.
9. Also named Minculpop. It was created by the regime in 1937 with the task of culturing all cultural life, except for the schools.
10. Their presence is attested by orders or writing concerning them. For example, from the end of the sixteenth century public authorities everwhere ordered them

to leave the country and in the middle of the nineteenth century Cesare Lombroso, one of the best known Italian criminal anthropologists, wrote about them in his book *L'uomo delinquente*.

11. It says, referring to the German laws, that the only "foreign people" in Europe are the Jews and the Gypsies. See Costamagna, C. - The entry for 'Razza' in Istituto dell'enciclopedia italiana: *Dizionario di politica* del PNF. - Rome, Year XVIII of the Fascist era (i.e. 1940).

12. *La difesa della razza*, anno IV, n.l, Nov. 5.

13. ACS (Archivio Centrale dello Strato), Min. Int. PS AAGGRR b.99 and 100. See also Emilia Romagna, op. cit., p.336.

14. ACS Min. Int., PS, series M/4, b.105.

15. Ibid.

16. Ibid.

17. Ibid.

18. Ibid.

19. Ibid.

20. Ibid.

21. Ibid.

22. Ibid. AAGGRR, II Guerra Mondiale, b.68.

23. Ibid.

24. Ibid.

25. Ibid.

26. Ibid. See also Emilia Romagna, op. cit., p.341.

27. A note by the General Division for Public Safety of the Salò government (see note 44 below) drawn up for the German Police two months after the Armistice recorded the existence of forty concentration camps in Italy. To these can be added those set up in the summer of 1942 in Friuli- Venezia Giulia for the people of Slovenia and Dalmatia on the orders of General Roatta to discourage the resistance movement of Tito's partisans. See Karpati, op. cit., above p.61.

28. Karpati, M. - "La politica Fascista verso gli zingari." In: *Lacio Drom* no.2/3, 1984. In 1987 the Mayor of Perdasdefogu denied absolutely that there had ever been a concentration camp in that place.

29. Karpati, ibid. A copy of the letter from the Police Superintendent of Fiume was sent to Mirella Karpati by Boris Pahor who was imprisoned with other Gypsies in Struthof.

30 Masserini, ibid.

31. Karpati, M. - "Il genocido degli zingari". In: *Lacio Drom* no.1, 1987.

32. Levak, Zlato. - "La persecuzione degli zingari, una testimonianza". In: *Lacio Drom* no.3, 1976. During the war Agnone was in the province of Campobasso. Today it is in Isernia.

33. Cited from Kenrick D. and Puxon G. - *Il destino degli zingari*. - Milan, 1975. There are a number of groups known as Sinti in Italy and north-west Yugoslavia.

34. Ibid.

35. Hudorovic, R. - "Il racconto di Rave". In: *Lacio Drom*, no.1, 1983.

36. Levakovic G. and Ausenda G. - *Zingari, vita di un nomade*. - Milan, 1975.

37. Masserini, op. cit.

38. *Rivista abruzzese di studi storici*, year VI no.1, 1985.

39. Karpati. *La politica fascista...* (see note 28).
40. Boursier, Giovanna et al. *Zigeuner, lo sterminio dimenticato.* Rome, 1996.
41. Karpati. *Zingari ieri.*
42. Boursier, op. cit.
43. Karpati. *La Politica fascista.*
44. The Saló Republic. La Repubblica Sociale Italiana, the new government installed by Mussolini at Saló in north Italy in September 1943, after the fall of Fascism in Italy and the Armistice signed between the new government of Badoglio and the Allies. The Saló Republic was only recognised by Germany and the Axis powers and was a puppet state controlled by the Germans. However, Bolzano and Alto Adige were annexed to Germany. In August 1944 the concentration camp at Gries was opened and continued until April 1945.
45. Masserini, ibid. Based on the papers in the local archives.
46. Karpati. *Politica fascista.*
47. Levakovic and Ausenda, op. cit.
48. Picciotto-Fargion, Liliana. - *Per ignota destinazione. Gli ebrei sotto il Nazismo.* - Milan, 1994.
49. To be published as Piasere, Leonardo. - *Italia Romani.* - Rome, 1998 and as the proceedings of the conference of the University of Teramo: *Concentration camps in Italy: from Internment to deportation.* - Teramo, 1998.
50. See the valuable book by Klaus Voigt. - *Il rifugio precario* - Florence, 1996 which was one of the first to try to clarify the questions of internment in the camps primarily before 1943. As Voigt writes, the difference between the types of internment was not substantial and depended on the number of persons imprisoned but in both cases the people concerned were prisoners without freedom.

II. Gypsies in the Austrian Burgenland.
The camp at Lackenbach
Erika Thurner

1. Göhring, Walter and Werner Pfeifenberger. - *80 Jahre Burgenland.* - Mattersburg, 1981; Karner, Stefan (ed.). Articles in *Das Burgenland im Jahr 1945*. Eisenstadt, 1985, especially Tobler, Felix. *Zur Verwaltung des Burgenlandes 1918-1948*, pp.38-48 and Schlag, Gerald. *Burgenländische Politik in den Jahren 1934-1938 und 1945-1946*, pp.49-65.
2. Dostal, Walter. -"Die Zigeuner in Österreich". In: *Archiv für Völkerkunde*. Vol. X.- Vienna, 1955. pp.1-14; Staudinger, Eduard G. - "Die Zigeuner im Burgenland während der NS-Herrschaft" in Karner, op. cit. - pp.149-64; Steinmetz, Selma. - *Österreichs Zigeuner im NS-Staat.*
    Vienna/Frankfurt/Zürich, 1966; Thurner, Erika. - "Nationalsozialismus und Zigeuner in Österreich" in the series: *Veröffentlichungen zur Zeitgeschichte 2*. Vienna/Salzburg, 1983 - pp.50-59.
3. The Burgenland newspapers fom the 1920s and 30s print the demands and reveal the atmosphere, e.g. Ödenburger Zeitung, Burgenlandwacht, Burgenländische Freiheit, see Thurner. *Nationalsozialismus*, p.52; Portschy, Tobias. - "Denkschrift betr. die Zigeunerfrage", August 1938 in *DÖW (Dokumente des Österreichischen*

Widerstands), Bibliothek 8085; Steïnmetz, Selma. "Die Zigeuner" in: DÖW (eds). *Widerstand und Verfolgung im Burgenland 1934-1945.* Vienna, 1979, pp.244-93.

4. For more details about the Nazi movement see Schlag, op. cit., p.52 ff. Portschy was a central figure, not merely carrying out policies but initiating them, before and during the Nazi era. In 1949 he was sentenced to 15 years imprisonment with a strict regime but was released in 1951. This, together with his holding on to the Nazi ideology and honouring Hitler, the Führer, make him a symbol of the neglected or failed denazification. See Steïnmetz Zigeuner, p.246.

5. Mulley, Klaus-Dieter. Zur "Eindeutschung" des Burgenlandes in: Karner op. cit.- pp.239-41.

6. For the ideological basis and the legal regulations for the persecution of the Gypsies, see Thurner *Nationalsozialismus* p.8 ff. And Döring, Hans-Joachim. - *Die Zigeuner im nationalsozialistischen Staat.* Vol.12 of Kriminologische Schriftenreihe. - Hamburg, 1964.

7. Döring, op. cit., Anhang 1 and 2; Steïnmetz. - *Österreichs Zigeuner.* Anhang III, p.51.

8. For the decrees concerning Lackenbach and a detailed history of the camp see Thurner, op.cit., p.60 ff.; Thurner, Erika. - *Kurzgeschichte des national-sozialistischen Zigeunerlagers in Lackenbach (1940-1945).* - Eisenstadt, 1984; also the translation of Thurner's 1983 book (see above note 2): *National Socialism and Gypsies in Austria.* Edited and translated by Gilya Garda Schmidt, The University of Alabama Press, Tuscaloosa, London, 1998.

9. Thurner. *Nationalsozialismus*, p.174 ff.; Documentation regarding five transports assembled in Austria for Lodz with altogether 5,007 persons were only recently discovered, hence the references in earlier literature to only two transports with 2,000 Romanies and Sinti. (Source: Jüdisches Museum Frankfurt, Ordner Ghetto Lodz 1940-1944, documents "Nicht-Juden im Ghetto", "Zigeunerlager", "Polenjugendverwahrlager", Dokument vom 13.11.1941.

10. Thurner. Nationalsozialismus, p.125 and Anhang XIX, XX, XXI.

11. For the Explanatory Circular for the Auschwitz Decree and Additional Decrees for the Alpen- and Donau-Reichsgaue, see Döring, op. cit., note 6 on p.156 and p.214 ff. and Thurner. Zigeuner in: DÖW (ed.). -*Widerstand und Verfolgung in Salzburg.* - Vienna, 1991.

12. More could be said about the different ideas of the Nazi party ideologists and officials as well as institutions such as the Rasse- und Siedlungshauptamt and SS-Ahnenerbe und Erbbiologische Forschungsstelle.

13. The sources suggest a prisoner complement of over 4,000. It is not known how many of the Lackenbach prisoners survived after deportation to other camps. At the end of March 1945 between 500 and 600 inmates were freed by the Red Army. For reparations see Steinmetz. *Zigeuner*, p.249; Thurner. - "Sinti und Roma wollen heute in Österreich leben" in: *Sturzflüge* 5/18.- Innsbruck, Feb. 1987, pp.53-63; Galanda, Brigitte. "Wiedergutmachung" in: Meissl, Sebastian and Klaus-Dieter Mulley. *Verdrängte Schuld, verfehlte Sühne, Entnazifierung in Österreich 1945-1955.* Vienna, 1986, pp.137-49.

14. Botz, Gerhard. Stufen der Ausgliederung der Juden aus der Gesellschaft in: *Zeitgeschichte* 14 Heft 9/10. Vienna/Salzburg, June/July 1987, pp.359-78; ibid. *Wohnungspolitik und Judendeportation in Wien 1938 bis 1945.* Vienna/Salzburg, 1975; Thurner *Nationalsozialismus*, p.59.

15. Botz. Stufen, pp.374-75.

196

III. The Internment of Gypsies in France
Marie-Christine Hubert

1. This study is based primarily on administrative documentation issued by the German authorities, mayors' offices, the Ministry of the Interior, the civilian police and military police, heads of internment camps and the Camps Inspectorate, housed at the National Archive in Paris and at regional archives (*Archives départementales*). The majority of these documents are not normally accessible to the general public, but can be consulted with special permission from the holding body; this is usually granted. Archival records are numerous, but incomplete.
2. Vaux de Foletier, François. - *Les Bohémiens en France au 19ème siècle*: Editions Jean-Claude Lattès, 1981. - p.180.
3. Challier, Félix. - *La nouvelle loi sur la circulation des nomades: loi du 16 juillet 1912*: Librairie de jurisprudence ancienne et moderne, 1913. - p.140.
4. Soulé-Limendoux, Henri. - *Ambulants, forains et nomades*: Imprimerie moderne, 1935. - p.79.
5. Delclitte, Christophe. - *Nomades et nomadisme: le cas de la France 1885-1912*, Master's Thesis in Political Science, Université de Paris VII, 1994. - p.81.
6. This legislation therefore bore no relevance to sedentary Gypsies, whom the French authorities did not see as a problem.
7. In the original, "*profession de commerçants ou industriels forains*". The weakness of the legislation stemmed from the fact that neither of the terms comprising category two was clearly defined, and was further complicated by category three covering, by default, those who did not fit into this nebulous classification.
8. This law remained on the statute books until 1969.
9. Vaux de Foletier, François. Op. cit., p.188.
10. Asséo, Henriette. - *Les Tsiganes : une destinée européenne*: Editions Gallimard Découvertes, 1994. - p.89.
11. Farcy, Jean-Claude. - *Les camps de concentration français de la Première Guerre Mondiale 1914-1920*: Editions Anthropos historiques, 1995. - p.63.
12. Farcy, Jean-Claude. Op. cit., p.100.
13. Farcy, Jean-Claude. Op. cit., p.65.
14. Indre-et-Loire regional archives, 4 M 221, September 16th 1939: correspondence between the mayor and the head of the local constabulary.
15. Indre-et-Loire regional archives, 4 M 218, October 22nd 1939.
16. "Metropolitan France" comprises the French mainland and Corsica.
17. The full texts of the decree of April 6th 1940 and of the circular of April 29th 1940 are available for consultation at the library of Etudes Tsiganes (2 rue d'Hautpoul, 75 019 Paris).
18. The text focuses on only two of these: the Occupied Zone and the Unoccupied, Free, or Southern (Vichy-run) Zone. The Coastal Zone – a mere ten to twenty kilometres wide, and administrationally an integral part of the Occupied Zone – is not indicated on this map. The remarks which follow are taken from Thalmann, Rita. - *La mise au pas. Idéologies et stratégies sécuritaires dans la France occupée*: Fayard, 1991.- pp.18-20.
19. Peschanski, Denis. - *Les Tsiganes en France 1939-1946* - Editions CNRS, 1994: p.41.
20. Bouches-du-Rhône regional archives, IV Y 4, Camp de Saliers.

21. Maximoff, Matéo. - *Dites-le avec des pleurs*: Editions Matéo Maximoff, 1993; *Routes sans roulottes*: Editions Matéo Maximoff, 1990.
22. National archives, 40 AJ 885/2.
23. Eure regional archives, 16 W 162.
24. National archives, 72 AJ 283, dossier A I N° 5, April 5th 1941, correspondence between General Von Stulpnagel and the General Delegate of the French Government to the Commandant of the Military Forces in France.
25. National archives, F^{1a} 3676. October 24th 1940, order of the district office.
26. Duméril, Edmond (with an introduction and annotations by Jean Bourgeon). - *Journal d'un honnête homme pendant l'Occupation juin 1940-août 1944*: Editions l'Albaron, 1990. - p.22.
27. National archives, 72 AJ 284. Maine-et-Loire.
28. Peschanski, Denis. Op. cit., p.28.
29. National archives, AJ^{40} 552 no.3.
30. In order to ensure the relaying of its directives the military administration set up four regional command structures, each with its own General acting as regional head, as follows: *Region A*: North-West (headquarters at Saint-Germain-en-Laye); *Region B*: South-West (headquarters at Angers); *Region C* (headquarters at Dijon) and Feldkommandantur Groß Paris (headquarters at Hôtel Meurice). The last-named included the *departments* of Seine-et-Marne and Seine-et-Oise until March 1941, when these were integrated into Region A.
31. National archives, 72 AJ 284, Maine-et-Loire, November 11th 1941, Proposals put forward by a high-ranking German official in Region B and reported by the mayor of Maine-et-Loire.
32. See Jacques Sigot's pioneering study. - *Un camp pour les Tsiganes... et les autres, Montreuil-Bellay 1940-1945*: Editions Wallada, 1983, 321 pp. Revised edition published 1994 under the title: *Ces barbelés oubliés par l'Histoire. Un camp pour les Tsiganes et les autres, Montreuil-Bellay 1940-1945*: Editions Wallada.
33. Mayenne regional archives, 265 W 2.
34. *The Secours National* (National Aid Agency) was set up by Marshal Pétain to assist persons experiencing health and/or social difficulties. It was equivalent to the Red Cross.
35. National archives, F^7 15312. Report by André Jean-Faure.
36. National archives, F^7 15100. March 9th 1942, Moisdon-la-Rivière camp, report by Doctor Aujaleu.
37. Yonne regional archives, 1 W 527. December 15th 1944.
38. Peschanski, Denis. Op. cit., p.64.
39. National archives, F^7 15106. Sarthe, 23 April 23rd 1941.
40. Yvelines regional archives, 300 W 81/1. Montlhéry camp 1940-42. The head of this camp was a police superintendent.
41. *L'Oribus* no.29, 1989, p.21. *L'Oribus* is a periodical; issue 29, under the title "Fils du vent et des barbelés", was entirely devoted to coverage of the internment of Gypsies in France.
42. National archives, 72 AJ 119. Doubs, May 8th 1942. Memo from the mayor.
43. The Todt Organisation was set up in 1940 by Fritz Todt, a German, General Director for Roads and Bridges, Minister with Responsibility for the Provisioning of Land Troops with Arms and Munitions and General Counsellor on Construction.

The organisation was responsible for constructing the fortifications and U-boat shelters of the Atlantic Wall, and for road construction and maintenance in the occupied territories from northern Norway to the south of France, as well as in Russia. It used local labour, either voluntary or requisitioned at the initiative of local Feldkommandanten. It employed a total of 217,000 in August 1941; by October 1942 this number had increased to 742,000. Speer, Albert. - *Au cœur du Troisième Reich*: Editions Fayard, 1971. Desmaret, Jacques. - *La politique de la main d'œuvre en France*: Editions P.U.F, 1946. - pp.176-77.

44. Evrard, Jacques. - *Histoire du STO : la déportation des travailleurs français dans le Troisième Reich*: Editions Fayard, 1972. - pp.70-77.

45. Pierre Laval, 1883-1945. French politician, head of the Vichy Government from 1942; shot for high treason by the post-War French government.

46. Evrard, Jacques. Op. cit., p.75.

47. Yonne regional archives, I W 509, February 27th 1943. Camp director's monthly report.

48. Yonne regional archives, I W 509, October 1943. Camp director's monthly report.

49. Loiret regional archives, 34 105, September 11th 1942. Correspondence between the German authorities and the mayor.

50. Vienne regional archives, 104 W 3, March 2nd 1943. Camp director's monthly report.

51. Oranienburg-Sachsenhausen Association. - *Sachso*: Editions Minuit / Plon, Terre humaine Collection, 1995. - p.40.

52. National archives, 72 AJ 286. Compiègne, report read by Mr. Lebosse to the War History Commission on November 23rd 1955. - *Mes prisons: Montluc, Fresnes, Romainville, Compiègne*, pages not numbered.

53. Yvelines regional archives, 300 W 81/1. Montlhéry camp 1940-42.

54. Berstein, Serge and Milza, Pierre. - *Histoire de la France au XXᵉ siècle*: Editions Complexe, 1995. - p.642.

55. National archives, F 3311. Internment of procurers, prostitutes and nomads.

56. Ibid.

57. Ibid.

58. Yonne regional archives, 3 M 15/26.

59. "Itinéraire exemplaire d'un Tsigane ordinaire", in *La Nouvelle République du Centre-Ouest* (local newspaper), Thursday April 5th 1991. The distance from Jargeau to Poitiers is some 400 km.

60. *Memorial Book, The Gypsies at Auschwitz-Birkenau*: Published by the State Museum of Auschwitz-Birkenau, KG Saur, 2 volumes, 1647 pp.

61. Gotovicht, José. - "Quelques données relatives à l'extermination des Tsiganes de Belgique" in *Cahiers d'Histoire de la Seconde Guerre Mondiale*. - Brussels, 1976.- pp.161-80.

62. Gotovicht, José. Op. cit., p.165.

63. *Liste des personnes arrêtées par l'autorité occupante en tant qu'Israélites ou Tziganes et déportées par les convois partis du camp de rassemblement de Malines entre le 4 août 1942 et le 31 juillet 1944*, published by the Belgian Ministry for Public Health and the Family, War Victims Commission, July 1st 1971, 6 volumes.

64. Z for Zigeuner – Gypsy.

65. Gotovicht, José. Op. cit., p.165.

66. Ibid.
67. Op. cit., p.168.
68. Ibid.
69. Op. cit., p.175.
70. As nomads frequently had no identity papers, it was common for them to be assigned different nationalities by the authorities.
71. Maine-et-Loire regional archives, 12 W 65.
72. There exists some doubt as to an additional four names.
73. Gotovicht, José. Op. cit., p.174.
74. Wormser-Migot, Olga. - *Le système concentrationnaire nazi 1933-1944*: Editions P.U.F., 1968. - pp.33-34.
75. Ducroquet, P. - *Statistiques de la déportation dans le department du Nord 1940-1944*. Committee of the Second World War, 1960, Table II. Breakdown by profession, no.23: Gypsies.
76. The German authorities found French legislation unsatisfactory in its restrictiveness. The offices of the field Commanders repeatedly reminded mayors that the "nomad" category "generally included caravan-dwellers displaying the ethnic characteristics particular to *Romanichels*" (National archives AJ[40] 885, no.2, *Zigeuner*, folio 3) and that nomads were "persons of the nomadic race, subject to the Nuremberg Laws" (Loiret regional archives: 34 105, September 11th 1942, letter from the Security Police to the local mayor).

IV. The Bulgarian Romanies during World War II
Elena Marushiakova and Vesselin Popov

1. For more details about the history of the Gypsies in Bulgarian lands see: Marushiakova, E. / Popov, V. - *Roma (gypsies) in Bulgaria*.- Frankfurt am main: Peter Lang Verlag, 1997.
2. Marushiakova, E. - "La religion et son role d'intégration et de ségrégation chez les Tsiganes" in *Etudes Tsiganes*, vol. 38, No.2 1992. - pp.31-37.
3. The Office of Strategic Services (the forerunner of the Central Intelligence Agency – CIA) Report on "Population Development of Bulgaria" written October 20th 1944. It shows data assembled about conditions in 1943. In: *Fifty Years Ago. Revolt Amid the Darkness. Days of Remembrance April 18-25, 1993*. Washington: U.S. Holocaust Memorial Museum, pp.255-65.
4. Newspaper *Dnes*, 13-14 August 1943; newspaper *Dnevnik*, 26 July 1943.
5. Newspaper *Dnes*, 16 August 1943; newspaper *Vecher*, 25 August 1943.
6. Newspaper *Tsiganite*, no.5, 17 March 1993.
7. Manush Romanov (formerly called Mustafa Aliev and Lubomir Aliev), a Sofia Gypsy and famous Gypsy activist in the 1940s and 50s, a theatre director. After the changes in 1990-91 he was member of parliament, an organiser and leader of one of the four national Gypsy organisations in Bulgaria – The Democratic Union of Roma.
8. Newspaper *Podkrepa*, no.25, 18 September 1990.
9. Marushiakova, E. / Popov, V (eds). - *Studii Romani*. Vol. I, Sofia, 1994, p.61.
10. Genov, D. / Tairov, T. and Marinov, V. - *Tsiganite v Bulgaria po patia na socialisma* [The Gypsy Population in Bulgaria on the way to Socialism]. - Sofia, 1968.

200

V. Gypsy deportations from Romania to Transnistria 1942-44
Michelle Kelso

ASB   Bucharest State Archives (Archivele Statului din Bucuresti)
IGJ   General Inspector of Constabulary (Inspectorat General al Jandarmeriei)
PCM   Presidency of the Council of Ministers (Presedintia Consilului de Ministri)
USHMM   United States Holocaust Memorial Museum

Unless otherwise specified, the English translations of Romanian sources in this chapter are the author's.

In the text "*jandarme*" has been translated "*constable*" and "*Prefect*" as "*Mayor*". The Prefect was a centrally appointed official responsible for a regional zone called a *prefetura*.

1.   A few of the historic and ethnographic works are: Kogalniceanu, Mihai. - *Desrobirea Tiganilor, stergerea privilegilor boieresti, emanciparea taranilor*: Editura Academiei RSR, 1976; Potra, G. - *Contributuini la istoricul Tiganilor din Romania*. Fundatia Regele Carol I, 1939; Ion Chelcea. - *Tiganii din Romania*: Editura Institutului Central de Statistica, 1944.
2.   See for example: Hillgruber, Andreas. - *Hitler, Regele Carol, si Maresalul Antonescu*: Humanitas, 1994; Watts, Larry. - *Romanian, Cassandra: Ion Antonescu and the Struggle for Reform 1916-1941*: Columbia University Press, 1993. Fisher-Galati, Stephen. - "*National Minorities in Romania 1919-1980: A Handbook*. Littleton: Libraries Unlimited, 1985, pp.190-215.
3.   Andreas Hillgruber. - *Hitler, Regele Carol, si Marsesalul Antonescu*: Humanitas, 1994, pp.47-48.
4.   ASB, Sabin Manuila XII 209, pp.1-3.
5.   ASB, IGJ, 121/1942, pp.5-7; 126/1942, pp.7-8.
6.   Ciuca, Marcel-Dumitru. - *Procesul Maresalului Antonescu Documente II*, Saeculum I.O., 1995, p.176.
7.   ASB, PCM, 42/1942, p.2.
8.   Ibid.
9.   Ibid., p.16.
10.   Ibid., p.6.
11.   Constables functioned as a rural police securing order in villages and small towns.
12.   ASB, IGJ, 13/1942.
13.   Ibid., p.32.
14.   ASB, PCM, 292/1941, p.3.
15.   Debate inside and outside of academic circles rages over Antonescu's willingness to deport the Jews. Moral implications aside, examination of correspondance between the two leaders illustrates a definite hesitancy on Antonescu's part to comply with German wishes to deport the Jews.
16.   ASB, PCM, 313/1941, pp.5-7.
17.   ASB, PCM, 156/1942, pp.1-4.
18.   ASB, PCM, 156/1942, p.2.

19. Ibid.
20. ASB, IGJ, 59/1942, p.359. Note: this is a copy of a decree.
21. Ibid.
22. ASB, IGJ, 95/1940, p.413.
23. ASB, IGJ, 130/1942, p.23.
24. ASB, IGJ, 127/1942, p.251.
25. Ibid., p.252.
26. ASB, IGJ, 130/1942, p.1.
27. Ioanid, Radu. - *Evreii sub Regimul Antonescu*. - Bucaresti: Editura Hasefer, 1977 - pp. 316-21.
28. ASB, IGJ, 130/1942, p.1.
29. Ibid, p.2.
30. Ibid.
31. ASB, IGJ, 126/1942, p.26.
32. Ibid.
33. Ibid.
34. Ibid., p.38.
35. ASB, IGJ, 126/1942, p.32.
36. Ibid.
37. Ibid., p.38.
38. ASB, IGJ, 126/1942, p.10.
39. Ibid., pp.61-62.
40. Ibid., pp.125-27.
41. Author's interview with Gheorghe Potcoava, August 1996.
42. ASB, IGJ, 126/1942, p.209.
43. Ibid., p.205.
44. Ibid., pp.213-14.
45. Ibid.
46. ASB, IGJ, 126/1942, p.233.
47. ASB, IGJ 166/1942, p.171, p.163.
48. ASB, IGJ, 121/1942, pp.336-37.
49. ASB, IGJ, 130/1942, pp.127-31.
50. ASB, IGJ, 43/1943, pp.260-62.
51. See note 27.
52. Author's interview with Ion Neagu, Romania, June 1995.
53. Author's interview with Constantina Pitigoi, June 1995.
54. Author's interview with Vasile Ionita, Romania, June 1995.
55. ASB, IGJ, 130/1942, p.118.
56. Ibid., p.117.
57. ASB, IGJ, 59/1942, p.305.
58. Author's interview with Ion Neagu, Romania, June 1995.
59. ASB, IGJ, 60/1943, p.116.
60. ASB, IGJ 130/1942, p.83.
61. Ibid., p.84.
62. ASB, IGJ, 130/1942, p.516.
63. Ibid., p.328.
64. Ibid., p.332.

65. Ibid., p.331.
66. ASB, IGJ, 130/1942, p.335.
67. Ibid., p.322-23.
68. ASB, IGJ, 77/1943, pp.47-48.
69. ASB, IGJ, 130/1942, pp.121-23.
70. Ibid.
71. Ibid.
72. Many local authorities wrote that unmarried women living with men should not be repatriated as this constituted low morality. They distinguished between "concubina" (a woman co-habitating with a man) and "nevasta/sotia" (wife) in their reports. Gypsies, however, classified a woman "wife" if she was married according to Gypsy custom, irrespective of a union's legality under Romanian law.
73. See note 27.
74. Author's interview with Rupita Gheorghe, Romania, August 1995, in collaboration with the USHMM.
75. ASB, IGJ, 59/1942, p.38.
76. Ibid, p.39.
77. Author's interview with Ion Neagu, Romania, June 1995.
78. ASB, IGJ, 130/1942, pp.530-31.
79. Ibid.
80. Ibid.
81. Ibid.
82. ASB, IGJ, 130/1942, pp.530-31.
83. Ibid, p.587.
84. Watts, Larry. - *Romanian Cassandra: Ion Antonescu and the Struggle for Reform 1916-1941*: Columbia University Press, 1993. - p.340.
85. Ibid.
86. ASB, IGJ, 86/1944, p.226.
87. Regional officers corrected this by adding "and non-nomads" when communicating instructions to the village constables.
88. ASB, IGJ, 86/1944, p.226.
89. Ibid.
90. Ibid., p.97.
91. Ibid., p.95.
92. ASB, IGJ, 86/1944, p.95.
93. Ibid., p.96.
94. Ion Gheorghe. - *Un Dictator Nefericit: Maresal Antonescu*: Machiavelli, 1996. - pp.333-39.
95. King Michael is Carol II's son, who was coronated after his father's abdication but did not actively participate in government from 1940-
96. Hillgruber, Andreas. - *Hitler, Regele Carol si Maresalul Antonescu: Relatiile Germano-Romane 1938-1944*: Humanitas, 1994.- p.260-61.
97. Author's interviews with survivors.
98. Romania granted German soldiers passage to German-controlled territory and many traversed the same paths as fleeing Gypsies.
99. Author's interview with Vasile Gheorghe, August 1995.
100. ASB, IGJ, 86/1944, p.295.

101. ASB, IGJ, 97/1944.
102. Ciuca, Marcel-Dumitru. - *Procesul Maresalului Antonescu Documente I.* Saeculum I.O., 1995. - p.1.
103. Ibid., p.17.

VI. The Soviet Union and the Baltic States 1941-44
Michael Zimmermann

1. Krausnick H. / H-H. Wilhelm. - *Die Truppen des Weltanschauungskrieges: Die Einsatzgruppen der Sicherheitspolizei und des SD 1938-1942.* - Stuttgart, 1981.- pp.141-50; Hilberg R. - *Die Vernichtung der europäischen Juden. Die Gesamtgeschichte des Holocaust* - Berlin, 1982. - p.208 f.
2. Ogorreck R. - *Die Einsatzgruppen und die "Genesis der Endlösung".* - Berlin, 1996.- pp.47-56, pp.161-75, pp.179-83, pp.217-22.
3. IfZ (Institut für Zeitgeschichte, Munich), MA 701/1, BdS, EK 3, Kauen 1.12.1941, Gesamtaufstellung der im Bereich des EK3 bis zum 1.12.1941 durchgeführte Exekutionen (Summary of executions), Bl. 31; BA (Bundesarchiv) Koblenz, R 58/217, EM (Ereignismeldung) 92, 23.9.1941, Bl. 299.
4. ND (Nuremberg Document) Fall IX, Nr. A 6-8, Bl. 669.
5. Krausnick ibid., p.158; ND Fall IX Nr.A 6-8, Bl.669-673.
6. ND-NOKW 2072 (281 Sicherungsdivision 23.6.1942); BA (Bundesarchiv) Koblenz R 58-217 EM 93, 24.9.1941; ZS (Zentralstelle der Landesjustizverwaltungzn Ludwigsburg) AR-Z 96/60, 81 1892-1894; EM 92, 23.9.1941, Bl.299; BA Koblenz, R 58-218; EM 119, 20.10.1941 Bl.239; ZS AR 72 a/60 Bl.34.
7. BA Koblenz, R 58-218, EM 119, 20.10.1941 Bl.239.
8. ZS, AR 72 a/60 Bl.34-36.
9. IfZ, Ge 01.05, 29 Ks 1/64/22 (7/63), Bl.93 ff.
10. IfZ, MA 701/1, BdS (Befehlhaber der Sicherheitspolizei), EK (Einsatzkommando) 3, Kauen 1.12.1941, Gesamtaufstellung der im Bereich des EK 3 bis zum 1. Dezember 1941 durchgeführten Exekutionen, Bl. 31; BA Koblenz, R 58/219 EM 150 2.1.1942, Bl. 364; BA Koblenz, R 58/221, EM 181, 16.3.1942 Bl. 90; BA Koblenz, R 58/221, EM 195, 24.4.1942, Bl. 402.
11. BA Koblenz, R 58/217, EM 92, 23.9.1941, Bl.299; BA Koblenz, R 58/221 EM 194, 21.4.1942, Bl.381 & 187ff.; ZS, AR-Z 96/60 Bl.1892-94, EG B 1.9.1942, Tätigkeits- und Lagebericht für die Zeit vom 16.8.-31.8.1942 (Action and situation report) Bl.1893; BA Koblenz, R 58/221, EM 194, 21.4.1942, Bl.382; ZS, AR 72 a/60, Bl.34-36; Kenrick D. / Puxon. G. - *Sinti und Roma, Die Vernichtung eines Volkes im NS-Staat.* - Göttingen, 1981.- p.104 (English title *The Destiny of Europe's Gypsies*).
12. BA Koblenz, R 58/217, EM 93, 24.9.1941, Bl. 321.
13. BA Koblenz, R 58/218, EM 119, 20.10.1941, Bl. 239.
14. ZS, AR 936/72 Bl. 8 ff.
15. BA Koblenz, R 70 Sowjetunion/15 Bl 69.
16. BA Koblenz, R58/218, EM 124, 25.10.1941 Bl. 300; ib. R 58/219, EM 148, 19.12.1941, Bl. 34; ibid. R 58/220, EM 172, 23.2.1942 Bl.416.
17. BA Koblenz, R 58/218, EM 111, 12.10.1941 Bl. 147 f.

18. BA Koblenz, R58/219, EM 135, 19.11.1941, Bl. 47-152 and EM 143, 8.12.1941, Bl.256-59.
19. BA Koblenz R 58/217, EM 93, 24.9.1941, Bl. 321.
20. ZS, AR-Z 96/60, Bl. 895ff.
21. Thus Einsatzgruppe C, BA Koblenz, R 58/218, EM 128, 3.11.1941, Bl.341.
22. BA Koblenz, R 58/217, EM 92, 23.9.1941 Bl. 299; ZS, AR 72 a/60 Bl. 34-36; IfZ, MA 701/1 BdS, EK 3, Kauen 1.12.1941 Bl. 31; BA Koblenz, R 58/219, EM 150, 2.1.1942, Bl. 364; ibid. R 58/218 EM 119, 20.10.1941, Bl. 239.
23. Hilberg, ibid., p.210f., 225f., 227.
24. ND Fall IX, Nr. A 6-8 Bl. 669-72; ND-NOKW 2072 (281 Sicherungsdivision 23.6.1942).
25. Krausnick, ibid., p.150-72.
26. This fantasy also had an extraordinary influence on the German army (ibid., p.217-23).
27. ND Fall IX, Nr. A 6-8 Bl. 672.
28. BA Koblenz, R 58/219, EM 150, 2.1.1942, Bl. 378. For the Krimchaks see Hilberg, op. cit., p.261
29. BA Koblenz, R 58/219, EM 145, 12.12.1941, Bl. 290.
30. BA Koblenz, R 58/220, EM 165, 6.2.1942, Bl. 316 and EM 170, 18.2.1942, Bl. 385; ibid. R 58/221, EM 178, 9.3.1942, Bl. 64; id. R 58/221, EM 184, 23.3.1942, Bl. 130 and EM 190, 8.4.1942, Bl. 268.
31. BA Koblenz, R 58/221 EM 190, 8.4.1942, Bl. 267; ND Fall IX, A 9, 81, 688.
32. For the murder of the Gypsies in Simferopol see ND Fall IX, A 54-55, Bl. 4761-85. The quote is from Bl. 4770.
33. IfZ, Ge 01.05, 29 Ks 1/64/ 22(7/63). Bl. 3ff.
34. Ibid.
35. ND Fall IX, A 54-55, Bl. 4761- 86.
36. Krausnick, ibid., p.217-78; Hilberg ibid., p.216-28.
37. The Order (Kdr.Gen.v.21.11.1941 - VII 1045/41-) is mentioned in the following documents: ND-NOKW 2077 (281 Sicherungsdivision 23.6.1942); ND-NOKW 2022 (281 Sicherungsdivision 24.3.43).
38. ND-NOKW 2072 (281 Sicherungsdivision 23.6.1942); ND-NOKW 2022 (281 Sicherungsdivision 24.3.1943).
39. Hilberg, ibid., p.248; Krausnick, ibid., pp.322-32.
40. Hilberg, ibid., pp.146-49, 212f., 262; Krausnick, ibid., pp.173-205; for Einsatzgruppe A ibid., pp.281-93, "Unterstellungsverhältnisse im Bereich von SS und Polizei im Nordraum (1942), ibid., p.637.
41. Lichtenstein H. - *Himmlers grüne Helfer. Die Schutz- und Ordnungspolizei im "Dritten Reich"*. - Cologne 1990; Krausnick, ibid., pp.167-70.
42. Krausnick, ibid., p.167-70; Hilberg, ibid. p.263f.; ZS, AR 871/63 Bl. 645ff.
43. For the order to kill Gypsies see ZS, AR 871/63 Bl.668-71.
44. ND-NO 5654, Jacob's letter 5.5.1942.
45. ND-NO 5665, Jacob's letter 21.6.1942.
46. ZS, AR-Z 871/63.
47. ZS, AR 8/80,81.87 with an example for 1944.
48. *Justiz und NS-Verbrechen*, vol.XIX. Amsterdam 1978, Nr.552, p.186ff., Landgericht Koblenz 21.5.1963, 9 Ks 2/62., KdS Minsk, p.257.
49. ZS, AR-Z 871/63 Bl. 669.

50. ZS, AR-Z 497/67 Bd. i Bl. 130.

51. ZS, AR-Z 497/67 Bd. II Bl. 139 HSSPF (Höherer SS- und Polizeiführer für das Ostland) 12.1.1942, Betr.: Zigeunerfrage, signed on his behalf by Jedicke (Generalleutnant der Polizei und SS-Gruppenführer).

52. ZS, AR-Z 497/67, Bd.II Bl.131; also BA Koblenz R 90/147 Bl.714 Abt.II Gesundheit u. Volkspflege II e Az.1 F, 4.12.1941, an den Höheren und Polizeiführer in Riga, signed Lohse.

53. ZS, AR-Z 497/67 Bd. II Bl.139, HSSPF für das Ostland 12.1.1942; BdO (Befehlshaber der Ordnungspolizei) für das Ostland 13.1.1942 an die KdO (Kommandeure der Ordnungspolizei) Litauen; KdO Litauen 21.1.1942, an Kommandeur der Schutzpolizei in Kauen, Kommandeur der Gendarmerie in Litauen in Kauen, SS- und Polizeistandortführer in Wilna; ibid. Bl.140 with the request of the SS- und Polizeistandortführers Libau to the SSPF Lettland 10.2.1942 concerning "Zusendung einer Abschrift der Anordnung des HSSPF f.d. Ostland v.12. I 42A z I a".

54. For the socio-psychological aspects see Browning C.R. - *Ganz normale Männer. Das Reserve-Polizeibataillon 101 und die "Endlösung" in Polen* - Reinbek, 1993. - pp.105-13.

55. ZS, AR-Z 497/67 Bl. 143: Auszugweise Abschrift an den SSPF Lettland, 19.1.1942.

56. This arises from a report of the KdO in Latvia, Karl Friedrich Knecht of 3.4.1942 (ZS, AR-Z 497/67 Bl.144, SSPF Lettland KdO. 1 a Nr. 800/42, 3.4.1942, Betrifft: Zigeunerfrage. Bezug: Meine Verfügung v. 11.3.1942).

57. BA Koblenz, 90/147, Bl.716-718, Reichskommissariat Ostland II Pol.St./Li.,an RMfbO, 2.7.1942, Betrifft: Zigeuner im Ostland.

58. Ibid. Bl.716. For the composition of the Latvian and Kurlandish Romanies see Kochanowski V. - *Some Notes on the Gypsies of Latvia* in: JGLS (*Journal of the Gypsy Lore Society* (3rd series) vol. xxv (1946) pts 1-2, pp.34-38, in particular pp.34-36, and pts 3-4, pp.112-16.

59. Ibid., pp.113-15.

60. ZS, AR-Z 497/67 Bl. 195-200, the statement of Dr Walter Alnor, former Commissioner for the Libau area 19.8.1969. Although the statement undoubtedly includes elements of denial, it seems reliable on the point in question. Whether Alnor adequately describes his role in the prevention of the killing is debatable.

61. ZS, AR-Z 497/67 Bl.143 f.

62. For Valmiyera ZS, AR-Z 101/67 especially p.231ff (testimony of Albert Karlowitsch) p.291ff. (testimony of Albert Belini); for Ayzpute ZS, AR-Z 497/67 p.149 (Kriegstagebuch des SS- und Polizeistandortführers Libau, entry for 21.5.1942); for Yelgava ZS, AR-Z 497/67 p.150f. and Abschlussbericht, p.11; for Bauska, p.159f. and Abschlussbericht, p.12; for Tukums p.157 and Abschlussbericht, p.11.

63. For Riga see ZS, AR-Z 497/67 esp. p.164 (testimony of Koslowskaja); for Valka see ZS, AR-Z 101/67 esp. p.127 (testimony of Brasmanis).

64. BA Koblenz, R 90/147, Bl.716-718, Reichskommissariat Ostland II Po.St./Li., to RMfbO 2.7.1942 Betrifft: Zigeuner im Ostland, p.716. According to this the number of Gypsies in Latvia in 1935 was 3,839.

65. In Kochanowski's articles we find some reference to the making of a distinction

between sedentary and nomadic Gypsies. According to Kochanowski, after the killing of the Romanies in Ludza, he went to the General Commissioner of Ostland in Riga and there lodged a bitter complaint that innocent people were being slaughtered. The Nazi in charge replied with a leer, "if you cannot prove to me that an adequate number of Gypsies are decent hardworking folk you will, every one of you, be exterminated. So with the collaboration of our own chief Janis Lejmanis, said Kochanowski, he began to compile a register of "honest Gypsies". (Kochanowski op. cit. p.114). It is not clear whom Kochanowski may have spoken to – with the Reichskommissariat Ostland, the Generalkommissariat Lettland or representatives of the SS and Police. For Lejmanis see Kochanowski, ibid., p.35 and p.114 as well as BA Koblenz R 90/147, p.716-18, Reichskommissariat Ostland II Pol.St./Li., an RMfbO 2.7.1942, betrifft: Zigeuner im Ostland, p.718.

66. BA Koblenz, R 90/147 Bl.704. Letter from eleven Frauenburg Gypsies. 12.3.1942 to "Herrn Hochwohlgeehrten Reichskommissar (Abschrift dem Herrn Hochwohlgeehrten Gebietskommissar Libau)". The forbidding of movement is documented not only for the Gypsies of Frauenburg but also for those from Talsen (BA Koblenz R 90/90 Schreiben Generaldirektion für Bildungs- und Kulturwesen 22.1.1943 an den Referenten für Schulangelegenheiten beim Generalkommissar in Riga; I Kult. S.10, 27.1.1943 an den Generaldirektor des Bildungs- und Kulturwesens, Riga; Schreiben an den Gebietskommissar in Libau 23.1.1943; ZS, AR-7 497/67 Bl.195-200, Aussage Dr Walter Alnor). Kochanowski says that after the shootings of summer 1942 he met Romanies in Dvinsk (Dünaberg), Riga, Tukums and Ragaciems, ibid., p.115.

67. *Der Prozess gegen die Hauptkriegsverbrecher vor dem Internationalen Militärgerichtshof Nürnberg 14. November 1945 - 1. Oktober 1946.* Nuremberg 1949. Bd.VIII, p.345 (English edition; *Trials of the Major War Criminals before the International Military Tribunal.*)

68. BA Koblenz, R 90/90. Schreiben Generaldirektion für Bildungs- und Kulturwesen, 22.1.1943; I Kult. p.10, 27.1.1943, an den Generaldirektor des Bildungs- und Kulturwesens, Riga; Schreiben an den Gebietskommissar in Libau, 23.1.1943.

69. BA Koblenz, R 90/147 Bl.704. Letter from eleven Frauenburg Gypsies. 12.3.1942.

70. Ibid.

71. IfZ, Fb 104/2 with a list of the Gypsies who were "specially treated". See also Krausnick op. cit., p.416 and BA Koblenz R90/147 Bl.755, D.R.f.d.O. Abt.IIIASO4G 701 1(1)Arbeitsgruppe Sozialversicherung, 23.10.1943 an die Abt. I Politik.

72. ZS, AR-Z 497/67 Bd. II Bl. 139, HSSPF für das Ostland 12.1.1942, Betr.: Zigeunerfrage, signed on his behalf by Jedicke 131.1.1942, to the SSPF-KdO Litauen, 21.1.1942, Kommandeur der Schutzpolizei in Kauen, Kommandeur der Gendarmerie in Litauen in Kauen, SS- und Polizeistandortführer in Wilna.

73. See however the comment in Kenrick/Puxon op. cit., p.102, concerning a transport to Auschwitz.

74. BA Koblenz, R 90/147, RMfdbO 11.6.1942 an den Reichskommissar Ostland.

75. BA Koblenz R 90/147 Bl.716-718, Reichskommissariat Ostland II Pol.St./Li., an RMfbO 2.7.1942, betrifft: Zigeuner in Ostland.

76. ND-PS 1133, Schreiben an Oberstleutnant Skowronek, Oberkommando des Heeres 31.7.1942.

77. Ibid.
78. BA Koblenz, R 90/147, Bl. 720f., RMfdbO 21.5.1943 Nr. I 925/43.
79. BA Koblenz, R 90/147 Bl. 753, BdS Ostland, 19.10.1943, Abt. V a 2 Tgb. 873/43G.
80. IfZ, MA 798, Bl.1402; Staatliches Museum Auschwitz-Birkenau (eds). - *Gedenkbuch. Die Sinti und Roma im Konzentrationslager Auschwitz-Birkenau.* - Munich/London/New York/Paris, 1993. - p.724-27. Register for the Gypsy camp (women) Nos 10,828-10,849.
81. For Volhynia see Ficowski J. - *The Polish Gypsies of Today* in *JGLS* (3rd series) vol. xxix (1950) pts 3-4, pp.92-102 (espec. p.92); for the Soviet Union except the Baltic, see Kenrick and Puxon. op. cit., p.135 (*The Destiny of Europe's Gypsies*, p.150).

Select bibliography

Note: This bibliography contains only books dealing with the topics covered in this volume and which have not already been listed in the bibliogaphy to the first volume *"From "Race Science" to the Camps, The Gypsies during the Second World War 1"*.

General

ALT Betty / FOLTS Silvia. - *Weeping violins: the Gypsy tragedy in Europe.* - Missouri: Thomas Jefferson University Press, 1996.

GILSENBACH Reimar. - "Die Verfolgung der Sinti - ein Weg, der nach Auschwitz führte. Vortrag zum Symposium Viereinhalb Jahre. Auschwitz 1940-1945!". In: *Feinderklärung und Prävention.* - Berlin: Rotbuch-Verlag,1988. - pp. 10-41.

GILSENBACH Reimar. - "Wie Lolitschai zur Doktorwurde kam. Ein akademisches Kapitel aus dem Völkermord an den Sinti". In: *Feinderklärung und Prävention.* - Berlin: Rotbuch-Verlag, 1988. - pp. 10 -134.

HOHMANN Joachim. -*Verfolgte ohne Heimat.* - Frankfurt am Main: Peter Lang, 1981.

ZIMMERMANN Michael. - *Verfolgt, vertrieben, vernichtet. Die Vernichtungspolitik gegen Sinti und Roma.* - Essen: Klartext Verlag, 1989.

ZIMMERMANN Michael. - *Rassenutopie und Genozid. Die nationalsozialistische "Lösung der Zigeunerfrage",* Hamburg, 1996.

Austria

STEINMETZ Selma. - *Österreichs Zigeuner im NS Staat.* - Vienna / Frankfurt / Zurich: Europa Verlag, 1966.

STOJKA Ceija. - *Reisenden auf dieser Welt. Aus dem Leben einer Rom-Zigeunerin.* - Vienna: Edited by Karin Berger, Picus, 1988.

STOJKA Ceija. - *Wir leben im Verborgenen. Erinnerungen einer Rom-Zigeunerin.* - Vienna: Edited by Karin Berger, Picus, 1991.

STOJKA Karl. - *A childhood in Birkenau.* - Washington: United States Holocaust Memorial Museum, 1992.

THURNER Erika. - "Nationalsozialismus und Zigeuner in Österreich". In: *Veröffentlichungen zur Zeitgeschichte Österreichs 2.* - Vienna / Salzburg, 1983. (English translation to appear as *Nazi-Fascism and Roma in Austria.* Tennessee, University of Knoxville.)

Bulgaria

MARUSHIAKOVA Elena / POPOV Vesselin. - *Ciganite v Bâlgarija*. - Sofia: Club 90, 1993. (English translation: *The Gypsies of Bulgaria*. - Frankfurt: Peter Lang, 1996.)

Czech lands

NEĆAS Ctibor. - *Andr'oda taboris. 1942-43*. - Brno: Masarykova University, 1987.

NEĆAS Ctibor. - *Ćeskoslovenśti Romové v Letech 1939-1945*. - Brno: Masarykova University, 1995.

NEĆAS Ctibor. - *Nemůžeme zapomenout, Našťi bisteras*. - Olomouc: University Palackeho, 1994.

France

BERNADAC Christian. - *L'Holocauste oublié. Le massacre des Tsiganes*. - Paris: Ed. France Empire, 1979.

PESCHANSKI Denis. - *Les Tsiganes en France 1939-1946*. - Paris: Editions CNRS, 1994.

SIGOT Jacques. - *Ces barbelés oubliés par l'Histoire. Un camp pour les Tsiganes et les autres. Montreuil-Bellay 1940-1945*. - Bordeaux: Wallada, 1983.

Italy

BOURSIER Giovanna / CONVERSO Massimo / IACOMINI Fabio. - *Zigeuner, Lo sterminio dimenticato*. - Rome: Sinnon, 1996.

KARPATI Mirella. - *Zingari ieri e oggi*. - Rome: Centro Studi Zingari, 1993.

MASSERINI Annemaria. - *Storia dei nomadi. La persecuzione degli zingari nel XX secolo*. - Padua: GB edizioni, 1990.

Romania

REMMEL Franz. - *Die Roma Rumäniens. Volk ohne Hinterland*. - Vienna: Picus, 1993.

USSR

NEILANDS Janis. "Lo Sterminio dei Roma in Lettonia". In: *Lacio Drom*. Nr. 1, 1995. - pp. 13-14.

Materials for teaching the Holocaust

Textbooks and reference books for pupils:

BROOMAN Josh. - *A Sense of History. The Era of the Second World War*. - London: Longman, 1993.

SUPPLE Carrie. - *From Prejudice to Genocide: Learning about the Holocaust*. - Stoke on Trent: Trentham Books, 1993.

Reference books for teachers:
BURLEIGH Michael / WIPPERMANN Wolfgang. - *The Racial State. Germany 1933-45*. - Cambridge: The University Press, 1991.

Teachers' resource packs:
Spiro Institute. - *Lessons of the Holocaust*. - London, 1998.

List of illustrations

p. 68   Diagram of internment camps for Gypsies internees at the Rivesaltes camp, 1940-46. From Hubert Marie-Christine. - Doctoral thesis, *Les tsiganes en France 1939-1946*, 1987.

p. 69   Numbers of nomads interned in France, 1940-46. From Hubert Marie-Christine. Ibid.

p. 71   French interment camps for nomads, 1940-46. Part of a map made by Jo Saville for the Association des Enfants Cachés, France, edition no. 8, March 1998.

p. 72   Plan of Moisdon-la-Rivière camp. National Archive, Paris: F 72AJ283AI2: January 27th 1941.

p. 73   Camp at Saint-Maurice-aux-Riches-Hommes (Yonne). The camp was set up in the courtyard of the disused village railway station at Saint-Maurice. National Archive, Paris: F^7 15 110: 1942.

p. 74   Main entrance to the Route de Limoges Camp at Poitiers (Haute-Vienne department). National Archive, Paris: F^7 15 109: January 1942.

p. 75   Barracks set aside for interned nomads, Poitiers (Haute-Vienne department). National Archive F^7 15 109: January 1942.

p. 76   The camp at Montreuil-Bellay (Maine-et-Loire department) in 1944. From Peschanski, Denis: *Les Tsiganes en France 1939-1946*. - Paris: Editions CNRS, 1994. Jacques Sigot Archives.

p. 77   Interior of a barracks at Mérignac camp (Gironde department). National Archive: F^7 15 099: February 1942.

p. 80   Interned children playing in front of the school building at Jargeau camp From Peschanski Denis. - op. cit. 1994. Archive of the Centre for Research and Documentation on Internment Camps and Jewish Déportation, Orléans (Loiret).

p. 84   Jean-Louis Bauer's political internee's identity card. Courtesy of Jacques Sigot Archives.

p. 96   Map of Transnistria. Courtesy of Art Expo, Bucharest.

p. 99   Percentage of Gypsies as compared to the total population in Romania by region from the 1930 census, compiled by the Central Institute of Statistics. Courtesy of the Bucharest State Archives.

p. 99   The number of Gypsies by province in rural and urban areas from the 1930 census for the Romanian territory in 1942, compiled by the Central Institute of Statistics. Courtesy of the Bucharest State Archives.

213

214

The Interface Collection

Interface: a programme

The Gypsy Research Centre at the Université René Descartes, Paris, has been developing cooperation with the European Commission and the Council of Europe since the early 1980s. The Centre's task is to undertake studies and expert work at European level; a significant proportion of its work consists in ensuring the systematic implementation of measures geared towards improving the living conditions of Gypsy communities, especially through the types of action with which it is particularly involved, such as research, training, information, documentation, publication, coordination etc., and in fields which are also areas of research for its own teams: sociology, history, linguistics, social and cultural anthropology...

In order to effectively pursue this work of reflection and of action we have developed a strategy to facilitate the pooling of ideas and initiatives from individuals representing a range of different approaches, to enable all of us to cooperate in an organised, consistent fashion. The working framework we have developed over the years is characterised both by a solidity which lends effective support to activities, and by a flexibility conferring openness and adaptability. This approach, driven by an underlying philosophy outlined in a number of publications, notably the *Interface* newsletter, has become the foundation of our programme of reference.

Interface: a set of teams

A number of international teams play a key role within the programme framework, namely through their work in developing documentation, information, coordination, study and research. With the support of the European Commission, and in connection with the implementation of the Resolution on School Provision for Gypsy and Traveller Children adopted in 1989 by the Ministers of Education of the European Union, working groups on history, language and culture - *the Research Group on European Gypsy History, the Research and Action Group on Romani Linguistics,* and *the European Working Group on Gypsy and Traveller Education* – have already been established, as has a working group developing a Gypsy encyclopaedia. Additional support provided by the Council of Europe enables us to extend some of our work to cover the whole of Europe.

Interface: a network

• these Groups, comprising experienced specialists, are tackling a number of tasks: establishing contact networks linking persons involved in research, developing documentary databases relevant to their fields of interest, working as expert groups advising/collaborating with other teams, organising the production and distribution of teaching materials relevant to their fields;

• these productions, prepared by teams representing a number of different States, are the result of truly international collaboration; the composition of these teams means that they are in a position to be well acquainted with the needs and sensitivities of very different places and to have access to national, and local, achievements of quality which it is important to publicise;

• in order to decentralise activities and to allocate them more equitably, a network of publishers in different States has been formed, to ensure both local input and international distribution.

Interface: a Collection

A Collection was seen as the best response to the pressing demand for teaching materials, recognised and approved by the Ministers of Education in the above-mentioned Resolution adopted at European level, and also in the hope of rectifying the overall dearth of quality materials and in so doing to validate and affirm Gypsy history, language and culture.

Published texts carry the *Interface* label of the Gypsy Research Centre.

- they are conceived in complementarity with each other and with action being undertaken at European level, so as to produce a structured information base: such coherence is important for the general reader, and essential in the pedagogical context;

- they are, for the most part, previously unpublished works, which address essential themes which have been insufficiently explored to date, and because they do so in an original fashion;

- their quality is assured by the fact that all are written by, or in close consultation with, experienced specialists;

- although contributions come from specialists, the Collection is not aimed at specialists: it must be accessible/comprehensible to secondary level students, and by teachers of primary level pupils for classroom use. The authors write clear, well-structured texts, with bibliographical references given as an appendix for readers wishing to undertake a more in-depth study;

- although contributions come from specialists, the Collection is not aimed at any particular target group: in an intercultural approach to education, and given the content of each contribution, every student, and every teacher, should have access to Gypsy/Traveller-related information, and may have occasion to use it in the classroom. The texts on offer, being the work of extremely competent contributors, may embody new approaches to the topics covered (history, linguistics etc.) and as such being of relevance not only to teachers, teacher trainers, pupils, students and researchers, but also social workers, administrators and policy makers;

- contributions may be accompanied by practical teaching aids or other didactic tools; these tools and materials are prepared by teams in the field, experienced teachers and participants in pilot projects. Their output is very illustrative of *Interface* programme dynamics : an association of diverse partners in a context of action-research, producing coordinated, complementary work, with a scope as broad as Europe, yet adapted to the local cultural and linguistic context;

- format is standardised for maximum reader-friendliness and ease of handling;

- the *Interface* collection is international in scope: most titles are published in a number of languages, to render them accessible to the broadest possible public.

A number of topics have been proposed, of which the following are currently being pursued:

- *European Gypsy history*
- *Romani linguistics*
- *Rukun*
- *Reference works*

Jean-Pierre Liégeois
Director, Interface Collection

217

Titles in the Interface Collection : a reminder

*The **Interface** Collection is developed by the Gypsy Research Centre at the University René Descartes, Paris, with the support of the European Commission and of the Council of Europe.*

1 • Marcel Kurtiàde
- *Širpustik amare ćhibǎqiri* (Livre de l'élève / Pupil's book) CRDP - ISBN : 2-86565-074-X
- Livre du maître / Teacher's manual, disponible en / available in : Albanian, English, French, Polish, Romanian, Slovak and Spanish. (Un numéro ISBN est attribué à chaque langue / each with its own ISBN).

2 • Antonio Gómez Alfaro
- *La Gran redada de Gitanos* PG - ISBN : 84-87347-09-6
- *The Great Gypsy Round-up* PG - ISBN : 84-87347-12-6
- *La Grande rafle des Gitans* CRDP - ISBN : 2-86565-083-9
- *La grande retata dei Gitani* ANICIA/CSZ : 88-900078-2-6
- *Marea prigonire a Rromilor* EA - ISBN : 973-9216-35-8
- *Die große Razzia gegen die Gitanos* PA - ISBN : 3-88402-199-0

3 • Donald Kenrick
- *Gypsies : from India to the Mediterranean* CRDP - ISBN : 2-86565-082-0
- *Los Gitanos : de la India al Mediterráneo* PG - ISBN : 84-87347-13-4
- *Les Tsiganes de l'Inde à la Méditerranée* CRDP - ISBN : 2-86565-081-2
- *Zingari : dall'India al Mediterraneo* ANICIA/CSZ : 88-900078-1-8
- *Τσιγγάνοι : από τις Ινδίες σιπ Μεσόγειο* EK - ISBN : 960-03-1834-4
- *Циганите: от Индия до Средиземно море* LIT - ISBN: 954-8537-56-7
- *Rromii: din India la Mediterana* EA - ISBN : 973-9216-36-6
- *Sinti und Roma: Von Indien bis zum Mittelmeer* PA - ISBN : 3-88402-201-6
- *Ciganos : da Índia ao Mediterrâneo* SE - ISBN : 972-8339-15-1

4 • Elisa Mª Lopes da Costa
- *Os Ciganos : Fontes bibliográficas em Portugal* PG - ISBN : 84-87347-11-8

5 • Marielle Danbakli
- *Textes des institutions internationales concernant les Tsiganes* CRDP - ISBN: 2-86565-098-7
- *On Gypsies : Texts issued by International Institutions* CRDP - ISBN : 2-86565-099-5
- *Текстове на международните институции за циганите* LIT - ISBN: 954-8537-53-2

6 • Bernard Leblon
- *Gitans et flamenco* CRDP - ISBN : 2-86565-107-X
- *Gypsies and Flamenco* UHP - ISBN : 0 900 45859-3
- *Gitani e flamenco* ANICIA/CSZ : 88-900078-8-5
- *Gitanos und Flamenco* PA - ISBN : 3-88402-198-2

7 • David Mayall
- *English Gypsies and State Policies* UHP - ISBN : 0 900 458 64 X

8 • D. Kenrick, G. Puxon
- *Gypsies under the Swastika* UHP - ISBN : 0 900 458 65 8
- *Gitanos bajo la Cruz Gamada* PG - ISBN : 84-87347-16-9
- *Les Tsiganes sous l'oppression nazie* CRDP - ISBN : 2-86565-172-X
- *Хитлеризмът и циганите* LIT - ISBN : 954-8537-57-5
- *Os Ciganos sob o domínio da suástica* SE - ISBN : 972-8339-16-X

9 • Giorgio Viaggio   • *Storia degli Zingari in Italia* ANICIA/CSZ : 88-900078-9-3

10 • D. Kenrick, G. Puxon   • *Bibaxtale Berśa* PG - ISBN : 84-87347-15-0

11 • Jean-Pierre Liégeois   • *Minorité et scolarité : le parcours tsigane* CRDP - ISBN : 2-86565-192-4
                                      • *School Provision for Ethnic Minorities : The Gypsy Paradigm* UHP - ISBN : 0 900 458 88 7

12 • K. Fings, H. Heuß,   • *Von der "Rassenforschung" zu den Lagern Sinti und Roma unter*
         F. Sparing   *dem Nazi-Regime - 1 —* PA - ISBN : 3-88402-188-5
                                      • *De la "science raciale" aux camps Les Tsiganes dans la Seconde Guerre mondiale - 1 —* CRDP - ISBN : 2-86565-186-X
                                      • *From "Race Science" to the Camps The Gypsies during the Second World War - 1 —* UHP - ISBN : 0 900 458 78 X
                                      • *Dalla "ricerca razziale" ai campi nazisti Gli Zingari nella Seconda Guerra mondiale - 1 —* ANICIA/CSZ : 88-900078-3-4

13 • Joint authorship   • *In the shadow of the Swastika The Gypsies during the Second World War - 2* UHP - ISBN : 0 900 458 85 2

14 • G. Donzello,   • *Un ragazzo zingaro nella mia classe* ANICIA/CSZ : 88-900078-4-2
         B. M. Karpati

Série Rukun / The Rukun Series :

• *O Rukun ʒal and-i skòla*, Groupe de recherche et d'action en linguistique romani
                Research and Action Group on Romani Linguistics   RB - ISBN : 2-9507850-1-8
• *Kaj si o Rukun amaro ?* Groupe de recherche et d'action en linguistique romani
                Research and Action Group on Romani Linguistics   RB - ISBN : 2-9507850-2-6
• *I bari lavenqi pustik e Rukunesqiri*, Groupe de recherche et d'action en linguistique romani
                Research and Action Group on Romani Linguistics   RB - ISBN : 2-9507850-3-4

Publishers' addresses

• **ANICIA** (with the *Centro Studi Zingari*)
Via San Francesco a Ripa, 62
I - 00153 - Roma

• **CRDP** — Centre Régional de Documentation
Pédagogique Midi-Pyrénées
3 rue Roquelaine
F - 31069 - Toulouse Cedex

• **CSZ** — Centro Studi Zingari (with the *Anicia*)
Via dei Barbieri, 22
I - 00186 Roma

• **EA** — Editura Alternative
Casa Presei, Corp. B, Et. 4
Piaţa Presei Libere, 1
RO - 71341 - Bucureşti 1

• **EK** — Editions Kastaniotis /
ΕΚΔΟΣΕΙΣ ΚΑΣΤΑΝΙΩΤΗ
11, Zalogou
GR - 106 78 - Athènes

• **LIT** — Editions Litavra /
за ИК »ДИТАВРА»
163А Rakovoki St
BG - 1000 - Sofia

• **PA** — Edition Parabolis
Schliemannstraße 23
D - 10437 Berlin

• **PG** — Editorial Presencia Gitana
Valderrodrigo, 76 y 78
E - 28039 - Madrid

• **SE** — Entreculturas /
Secretariado Coordenador dos Programas
de Educação Multicultural
Trav. das Terras de Sant'Ana, 15 - 1°
PT - 1250 - Lisboa

• **UHP** — University of Hertfordshire Press
College Lane - Hatfield
UK - Hertfordshire AL10 9AB

• *Rukun series distributed by :*
RB — Rromani Baxt
22, rue du Port
F - 63000 - Clermont-Ferrand

• *distribution in Ireland:*
Pavee Point Travellers Centre
6 North Great Charles Street
IRL - Dublin 1